Arthur Scratchley

On average Investment Trusts and Companies dealing with Stock Exchange Securities

Part I - IV

Arthur Scratchley

**On average Investment Trusts and Companies dealing with Stock Exchange Securities**
*Part I - IV*

ISBN/EAN: 9783337153496

Printed in Europe, USA, Canada, Australia, Japan

Cover: Foto ©ninafisch / pixelio.de

More available books at **www.hansebooks.com**

DIVISION VI. *of Treatise on Associations for Provident Investment.*

ON

# AVERAGE INVESTMENT TRUSTS

AND

## COMPANIES DEALING WITH STOCK EXCHANGE SECURITIES,

*Exemplified in*
{
*Foreign and Colonial Government Investment Trusts;*
*Guaranteed Securities Trusts;*
*Municipal Securities Trusts;*
*Railway Share and Debenture Trusts;*
*Gas and Water Trusts;*
*Subscription Trusts, etc., etc.;*
}

BEING A

*Practical Guide to their Formation and Management,*

WITH

**An Exposition of the financial principles involved in Stock Exchange Securities and Foreign Government Loans, and of the errors in some Trusts;**

AND

TABLES ON COMPOUND INTEREST, SINKING FUNDS AND DRAWINGS.

BY

## ARTHUR SCRATCHLEY, M.A.,

*Of the Inner Temple, Barrister-at-Law,*
*Formerly Fellow and Sadlerian Lecturer of Queens' College, Cambridge;*
*One of the Examiners in 1850 and 1851 of the Institute of Actuaries;*
*Consulting Actuary to the Tithe Redemption Trust,*
*Corresponding Member of the Central Commission of Belgium on Statistics.*

Parts I.—IV.

LONDON:
SHAW AND SONS, FETTER LANE, FLEET STREET, E.C.
Law Printers and Publishers.

1875.

*⁎* The Author will feel obliged to Secretaries, Managers, and others who will forward to him any Reports, or other Documents which may be useful to add to the materials collated in the present volume.

*The following Parts will be published shortly :—*

PART — V.—OF PUBLIC DEBTS, *continued.* — The Rearrangement of Foreign Debts.

„  VI.—OF EXPENDITURE TRUSTS.

„  VII.—OF OTHER TRUSTS (Colonial, &c.) not dealing with Stock Exchange Securities.

„  VIII.—LAW NOTES, and Alphabetical Digest of Cases.

„  IX.—OF RAILWAY SECURITIES,—MUNICIPAL SECURITIES, ETC.

# NOTICE.

When advising on matters connected with Joint Stock Companies, we have frequently had occasion to remark the want of a work on the principles and practice of those which invest in Stock Exchange Securities.

The object of this publication is to point out the legal and financial elements involved in the constitution of such associations, and to show how united action in dealing with Stock Exchange Securities may advantageously be substituted for individual venture.

A person, who starts with the intention of purchasing stock for investment, is too often led on to speculation—an evil that has been growing up of late years to an alarming extent. It has also been fostered by the custom of the Stock Exchange, which allows persons to buy stock without having sufficient money to complete the purchase, in the hope of a profit by a rise in prices, or to sell without having any stock to deliver, in the fancied prospect of a gain by buying back at a fall; the results usually happening adverse to their expectations.

The House of Commons Foreign Loans Committee of 1875 has recently published the results of its inquiries and removed any doubts as to the propriety of the Legislature interfering in such matters. The public recognizes that a service of the most useful kind has been rendered by the light thrown on the operations of the Stock market.

Parliament might possibly have inquired with advantage into the circumstances attending the issue of other Foreign Loans, but the cases taken are typical enough and exhibit the general character of the system. Circumstances are changed, however, and the history of the past, with its details of recklessness and waste, is not likely for some years to be repeated.

The uncertainty attending individual dealings with Stock Exchange Securities is forcibly exemplified by the recent collapse in the payment of the Turkish Debt, following as it has done almost immediately on the minor failure at Uruguay. These additions to the list of Defaulting States, which we have given in Part III., though not unanticipated by the experienced few, have in respect to Turkey fallen with sudden severity on the investing public. The moral they show is, that no such investments can be regarded as other than speculative, unless spread over a large range of Securities, and as we have pointed out in Chapter III., Part I., it is wrong, or at all events unwise, to pay away apparent profits in the earlier years of any Trust, when a long period of its future existence has yet to be provided for.

By these disastrous events the further lesson will be taught that a better chance of profit on money is to be found in the wide field of Home investments, or at least in those which afford tangible property as a guarantee rather than the promises of Governments, that may have the will but not the power or means of performing what they undertake.

In this publication, Trust Associations, or Average Investment Funds, have, with a view to simplicity, been separated into three classes according as they are constituted—

(1) *by a Deed of Trust,*

(2) *by incorporation as Companies with a capital in shares,*

(3) *or as Subscription Trusts working mainly with the small subscriptions of members.*

This last kind having much to recommend it if conducted after the manner of the best class of Building Societies, which have been so successfully developed in this country.

We have to acknowledge the valuable assistance we have received from Mr. Edward A. Scratchley, of Lincoln's Inn, in the analysis of the various Trusts and statistical facts furnished.

2, PLOWDEN BUILDINGS, TEMPLE,
*November,* 1875.

POSTSCRIPT TO

MR. SCRATCHLEY'S PRACTICAL TREATISE ON *Average Investment Trusts and Companies dealing with Stock Exchange Securities,* December, 1875.

---

The decree of the Turkish Government, by which the payment of a portion of the amount becoming due for Interest and Sinking Fund on the public debts of that country is suspended, having been issued as the sheets of this work were passing through the press, the following concise view is appended of the Redeemable loans raised by Turkey from 1854 to 1871 inclusive (but exclusive of the ordinary 5 per cent. debt of 1865, the Guaranteed loan of 1855, and the loans after 1871).

It shows some remarkable facts :—

1st.—That, although the total Nominal amount of these Redeemable loans was £59,932,040, the money which Turkey actually received at the issue prices was but £39,811,581. The Bonus thus given on the bonds being over 20 millions.

---

[* Messrs. Shaw and Sons, Fetter Lane, London, 1875, price 6s.]

## STATE-

The Loans to Turkey effected before 1872 and Bonds not being considered fully The Guaranteed Loan of 1855 and the General

| Year of Loan. | Nominal amount of Loan issued. | Prices of issue per cent. | Dividend per cent. | Sinking Fund per cent. | Year by Contract for last repayment. |
|---|---|---|---|---|---|
| 1854 | £ 8,000,000 (*Mr. R. B. Martin.*) | £ 80 | £ 6 | £ 1 | 1889 |
| 1858 | 5,000,000 | 85 and 62½ | 6 | 1 | 1892 |
| 1860 | 2,009,820 (*Mr. R. B. Martin.*) | 62½ | 6 | 1 | 1896 |
| 1862 | 8,000,000 (*Mr. R. B. Martin.*) | 68 | 6 | 2 | 1886 |
| 1863-4 | 8,000,000 (*Mr. R. B. Martin.*) | 72 and 68 | 6 | 2 | 1886 |
| 1865 "Muttons" | 6,000,000 (*Mr. Eyken.*) | 65½ | 6 | 2.44 | 1886 |
| 1869 "Cohens" | 22,222,220 (*Mr. Eyken.*) | 60½ | 6 | 1 | 1902 |
| 1871 | 5,700,000 | 73 | 6 | 1 | 1905 |
|  | 59,982,040 |  |  |  |  |

[Against any special figures the names of the latest authorities are inserted, namely, the chairmen of the meetings recently held. The total cost of each loan would appear somewhat higher if the discount at the time of issue and interest for fractions of bonds undrawn each year were included.]

MENT OF
redeemable at par. The later ones are omitted, the placed with the Public.
5 per cent. debt are also not included.

| Money Turkey received on each Loan at price of issue. | Total money remitted by Turkey on each Loan up to the present time, reckoned only from the date of the first drawing inclusive. | Reduced amount Turkey would still owe on each Loan if the money it actually received had been an ordinary *borrowing at 6 per cent. without Bonus. | Amount still due by Turkey, represented by the discounted values of the remaining annuity repayments, covering Dividend and Sinking Fund, which it has covenanted to pay. |
|---|---|---|---|
| £ | £ | £ | £ |
| 2,400,000 | 3,885,000 | 266,034 | 1,995,759 |
| 3,500,000 | 5,425,000 | 73,605 | 3,728,351 |
| 1,256,138 | 1,688,244 | 131,792 | 1,667,237 |
| 5,440,000 | 8,000,000 | [Nothing due but overpaid 276,813] | .5,099,813 |
| 5,680,000 | 7,680,000 | 529,800 | 5,261,955 |
| 3,980,000 | 4,810,800 | 531,688 | 4,163,522 |
| 18,444,443 | 8,555,553 | 8,648,688 | 20,824,547 |
| 4,161,000 | 1,197,000 | 3,685,561 | 5,524,937 |
| 39,811,581 | 41,241,597 | 13,867,118† | 48,266,121 |

[\* The money actually advanced carrying 6 per cent. interest, from which is deducted the repayment annuity, remitted each year, by a debtor and creditor account.]

[† In this column the Loan of 1862 is omitted in the casting, as at 6 per cent. without Bonus it would be overpaid.]

2nd.—In repayment of these advances up to the present time £41,241,597 has been remitted by Turkey for dividends and sinking funds, reckoning only from the respective dates at which the first drawing occurred on each loan.

3rd.—Nevertheless by the contracts there is still a debt of £48,266,121 outstanding; this being the equivalent discounted value of the repayments that Turkey has to make for the various unexpired terms of years.

The unsatisfactorily heavy nature of these contracts becomes very striking when the amount, yet to be paid in respect to any one of these loans, is compared with what would be due, if the transaction had been an ordinary advance at 6 per cent. interest per annum on the actual money lent to Turkey, without any Bonus.

Taking as an example the 6 per cent. loan of 1865 (termed the " Muttons ")—on which Turkey received £3,930,000 cash, while bonds were issued for £6,000,000 —the table shows that the amount already remitted by Turkey on that loan is close upon five millions (£4,810,800), and that as a mere 6 per cent. debt the balance still owing would be but £531,688; whereas the outstanding debt by its contract is still £4,163,522.

Viewed in the same manner, the total amount, which Turkey would owe now on these Redeemable loans, would be under 14 millions (£13,867,118.)

# CONTENTS.

|  | PAGE |
|---|---|
| NOTICE | v |

## PART I.
### PRELIMINARY OBSERVATIONS.

Section 1.—Origin of Trust Associations - - - - - - - 1
                Nature of Trust Associations - - - - - - 2
„ 2.—Opinions of Public Writers and Others - - - - - 3
                Bondholders Committee's Report - - - - - 5
„ 3.—Of the usefulness of Trust Associations - - - - - 7
                Amounts of Public Securities - - - - - - 8
                Fixed and Variable Dividends - - - - - 9
                Evils of Speculation - - - - - - - 10

### PART I. (*continued*).
#### CHAPTER I.—*The Original Trust.*

Section 1.—The Prospectus of 1868 - - - - - - - 12
„ 2.—The first Contract and subsequent Issues - - - - 15
                Fluctuation in Prices - - - - - - - 16
„ 3.—Progress of the Original Trusts - - - - - - 18
                Report of the fourth issue in 1875 - - - - - 19
                Report of the fifth issue of 1875 - - - - - 20

#### CHAPTER II.—*Of Existing Trusts.*

Section 1.—Names with details of Capital and leading features - - 21
                Names of Trustees and Directors - - - - - 22
„ 2.—Rate of Profit reported - - - - - - - - 34

CHAPTER III.—*Of some Defects in Existing Trust Associations.*

|  | PAGE |
|---|---|
| Section 1.—Objections to a Premature System of Drawings | 39 |
| „ 2.—Of Reserve Funds and Contingencies of Loss | 40 |
| „ 3.—Of the Unequal Effect of Drawings when of Fixed Amounts | 42 |
| „ 4.—Of the wide field for "Trust" operations | 44 |
| Necessity for Reserves | 45 |
| Extent of Public Securities | 46 |

# PART II.

## OF THE PRINCIPLES OF NEW TRUST ASSOCIATIONS.

CHAPTER I.—*Plan of a Trust Company with Shares.*

Section 1.—The —— Debenture Trust Company (Limited) - - - 51

CHAPTER II.—*Of New Trusts (continued).*

| | |
|---|---|
| Section 1.—Subscription Trusts with or without Share Capital | 56 |
| „ 2.—Of the rate of Premium charged in place of Interest and of Valuations | 59 |
| „ 3.—Regulations of Subscription Trusts | 60 |
| Debenture Funds | 60 |
| Certificates | 61 |
| Security to Subscribers | 63 |
| Formation of Funds | 63 |
| Securities | 63 |
| Remarks | 64 |
| „ 4.—Other provisions of Subscription Trusts | 65 |
| Of Advances and Investments | 65 |
| Principal Clauses :— | |
| Members | 66 |
| Funds | 67 |
| Loans | 67 |
| Profits | 68 |
| Transfers | 68 |
| Withdrawals | 69 |

Section 4.—Principal Clauses—*continued*.

|  | PAGE |
|---|---|
| Votes | 69 |
| Officers | 70 |
| Directors | 70 |
| Accounts | 71 |
| „ 5.—Future Subscription Trusts | 72 |
| Modifications recommended | 72 |
| „ 6.—Of Tontine Bonuses and Subscription Shares | 73 |
| „ 7.—Of some Special kinds of Trusts that may be formed with advantage | 75 |
| Real and Leasehold Property Investment Trusts | 75 |
| Annuity Trusts | 76 |
| Deferred Securities Trusts | 76 |

CHAPTER III.—*Of New Trusts (continued)*.

Section 1.—Of the kind of Share Capital for Trusts, of Preferred and Deferred Shares, and of Trusts Limited by Guarantee - 76
Share Capital Redemptions - 78
„ 2.—Of the Privileges of Founders and Expenses of Management 79
„ 3.—Of Erroneous Dividends and Deposits - 80
Public Securities, Investment Companies, and their Profits 81

## PART III.

### THE DEBTS OF NATIONS.

CHAPTER I.—*The Debts of Nations*.

Section 1.—Their Amount and recent Progress - 87
Summary of their Total Indebtedness - 88
„ 2.—Foreign Loans on which Default has been made - 90

CHAPTER II.—*Particulars of the Debts, Population, Area, Imports and Exports, etc., of each Country*.

Summary of the Fluctuations in the prices of Consols from 1730 to 1875 - 93

# PART IV.

## OF THE TERMS ON WHICH FOREIGN DEBTS HAVE BEEN CONTRACTED, AND THE FINANCIAL PRINCIPLES INVOLVED.

### Chapter I.

| | PAGE |
|---|---|
| Section 1.—Of Sinking Funds, Loan—Repayments and Drawings | 129 |
| Sinking Fund Table | 130 |
| Practical Rules for calculating the same | 131 |
| Misconception as to Sinking Funds | 134 |
| As to a "51 years" Repayment by Drawings Table | 135 |
| ,, 2.—Of Foreign Debts, with illustrations of the cost thereof to the State borrowing | 137 |
| Specimens from the Turkish and Egyptian Loans | 138 |
| The terms of the Egyptian Loan of 1868 examined | 139 |
| ,, 3.—As to Profit to Lenders | 140 |
| ,, 4.—On the cost to borrowing States (*continued*) | 142 |
| The Turkish "Muttons" Loan of 1865 examined | 142 |
| The Turkish "Cohen" Loan of 1869 | 142 |
| Reckless nature of Foreign borrowings | 143 |
| Of Lottery-drawings | 145 |
| Further note on the cost of the Egyptian Loan of 1868 | 146 |
| Particulars of some Loans expensively contracted | 147 |
| Of the Usurious terms involved | 148 |
| ,, 5.—Alternative measures proposed | 149 |
| Note on Foreign and Municipal Lottery Loans | 150 |
| Popularity of Drawings | 150 |
| Of the Doubling of Money at 10¼ per cent. | 151 |
| Saving to Egypt if the 1868 Loan had been redeemable in 18½ years instead of in 30, with a dividend stock paying 6 per cent. and Bonus | 152 |

### Chapter II.—*Of Dividends and Drawings in Foreign Stocks.*

| | |
|---|---|
| Section 1.—The relative values of Dividends and Drawings | 153 |
| Table showing the value of Dividends and Drawings | 154 |
| Comparison of Market prices with the same | 155 |
| ,, 2.—As to Stocks at a Premium which are redeemable at par | 156 |
| Table showing the values of the same | 158 |

CONTENTS. xiii

PAGE

Section 3.— On the effect of the surplus of Dividends, over a security rate of 4 per cent. per annum, in replacing Capital paid for Stocks - - - - - - - - - - 159
  Table showing the same - - - - - - 160
   Illustrations of Capital returned by surplus dividends 161

CHAPTER III.—*Tables (continued)*.

Section 1.—Memoria Technica Tables - - - - - - - 163
  Property of the number 70 and the Doubling of money - 163
  Table showing the accuracy of the Rule - - - - 163
  Doubling periods - - - - - - - - 164
  Savings Fund Table - - - - - - - 165
„ 2.—Suggestions with respect to Loans - - - - - - 165
  Alternatives for raising money at par on temporary or perpetual Stocks, so as to produce either fixed or increasing incomes - - - - - - - - - 166
„ 3.—Of the present values of Decreasing and Increasing Annuities 167
  Rules for calculating the same - - - - - 167

*b* 2

# LIST OF TABLES.

### 1st. SERIES.

### I. SINKING FUND TABLE.

*Showing the annual Sinking Fund (set aside in equal parts at the end of each half-year) which will amount to £100 at various rates of interest.*

### II. "51 YEARS'" DEBENTURE REDEMPTION TABLE.

### III. TABLE

*Showing the* VALUES OF BONDS *carrying £6 and £7 dividends a year respectively, with £100 par value receivable by Drawings at the end of uncertain periods of years. [Discounted half-yearly at 6 and 7 per cent. per annum respectively.]*

### IV. STOCKS AT A PREMIUM.—TABLE

*Showing the prices of Stock, corresponding to the rate of interest desired to be made on Stocks above par, and which produce half-yearly dividends at 5, 6, and 7 per cent. per annum. The Stock being redeemable at par or £100.*

### V. SURPLUS OF DIVIDENDS OVER 4 PER CENT.—TABLE.

*If £100 be laid out in a purchase of Stock producing equal Dividends half-yearly, and the surplus of Dividends over £4* INTEREST *be applied half-yearly to write off Capital, then the amounts of Capital returned will be according to the amount of Dividend received for the £100.*

## "MEMORIA TECHNICA" TABLES.

### VI. Table

Showing the periods in which £100 or any other sum will double itself by the Rule dependent on the Number 70.

### VII. SAVINGS FUND TABLE

Showing the *savings* per *annum* invested half-yearly, which will amount to £100 at the end of any number of periods, using the accurate time in which a *single* sum of money would double, according to the rates of interest at which they are laid out half-yearly.

---

### 2ND SERIES.

TABLES FOR AN AVERAGE INVESTMENT TRUST, WITH SHARE CAPITAL; AND ISSUING BONUS INVESTMENT BONDS AND BONUS INVESTMENT CERTIFICATES.

*These Tables are calculated on the basis of Bonds and Certificates of £100 each, but in many cases Bonds and Certificates of £25 and £30 each may be found more convenient.*

#### CLASS A.—Bonus Investment Bonds.

TABLE *showing how a Trust with a Fund of* £100,000, *making* 6 *per cent. per annum, clear of expenses, and paying* 4 *per cent. to the Bondholders, could after* 8 *years pay off* 70 *Bonds a-year, the Bonds drawn getting* £120. *A considerable surplus will remain, from the Compound Interest not included, available for residuary Allotments to the Shareholders.*

LIST OF TABLES.   xvii

### CLASS B.—Bonus Investment Bonds.

TABLE *showing how a Trust with a Fund of* £100,000, *making* 6 *per cent. per annum, clear of expenses, and paying* 4½ *per cent. to the Bondholders, could after* 7 *years pay off* 70 *Bonds a-year, commencing at* £115 *per Bond, and increasing* £1 *for each year's delay. The Bonds drawn in the last* (21st) *year getting* £128. *A considerable surplus will remain, from the Compound Interest not included, available for residuary Allotments to the Shareholders.*

### CLASS C.—Doubling Accumulative Bonds.
### With Contingent Bonuses.

TABLE *showing how a Trust, which makes only* 5 *per cent. clear of Expenses, could, out of an Accumulation at Compound Interest, return* £200 *for each* £100 *Bond, by Annual Drawings commencing at the end of the* 10th *Year. If the Trust made a higher rate clear of Expenses, it could set aside the Surplus towards* TRIENNIAL *Allotments of Additional Contingent* BONUSES. *The Table is given on the basis of* £100,000 *Fund in* 1,000 *Bonds of* £100 *each returnable by* £200,000 *drawn at the rate of* 100 *Bonds a Year.*

### CLASS D.—Bonus Investment Certificates.
### Realisable by Monthly or other Periodic Subscriptions.

TABLE *showing the Amount that may be received back in* PRINCIPAL AND INTEREST (*accumulated half-yearly at* 4 *per cent. per annum*), *at end of different terms of years, for* £100 *paid in, apart from the Bonuses to be allotted at Triennial Valuations of Profits, but payable on completion of the Certificates.*

## 3RD SERIES.

The following Tables are extracted from the *Building Society Treatise* as likely to be of service in "Trust" operations:

### TABLE I.

*Showing the Decimal corresponding to every Penny in the Pound.*

### TABLE II.

*Showing the sum per Pound to which a Rate of Interest per cent. is equivalent.*

### TABLE III.

*Showing the RATE OF INTEREST obtainable from £3 per cent. stock for £100 cash invested according to the price of the day.*

### TABLE IV.

*Showing the Amount to which £100 Principal will increase at various Rates of Compound yearly Interest.*

### TABLE V.

*Showing the Rates of Interest payable only once a-year, which are equivalent to nominal annual rates of Interest actually paid at frequent intervals in each year.*

### TABLE VI.

*Showing the nominal Annual Rates of Interest paid momently, which are equivalent to rates paid at the end of each year.*

## TABLE VII.

*Showing the Amount to which £100 will increase at Compound Interest, according as it is paid yearly, half-yearly, quarterly, or momently. [See Table IV.]*

## TABLE VIII.

*Time in which Money will double itself at Simple or Compound Yearly Interest.*

## TABLE IX.

*Showing the present Value of £100 payable at the end of any number of Years, at various Rates of Interest.*

## TABLE X.

*Showing the Amount to which an Annuity of £100, paid at the end of each year, will accumulate at Compound Interest.*

## TABLE XI.

*Showing the present Value of an Annuity of £100 payable at the end of each Year.*

## TABLE XII.

*Showing the yearly annuity which £100 will purchase for a given number of Years.*

## TABLE XIII.

*Present value and amount of £100 payable at end of any number of years at 2½ per cent. and 3½ per cent.*

*Present value and Amount of an Annuity of £100 payable at end of each year at 2½ per cent. and 3½ per cent.*

## TABLE XIV.

*Present value of an Annuity of £100 per annum, for a given number of years certain, supposing the Purchaser to take out of the annuity 5 per cent., 6 per cent., or 7 per cent. per Annum as Interest on his Purchase Money, while he is enabled to Re-invest the Surplus of the Annuity beyond the Interest, so as to make 3 per cent., 4 per cent., and 5 per cent. thereon, in order to replace the Purchase Money by the end of the number of years.*

## TABLE XV.

*Specimen of Deposit Tables, for Savings Banks and Industrial Associations, showing—*

1.—The Amount to which a Deposit of £100 will accumulate at the end of any number of years up to 10.

2.—The Amount to which a Deposit of £10 per annum will accumulate at the end of any number of years up to 10.

## TABLE XVI.

*Extract from the Tables of Logarithms.*

## TABLE XVII.

*English Life Table No. 3. Interest 3 per cent.*

(Calculated by the Registrar-General from the Returns for 17 Years.)

# AVERAGE INVESTMENT TRUST ASSOCIATIONS.

### PART I.

PRELIMINARY OBSERVATIONS.

Section 1.—*Origin of Trust Associations.*
　 „　2.—*Opinions of Public Writers and Others.*
　 „　3.—*Of the Usefulness of Trust Associations.*

Section 1.—*Origin of Trust Associations.*

ART. 1.—Until the year 1844 specific comprehensive legislation for *Joint Stock Companies* was unknown in this country. They were still subjected to the doctrines of the old unwritten law relating to partnerships, and unless they had obtained incorporation by the expensive and exceptional process of a Charter or an Act of Parliament, each member was considered an individual partner, responsible, to his last shilling and his last acre, for the whole of the debts of the partnership and for every Act committed on its behalf by any other member. It is only since 1856 that the English Legislature (imitating tardily the law-makers of the Continent and America) has recognized the possibility of a *Limitation of individual liability* to losses on the part of a person entitled to receive any portion of the profits of a venture, and the year 1862 saw the passing of a comprehensive measure for the regulation of public companies, which has rendered the incorporation of subscribers to any business purpose, with limited liability, so simple and easy a matter, that every day fresh companies are started and new applications of the power of association devised. The system of Limited Liability, in a modified form, has also been made applicable to private partnerships by the Act of 1864, which enables a lender to share in the *profits* of a concern without being liable to lose more than the money invested.

2.—In addition to these above, other special Acts have been passed, professedly designed for the industrial classes, under which societies (such as we have described in previous divisions of this treatise) are required to be registered.

Among them a statute of the year 1871, and another of 1874, have for their object the enabling of provident persons to fructify their small savings by aggregation, with the view of investing them in houses or land, and those Acts confer several advantages on societies established under them.

3.—It is, however, to the Joint Stock Companies' Acts of 1862 & 1867, that this, the 5th division of our Treatise on *Associations for Provident Investment*, refers, especially in respect to "Trusts" for obtaining profits from investments in general securities, including those dealt in on the Stock Exchange.

These Trusts bear different names, such as "*Foreign and Colonial Government Trusts*"—"*Guaranteed Securities Trusts*"—"*Railway Share and Debenture Trusts,*" &c.; but they all tend to the same purpose, and are "Average Investment Funds," operating so as to give to their members an average profit, from a variety of securities.

4.—The causes, which have given rise to the formation of these Trusts, may be briefly described as efforts made to afford to individuals the benefits arising from co-operative action in their investments, and some protection against the losses to which purchasers are exposed who buy stocks or general securities in an isolated manner,—losses which they frequently do not apprehend until they subsequently find it necessary to realize at a time when some particular Stock is depressed in value.

5.—The propriety of enabling persons of limited means to invest— in Government and public securities, paying remunerative dividends — through the agency of Average Investment Funds, was warmly advocated by that eminent lawyer, the late Lord Westbury, who, with other persons of standing, founded the first *" Foreign and Colonial Government Investment Trust"* in 1868.—His view was, that, whether a man has a large or small sum to invest, he runs the risk of making a mistake in his individual purchase from not understanding the peculiarities of the Stock; whereas, if he subscribe to a general fund, which (assisted by the advice of persons of experience in such matters) would divide its purchases carefully among a selected variety of investments—each member would derive greater benefit with much security from loss by the distribution of the risk over a large average.

*Section 2.—Opinions of Public Writers and Others.*

ART. 6.—There is a remarkable concordance of opinion both of public men of weight in financial matters, and of the journals which treat specially of such subjects, as evidenced by the following extracts :—

I.—Mr. Ray, the experienced manager of an important Trust, observes— " Many persons believe that 3 per cent. Stock in the English Funds is the best of all investments, yet they seek to obtain a larger interest.

" The great principle involved is *how to obtain a high rate of interest with the utmost possible security.*

" There are many people to whom the profitable investment of their small capital is of vital importance. They may be, and many are, entirely dependent on the interest ; in such cases 3 per cent. from Consols would be a meagre pittance, insufficient even for support, and many a heart would be gladdened if an increased interest could be obtained and the capital remain safe.

# OPINIONS OF WRITERS.

"*It should be borne in mind, however, that if investments bearing a high rate of interest are touched at all, it should be on a system to divide and sub-divide them so as to secure an average.*

"*It is obvious that people with a small amount to invest cannot secure the advantages of high interest and that safety which is afforded by a combination of various Securities, and it is questionable whether investors of anything under £10,000 can secure equal advantages to those offered by the principle of co-operation in investments carried out by Trusts and companies established for that purpose.*

"The principle of co-operation in investments by means of Trusts may be summed up thus :—Investors place their money in the hands of trustees, who use their experience and knowledge for the purpose of investing in a number of Securities so as to secure an average. The cost of management of the Trusts is generally limited to one-half per cent. on the amount subscribed, and this is really the cost to the investor for an insurance of a fixed interest, and of the greater security and profit derived from a greater number of investments than would be within his reach."

II.—"Trust" Associations are described by *Herapath's Journal* as having for object to place the investor of moderate means on the same footing as the large capitalist, by diminishing the risk of investment over a number of different Stocks, and reserving a portion of the extra interest as a sinking fund to pay off the original capital.

"Thus a capitalist investing a given sum in several Stocks, and using ordinary prudence, will, in a limited number of years, and by the plan indicated, have received back his original capital, in addition to a high rate of interest on his investments. To secure this object a Trust is formed, composed of persons who have subscribed an aggregate sum, which is lodged with the Trustees for the purchase of certain Securities specified in a Schedule annexed to the Trust Deed, the Trustees first deducting from the amount subscribed the cost of such purchase and all preliminary charges and expenses of the formation of the Trust. Certificates are then issued to the amount subscribed, each certificate being of the nominal value of £100, but issued at a prescribed discount, and to each certificate are attached coupons for interest for 25 years. In addition to, and part of these certificates, is also delivered a coupon of reversion, one such being issued with each certificate.

"The annual income of the scheduled Securities and moneys arising from the payment or redemption of same is applied under a Trust to the following purposes :—First, in payment of all expenses, incidental to the Trust, during the preceding year. Secondly, in payment of the interest on the nominal amount to the certificate holders, and thirdly, in the redemption at par of so many of the certificates as the surplus fund shall be competent to redeem. A drawing by lottery of the certificates to be redeemed is held annually, and due provision is also taken in the deed to meet any possible contingency arising from a deficiency to pay interest.

"Well administered and with a judicious selection of Securities by the trustees, Trusts are sure to prove successful undertakings. The extension of the principle to other classes of security than those embraced by the original scheme, makes it pretty evident that the introduction of this new financial element is looked upon with favour by investors.

"Whilst the sound principles adopted by the Foreign and Colonial Government Trust are adhered to, and every approach to speculative operations excluded, we believe that the Trust system is capable of almost unlimited extension, especially where the trustees are men of integrity and financial experience."

III.—In their first Annual Report, the Council of the *Corporation of Foreign Bondholders* (which numbers among its members financial notabilities of the highest rank, and is under the guidance of Mr. Hyde Clarke) remarked that:—

"Trusts offer, in conjunction with private investments, a useful mode of averaging operations in the case of the wealthier classes, while to small capitalists they give the means of making a safe beginning.

"As nothing can be more inadvisable than to stake all in one or two loans, the small holder prefers to resort to a Trust company. One result of the Trust companies is to spread a knowledge of such investments among the community, and this must greatly stimulate the employment of capital for such purposes. Some suppose that such engagements favour reckless speculation, but the experience of Holland is now found to meet with confirmation in this country, that the holders of Securities having high interest are led to cultivate habits of saving. Thus they not only provide against contingent hazards, but become accumulators of capital. A casual disaster arrives as a timely warning not to dissipate the promising income even of an old established Stock.

"The organisation of these large companies being conducted with intelligence, exercises a very great and salutary influence which will be the more felt in the future. As they are able to take a leading part in operations, they will be able to encourage the more deserving proposals for obtaining money by public subscription.

"The occasions which arise for co-operation with the Council and Committees give the general body the advantage of the counsel and assistance of the men of standing and ability who are engaged as Trustees or otherwise in the conduct of the affairs of these large institutions.

"It will be noticed that great corporations are growing up, which in their sympathies must be altogether allied with the bondholders, and give a new element of stability to the general body, and which even the co-operation of large individual bondholders did not so well afford."

IV.—The *Financier* warmly advocates the system of "Trusts":—

"The investor of the present day in many respects is in a much more favourable position for laying out his money safely and profitably than the investor of a few years ago. His wants are very much better provided for, both as regards the variety and the quality of the Securities offered to him. As regards investments, he has facilities for obtaining information which did not exist ten years ago. And he is unquestionably far shrewder and more careful in making his selections. The introduction of an entirely new form of investment within the last six years has undoubtedly met the requirements of a large class of persons, and has probably been the means of profitably employing money which would otherwise have been employed in some less secure manner. The rate of interest returned is so high that, except in the way carried out in this kind of investment, no Stock can be expected to return it without an amount of risk which a large class of investors would not be justified in accepting, although in a measure compelled to do so for the sake of obtaining a needed amount of income. The investments to which we refer are those known as 'Trusts.' The original idea has been gradually extended in different forms, until there are now few kinds of Stock dealt in on the Stock Exchange to which it has not been applied. The appreciation of these Trusts by the public is shown by the fact that most of them are quoted at prices very considerably above those at which they were originally issued.

"The investors to whom these Trusts are chiefly a boon are that very numerous class who require a return of more than 4 per cent. on their capital, but to whom a practically secure income is also of the utmost importance."

The *Financier* further observes that, "The investments which can now be purchased to pay 5 or 6 per cent. are of quite a different character to that required by the class of persons *who want absolute security* with a higher rate of interest than they know how to obtain. There are, indeed, a certain number of Securities which may be purchased to pay 5 per cent., and which are undoubtedly sound *bonâ fide* investments ; but there is risk attached to them, magnified by prejudice to undue proportions. These Securities are chiefly 'Foreign Government Loans' of the best class, 'American Government' and 'Railway Securities,' 'Foreign Railway Obligations,' and some others.

"From the increase in Investing Capital, Home Securities cannot be purchased to pay even 5 per cent., unless the shares of Joint-Stock Companies be selected, which are rarely entitled to favour. Colonial Government Bonds were formerly a favourite investment, being to some extent connected with the country, but now these Securities have risen to prices at which the return is less than 5 per cent.

"Investors who now require 6 per cent. for their money must incur *some* risk, and the risk to individuals now is perhaps greater in proportion to the rate of interest than it was formerly.

"The Trusts in many cases have valuable reversions attached to them, which become payable when the whole of the certificates have been paid off. In the cases where the market values of the Trusts are above par, it is of course a disadvantage for a holder to be paid off at par, and investors who purchase at prices above par must allow for this in calculating the return on their money. For persons who have not the necessary knowledge and experience to make a selection of a number of Stocks for themselves on this plan, the Trusts are most appropriate and useful."

---

*Section 3.—Of the Usefulness of a Trust.*

ART. 7.—The usefulness of an *Average Investment Trust* to inexperienced individuals is suggested indeed by noticing the great increase in Stock Exchange securities of late years.

This is shown by the *London Daily Stock and Share List*, issued "under the authority of the committee of the Stock Exchange," which, in consequence, is commonly called the *Official List*, and has two or three times been enlarged within a very few years. Twenty years ago the *Stock and Share List* consisted of but one page, while it now has four.

The list, as it now appears, presents a very large number of various kinds of securities, many of which it would have been almost impossible to have thought of twenty years ago. The amount is of astounding magnitude. From the *Economist* can be reckoned an approximate total as follows :—

|  |  | £ |
|---|---|---|
| 1. British Government Securities | - - - | 779,283,245 |
| 2. Foreign and Colonial Government Securities | - | 2,388,032,586 |
| 3. Railway Companies - - - - | - | 1,258,840,146 |
| 4. Banking ,, (subscribed capital) | - - | 170,182,672 |
| 5. Finance ,, ,, ,, | - - | 27,312,610 |
| 6. Insurance ,, ,, ,, | - - | 79,633,632 |
| 7. Mining ,, ,, ,, | - - | 21,062,745 |
| 8. Miscellaneous ,, ,, ,, | - - | 205,441,430 |
| 9. Trust Associations ,, ,, | - - | 32,131,640 |
|  | Total | £4,961,920,706 |

8.—The same authority observes, that the *different kinds* of Stocks are also very numerous, making it very difficult for an investor with this immense variety before him, even if he be possessed of a fair knowledge of such matters, to make a wise selection, while, in the case of ordinary persons, almost entirely destitute of any such knowledge, the task is nearly a hopeless one. The *Economist* further adds :—

"A little knowledge is a dangerous thing. This is certainly true with regard to persons who, knowing a little about the 'ins and outs' of Stock Exchange dealings, enter into purchases on vague and uncertain grounds. Purchases based on the probable course or present condition of the Stock Markets, irrespective of the merits of any particular Security, must always be most uncertain and hazardous; and when based on the condition, or apparent condition, of the market for some one Stock regardless of its merits, can very rarely be successfully carried out by anyone outside of the Stock Exchange."

9.—The able financier, who writes in the journal of that name, makes some important comments on securities yielding *variable* rates of dividend. He remarks that persons, whose incomes are such that a decrease is to be carefully avoided, require securities that pay *fixed* rates of interest. Sometimes they imprudently embark in stocks that pay " Variable " dividends, but which have so long continued to pay the same rate of interest year after year that they have at length come to be regarded as paying " Fixed " dividends.\* Fluctuations, however, arise from many different causes, according to the nature of the enterprise represented. If the Income is to be secure, many classes of stocks must be avoided. Most of the trouble and many of the losses arising from investments made in securities unsuited to the requirements of particular cases, have proceeded through purchases having been made at times when appearances strongly favoured the idea that everything was particularly safe and smooth. People do not, in questions of investment, go against the opinion of the great majority of the dealers and operators; on the contrary, they generally follow that opinion. This opinion being sometimes wrong, investors who have left their legitimate securities to follow a reputed " certainty " in some other direction, become heavy losers.

10.—On the other hand, financial mutability is increased by the periodical influences of the commercial cycle. There is a conspicuous alternation in trade (whatever may be the reason) between periods of prosperity and periods of adversity. According to the common saying there are " five fat years in the money market and five lean years." The *Financier* observes :—

" If then things go the reverse of smoothly for such a concern—the value of Money being maintained at a high level, Trade being slack, there being perhaps a War, or other events affecting trade unfavourably—then the result is that the Income derived from this class of investments diminishes, and their value falls in the market.

" If the investors, who purchased these Stocks, were wealthy capitalists, or an associated body like a Trust, they would probably wait until circumstances were more favourable for the enterprise. But if they be persons who require

---

[\* A notable instance of this was presented in 1875 by the large losses experienced by the leading Joint Stock Banks through deception in respect to bills discounted.]

a *regular* income from the money so laid out, whether the results gave a profit or a loss, the transaction could not be considered as a proper and legitimate one even *for them*, but would more correctly be described as a rash speculation. But, supposing the income to be reduced, and the capital invested lowered in value, it is evident that the individual holder's condition would be a sad one. His income, which before was not large, is reduced, his capital—for the time at least—partly lost, and, in addition, he is beset by doubts and fears as to what is best to be done—whether he had better sell at once, or wait for the chance of the Stock recovering."

11.—It is the common practice for investors to judge of the probable income to be derived in the future by taking the dividends paid for the last few years as the basis of their calculations. Estimates made on this plan must, of course, have a great deal of uncertainty about them, and they are rarely sufficiently probable to justify the class of investors referred to in laying out their money in stocks that yield variable dividends. However safe the income from such sources may appear to be, there are so many contingencies that may arise to falsify the most careful calculations, that it can never be regarded as other than uncertain, and as partaking in a great measure of a speculative character. The cause which reduces the income, of course, also lowers the Market Value of the capital from which the income is derived; and so, at the same time, the income falls off, and the capital can only be exchanged into another investment at a great sacrifice.

The evils of speculation have been thus exposed :—

"If some investors think twice before they take their money out of the English Funds and employ it in more remunerative Securities, there are others who are much too anxious to select Speculative Investments in preference to sound and steady ones. There is a very large class of people who yearly fritter away their savings on the Stock Exchange. Many of these people, indeed, not only lose their savings, but partially or altogether ruin themselves. Nothing, apparently, but sharp experience will teach them the folly of Speculating, and the certainty of ultimate loss arising from their operations. It is chiefly amongst people of moderate means, and who have accumulated small amounts by savings from their businesses, trades, or salaries, that the class of Speculators to which we refer are generally to be found. The mistake is commenced by the savings being transferred from the English Funds into some Speculative Security, with the idea that the amount may be increased by a rise in price. The sum is too small to render the difference in the rates of interest of any importance. This step once taken, the operator becomes in spirit a Speculator, and it is probably not long before he discovers that it is quite as easy to buy without having the money to pay for the Stock, as it is to confine his purchases to the extent of his spare money. A rise of 1 per cent. perhaps gives him a profit of £5 on the £500 Stock he has bought and taken up; within a few days, if so, his thought is, 'If I had had £5,000 instead of £500, I should have made £50 instead of £5!' After that, he soon becomes a confirmed Speculator, probably dealing in more thousands of Stock than he has hundreds of pounds. His ultimate ruin, unless he has sense enough to leave off before he has lost everything, could never for a moment be a matter of doubt."

12.—Apart from the certainty of loss, resulting from inexperience, it has become obvious of late years that some sort of co-operative protection is very requisite to protect the individual against associated speculators. These associations of unscrupulous persons are formed with the design of depressing as "Bears" or raising as "Bulls," the prices of stocks far out of the range of their legitimate fluctuation, whether with regard to their intrinsic merit, or the state of the money market.

PART I.—*continued.*

CONTENTS.

CHAPTER I.—*The Original Trust of* 1868.
,, II.—*Names and Details of other Existing Trusts.*
,, III.—*Of some Defects in Existing Trusts.*

CHAPTER I.

THE ORIGINAL TRUST.

*Section* 1.—*The Prospectus of* 1868.

ART. 13.—The first Trust of any importance for the purpose of buying Stock Exchange Securities was founded in 1868, when the following Prospectus appeared on the 21st March :—

" The Foreign and Colonial Government Trust, in Certificates of £100 each, bearing 6 per cent. interest. To be issued at £85.

" I.—The object of this Trust is to give the *investor of moderate means the same advantages as the large Capitalist,* in diminishing the risk of investing in Foreign and Colonial Government Stocks, by spreading the investment over a number of different Stocks, and reserving a portion of the extra interest as a Sinking fund to pay off the original capital.

" A capitalist, who at any time within the last 20 or 30 years had invested, say £1,000,000 in ten or twelve such Stocks, selected with ordinary prudence would, on the above plan, not only have received a High rate of Interest, but by this time have received back his original capital by the action of the Drawings and Sinking fund, and held the *greater part of his Stocks for nothing.*

" Some parties, believing it would be a convenience to the public if such a mode of Investment were made generally accessible, have made arrangements by which well selected Government Stocks, to the value of £1,000,000 sterling, will be placed in the names of the following Trustees, viz.:—

" The Right Hon. Lord Westbury ; The Lord Eustace Cecil, M.P.; G. M. W. Sandford, Esq., M.P.; George Woodhouse Currie, Esq. ; and Philip Rose, Esq."

# THE PROSPECTUS OF 1868.

" II.—The following Stocks, being all Dividend-paying Stocks of Foreign or Colonial Governments, currently dealt in on the London Stock Exchange, have been selected for the Investment, viz. :—Austrian, Australian, Argentine, Canadian, Brazilian, Chilian, Danubian, Egyptian, Italian, Nova Scotian, Peruvian, Portuguese, Russian, Spanish, Turkish, and United States Ten-Forties payable in gold; not more than £100,000 *being invested* in the Stock of any one Government.

"These Stocks will be made over to the Trust at the prices quoted in the *Official List* of 18th March, as certified by two eminent Brokers, plus £2. 10s. for each £100 of Stock, for which all expenses of the purchase and issue, including stamps, &c., have been undertaken.

" The prices and specific amounts of each Stock are specified in the Schedule to the Contract and Trust Deed.

" The average rate of Interest of the Investment in the above Stocks is 8 per cent., and a large number of them, purchased considerably below par, will be repayable by Drawings at par, within the period of the Trust.

" Against this investment of £1,000,000 will be issued 11,765 Certificates of £100 each, with half-yearly Coupons bearing £6 per cent. interest payable at the Banking-house of Messrs. Glyn, Mills, Currie, and Co., 1st March and 1st September, the first Coupon falling due on 1st September next.

" *The Price of Issue will be £85 per cent., thus yielding an Annual Interest of 7 per cent., without reckoning the advantage of being repaid at par, and without including the value of the Reversion of the Stocks purchased.*

" The Excess of Interest, after paying the 7 per cent. interest to the Subscribers (on their £85), and the amount received from Drawings, will, after payment of Expenses, be applied as a Sinking fund in repaying the Certificates at par by annual Drawings, which are to be made in the presence of a Notary Public in the month of February in each year."

" III.—According to a Table prepared by an Actuary the whole of the 11,765 Certificates will, in all probability, be thus paid off in 24 years, and there will remain Stocks to the amount of £909,409, nominal capital, for distribution as a Reversion : accordingly the Trust will be wound up as soon as all the Certificates have been drawn, or at the end of 24 years, whichever shall first happen; the remaining Stocks being then sold, and the remaining Certificates, if any, paid off.

" In addition to the Coupons for the Half-yearly Interest, a Coupon, representing the Share accruing to the Certificate holder in the above Reversion, will be attached to each Certificate. This Coupon of Reversion will be retained by the holder when his Certificate is drawn.

"The arrangements thus made will secure the following advantages to the Subscribers:—
1. *Interest at 7 per cent. on the amount subscribed.*
2. *A Bonus of 15 per cent., by the repayment of Capital at par within 24 years.*
3. *A Reversion, calculated [if the above £1,000,000 be all invested], at upwards of £900,000 nominal capital, eventually divisible among the Subscribers.*

" If by the default or delay of any Foreign Government the Dividends and Drawings received in any year should be insufficient to pay the full amount of Interest on the Certificates, the Deficiency will form a first charge upon the subsequent Receipts, subject only to the annual allowance for expenses."

" IV.—The object being to give the fullest confidence in the security of the Trust fund, the Stocks will remain, under the control of the Trustees, at the Bank of Messrs. Glyn, Mills, Currie, and Co., till the termination of the Trust, and the Trustees will be empowered to draw Dividends, receive Capital repaid &c., and apply the amount received in Interest and Sinking fund according to the Trust Deed.

" A power of sale, under special circumstances, will be vested in the Trustees and a Committee of Certificate-holders, to be chosen at general meetings, held annually for the purpose, and for receiving a report and accounts from the Trustees. Auditors at the same time will be appointed to make periodical inspections of the Securities of the Trust, and any vacancies in the Trust will be filled up.

" *The ordinary expenses of management of the Trust are limited to a sum not exceeding £2,500 per annum. No other expenses can be undertaken without the assent of the Certificate-holders' Committee.*"

" V.—Within two months after the closing of the Subscription a General Meeting of the Certificate-holders will be convened, for the purpose of appointing a Committee, in terms of the Trust Deed.

" Application must be made on the annexed form, accompanied by a deposit of £10 per cent.

" In cases where no Allotment is made the Deposits will be returned without deduction, and where the Certificates allotted are less than the number applied for the surplus Deposits will be credited towards the allotment.

" Payments to be made as follows:—

| | |
|---|---|
| On application | £10 |
| On Allotment | 5 |
| 15th April | 25 |
| 15th May | 25 |
| 15th June | 20 |
| | £85 |

"Subscribers may anticipate their payments on the days when any of the instalments fall due, being allowed a discount at the rate of £4 per cent. per annum."

"VI.—The Contract provides for the delivery of the Stocks on the 30th March from which date the account will bear Interest at £4 per cent. per annum until the purchase is completed.

"Provisional Certificates will be issued on Allotment, and the final Certificates with Interest Coupons attached, and also the Coupons of Reversion, will be issued immediately after payment of the final Instalment.

"As *the principle of the measure* does not depend on the amount subscribed, if *a substantial part* only of the £1,000,000 should be allotted, the arrangement will be carried out with a *pro ratâ* reduction of the amount of each Stock made over to the Trust.

"As the payments are received from the subscribers by the Bankers, they will be exchanged for Stocks, to be handed over to the Trustees."

---

*Section 2.—The first Contract and subsequent Issues.*

ART. 14.—The *contract* for the first issue of this Trust was according to the following Schedule:—

| Description of Stock. | Amount of Stock. | Price at which Stock was sold to the Trust. |
|---|---|---|
| Argentine 6 per cents. | £52,900 | 75½ |
| Austrian 5 per cents. | 88,200 | 68 |
| Brazilian 5 per cents., 1865 | 46,800 | 74¾ |
| Chilian 6 per cents. | 54,600 | 91½ |
| Chilian 7 per cents. | 50,200 | 99½ |
| Danubian 8 per cents. | 83,200 | 72 |
| Egyptian 7 per cents., 1864 | 55,400 | 90¼ |
| Egyptian Railway Loan 7 per cent. | 53,300 | 94 |
| Italian 5 per cents., 1861 | 201,000 | 49¾ |
| New South Wales 5 per cents. | 15,100 | 99 |
| Nova Scotia 6 per cents. | 34,700 | 102¼ |
| Peruvian 5 per cents. | 124,200 | 80½ |
| Portuguese 3 per cents. | 119,700 | 41¾ |
| Russian Anglo - Dutch Bonds Fl. 1,070,000 | 90,682 | 88¼ |
| Spanish New 3 per cents. | 259,590 | 38½ |
| Turkish 5 per cents. | 166,000 | 36⅛ |
| Turkish 6 per cents. | 69,200 | 57¾ |
| United States 10-40 Bonds | 36,225 | 68⅞ |
| Total | £1,600,997 | |

15.—Only\* £588,300 of the above was issued, in Bonds at 85 per cent. The amount (July, 1874), was reduced by Drawings to £417,600. In subsequent years new issues were made in this Trust, and the figures put together stand thus :—

| | £ | | | | | | | | | |
|---|---|---|---|---|---|---|---|---|---|---|
| 1868. | 588,300 | in shares of | £100 | bearing | 6 | per cent., | issued at | 85, | highest price in 1875. | 104 |
| 1870. | 600,000 | ,, | £100 | ,, | 5 | ,, | ,, | 80 | ,, ,, | 94 |
| 1871. | 1,000,000 | ,, | £100 | ,, | 6 | ,, | ,, | 92 | ,, ,, | 100 |
| 1872. | 500,000 | ,, | £100 | ,, | 6 | ,, | ,, | 95 | ,, ,, | 105 |
| 1872. | 750,000 | ,, | £100 | ,, | 5 | ,, | ,, | 88 | ,, ,, | 92 |
| | £3,438,300 | | | | | | | | | |

In each Trust the management expenses were restricted to £2,500 a year, or £12,500 a year for the whole; also in order to fix the amount *of preliminary expenses*, a contract was entered into by which every expense was guaranteed, (including advertisements, *ad valorem* and other stamps, legal and all other expenses, and the costs of purchasing the stocks) at a commission of 2½ *per cent. on the nominal amount of stocks purchased* in the first issue, and from 1½ to 2 per cent. in the later issues.

---

\* *Fluctuation in Prices.*

[1.—As a specimen of fluctuation in prices, the Turkish 5 per cent. Stock was fixed at the price of 36½ on the 21st March, 1868, when the first issue of the Trust was brought out. They rose to 53 in Midsummer, 1873, and at March 1874, they fell to 39½.—During 1866, Turkish Bonds of 1862 touched 48, and the following year they recovered to 65.

2.—Another instance of extreme fluctuation is shown in Mr. Cracroft's valuable chart of the course of the Italian 5 per cent. Stock, which was issued in 1851 at 85, and rose to 103 in 1852, was 94 in 1853, fell to 40 in 1867, was 47 in 1870, and rose to 71 in May, 1875. During the panic of the year 1866 this Italian Stock fell to 35¼, and recovering to 40 in the following year it touched 54⅝.

3.—The fluctuation in prices of other Foreign Government Securities have been very considerable during the last ten years, and it is only lately that the holders have seen a prospect of a recovery of what looked a serious loss in the years 1865 and 1866. During 1870, Portuguese bonds were marked 25, and the following year 39. Russian Five per Cents. 1870 touched 78½, and in 1871 91¾. Colonial Government securities, also, have risen steadily, and perhaps the reason of this may be traced to the fact that, while colonial loans have been raised to prosecute works of improvement, foreign loans have been largely negotiated for the mere purpose of covering deficits.

The following are fourteen years' prices of Government Stocks (from the official lists) :—

| | July 3, 1862. | July 3, 1867. | July 2, 1872. | July 1, 1875. |
|---|---|---|---|---|
| Consols | 91¾ | 94½ | 92½ | 93⅝ |
| India 5 per Cents. | 108½ | 110 | 109 | 106½ |
| Canadian 6 per Cents. | 106 | 97 | 107 | 105½ |
| New South Wales 5 per Cents. | 99 | 89 | 104 | 102½ |
| Victoria 6 per Cents., 1883 | 107 | 109 | 115 | 111½ |
| Brazilian 4½ per Cents. | 90 | 65 | 90 | 97 |
| Buenos Ayres 6 per Cents. | 95 | 82 | 100 | 89 |
| Chilian 4½ per Cents. | 84 | 70 | 90 | 83 |
| Dutch 4 per Cents. | 101 | — | 88 | 100½ |
| Do. 2½ per Cents. | 64 | 54 | 57 | 64¼ |
| Italian 5 per Cents. | 70 | 49 | 68 | 72½ |
| Mexican 3 per Cents. | 28½ | 16 | 15 | 14½ |
| Portuguese 3 per Cents. | 45½ | 41 | 41½ | 53 |
| Russian 5 per Cents. | 96 | 87 | 93 | 102 |
| Do. 3 per Cents. | 59 | 54 | 63 | 72 |
| Spanish 3 per Cents. | 55 | 36 | 30 | 19 |
| Sardinian 5 per Cents. | 82 | 71 | 78 | 86 |
| Turkish 6 per Cents., 1854 | 84 | 79 | 89 | 89 |
| Do. 6 per Cents., 1858 | 71 | 58 | 70 | 61 |
| United States 5 per Cents., 1874 | 76 | — | 91 | — |
| Venezuela 3 per Cents. | 24 | 21 | 19 | 8 |

4.—Fluctuation even in the English Funds occurs within wide limits.

Taking the result of an investment in the English Funds made about ten years ago. The average price of Consols for the year 1864 was 89½. An investment made at that price would pay interest at the rate of £3. 7*s*. per cent. The investor will of course have received this rate during the ten years with regularity, and without any anxiety as to its receipt or as to the safety of his capital. Were the capital now to be realised, there would be a profit of 5¼ per cent. on the amount of stock. At one period of the ten years, however, the stock might have been sold at 96¼, which would have given a profit of 6¾ per cent.; and at another time it was worth in the market only 84½, which showed an apparent loss of 5 per cent.

So in Railways, London and North-Western Railway Stock fell to 112¾ in 1866, and rose to 125 in 1867. National Discount Shares, after receding to 2 prem. in 1866, rose to 10 prem. in 1867. Midland Railway Stock rose from 119 in 1870 to 140 in 1871. And London, Chatham, and Dover Railway Stock advanced from 11½ in 1870 to 28 in 1871.]

## Section 3.—*Progress of the original Trusts.*

ART. 16.—The Certificate Bonds of the five different issues of the "*Foreign and Colonial Government Trust*" have well maintained their prices, although the securities with which these trusts are concerned have, with very few exceptions, occasionally fallen heavily in value, and several governments have ceased to pay the interest due. It affords proof that the system of averaging investments is a sound one, and that these particular trusts have not been drawn into the circle of speculation. They show that a trust can secure to its members an "Average" income without the risk attending isolated purchases.

17.—The Report of the *First* Foreign and Colonial Government Trust in March 1874, illustrates this:—

"The gross receipts for the year were £36,874, including £25,627 received as interest on Securities held by the Trust, and £11,091 from Government Drawings.

"The payments were £25,956 as interest, at 6 per cent., on 4,266 certificates, including the coupons due on the 1st March; £9,000 for redemption of 90 certificates at par; £2,276 for expenses of the Trust, leaving a balance of £3 to be carried forward. It may be observed that the only default at that time was in respect of *Spanish* 3 per cent. Stock, no interest having been received for the June or December coupons; the arrears then were £3,211, and have augmented by the non-payment of Spanish Dividends since."

The seventh annual general meeting of the 1st issue of the Foreign and Colonial Government Trust was held in 1875, Mr. G. W. Currie in the chair, who said that :—" Of the 5,883 certificates issued to the public at 85, 1,745 had been drawn and paid off, partly from the surplus income, but mainly from the proceeds of drawn bonds. To pay off these 1,745 certificates at par, had required £174,500, and as the certificates were issued at 85 and were paid off at 100, the certificate-holders, whose bonds were drawn, had received £26,175 as premium, in addition to the interest which had been regularly paid."

18.—At the Meeting in 1875, of the shareholders of the Fourth Issue, the Chairman, Mr Currie, said :—

"The feature in the report which principally called for attention was the Securities in default, which were the Alabama Eight per Cent. State Bonds, 1870; the City of Mobile Eight per Cent. (Alabama); Louisiana Eight per Cent. State Bonds; Louisiana Six per Cent. State Bonds; and Spanish Three per Cents. These were serious defaults, and he did not know that the Trustees could give more information upon them than was accessible to the public at large. As regarded the *Spanish*, after arrangements with successive Finance Ministers, an arrangement had been come to, the nature of which was probably known to all the bondholders. Under that agreement the bondholders, for every £100 overdue coupons, would receive about one-third in Rio Tinto Pagarés, and the other two-thirds in Three per Cent. Spanish Stock at 40—a composition which, it was considered, would give about 10s. or 12s. in the pound. As regarded *Alabama*, the Trustees had learned that commissioners had been appointed by the Legislature to inquire into the indebtedness of the State (of which they profess themselves ignorant), and those commissioners were empowered to draw up a plan for compromise, which would have to receive the sanction of the Legislature. The number of the bonds held by this Trust had been sent over there. As regarded *Louisiana*, the debt of that State was in an *unsatisfactory* state at present. There was a proposition made some time since, which amounted to nothing less than confiscation, and no further proposition had since been made; but he would express his own confidence that these unpaid sums would not permanently remain unpaid. He could not believe that in a country with such a power of extension and undeveloped wealth, with room for an industrious and growing population, and where the people were of English descent, that the State creditors would be allowed to be permanently thrown over. The Republican party now seem to be supplanted by a party with more moderate views, and he hoped their return to power would be accompanied by a return of that justice which was characteristic of Anglo-American communities. *In spite of these defaults, the Trustees had paid the interest in full together with the expenses, and drawn fifty-three certificates during the year, which had been paid off at par.* If the Spanish composition turned out to be 10s. in the pound, it would yield £1,500, which would be sufficient to draw fifteen more certificates. If all the Securities had been paid in full, the income would have been £4,099 more than it had been during the past year. If that had been achieved, there would have been a margin of income over the amount required to pay the interest on the Securities of £1,856, instead of which the accounts showed that there had been a deficiency of about £2,240, which had to be made up out of the annual drawings. This might be considered, to some extent, as borrowed from capital. This Trust was founded in 1872, and was divided into 5,000 certificates, 174 of which had been drawn at par, the holders of which had received £870 in dividends. As regarded the future, he did not think anything had happened to invalidate the principle upon which the Trust was founded in 1872; on the contrary, the fact that they had been able to do what they had done, in spite of the temporary default in two or three of the Securities, showed the soundness of the principle upon which the Trust was founded."

19.—At the meeting of the Shareholders of the Fifth Issue, the Chairman stated that:—"The income from the Securities had been sufficient to pay the interest on the certificates and all expenses, and showed a surplus of £2,500. Seventy-four certificates had been redeemed at par. The revenue account showed that the income for the year was £47,114. The reserve for the half-year ending December 15 last was £18,708.

"He congratulated the certificate-holders on the highly satisfactory condition of the Trust. The surplus of income alone, without taking into account the drawings, had been £2,500 over the sum required for the expenses of the Trust; but in that £2,500 there was a sum of £800 not properly belonging to the receipts of the year. Deducting this, however, there was an actual surplus of £1,700. The only default in the Securities of the trust was on the Spanish Three per Cents., amounting to £3,034. The actual arrear in Spanish Three per Cents. amounted to £6,069. The Trust originally consisted of 7,500 certificates, issued at 88; and although they had not been at work two complete years, they had drawn ninety-one certificates which had been paid off at par. The holders of these certificates had, therefore, received among them a bonus of £1,092. Notwithstanding the default on the Spanish investments, the actual selling value of their Securities was many thousand pounds more than when the investments were made. The £70,000 invested in the 5 per cent. French Rentes showed a rise in value of rather more than £11,000. It was quite clear, however, that if the events went on smoothly in France a large profit would be realised."

CHAPTER II.

OF EXISTING TRUSTS—*continued.*

*Section 1.—Names with Details of Capital and Leading Features.*

ART. 20.—Since 1868, several other *Average Investment Funds* have been established. Some under the legal form of trusts, while in others registration under the companies' acts has been preferred, and they have become " Limited Liability Associations," the impression being that the latter is generally the best form for the management, as there are dangers to trustees lurking behind their legal status, which may hereafter prove serious, should any neglect or mistake in carrying out its provisions be found to have occurred.

The following is a list of all the more important Trust Associations. It shows by the magnitude of capital invested, and by the high standing of the Trustees and Managing Committees, the increasing confidence entertained in these undertakings :—

*Names of Trustees and Managing Committees.*

| Name. | No. of Trusts to which each belongs. | Name. | No. of Trusts to which each belongs. |
|---|---|---|---|
| Abraham, A. B., Esq. | 1 | Brady, Sir Antonio | 1 |
| Alderson, E. P., Esq. | 1 | Bremner, John A., Esq. | 1 |
| Anderson, Sir James | 2 | Brown, John, Esq. | 1 |
| Andrew, W. P. Esq. | 1 | Burton, James, Esq. | 1 |
| Barlow, Arthur P., Esq. | 1 | Calhoun, P. C., Esq. | 1 |
| Barnard, Geo., Esq. | 1 | Callender, Wm. R., Esq. | 1 |
| Bayman, R. Esq. | 1 | Cater, John, Esq. | 1 |
| Beadon, Sir Cecil, K.C.S.I. | 1 | Cecil, Lord Eustace, M.P. | 2 |
| Bennoch, F., Esq. | 2 | Clerihew, Geo., Esq. | 1 |
| Best, Capt., the Hon. | 1 | Clews, Henry, Esq. | 1 |
| Bentinck, G. C., Esq., M.P. | 1 | Cox, T. H., Esq. | 1 |
| Beer, Julius, Esq. | 1 | Currie, G. W., Esq. | 2 |
| Blane, Sir Seymour, C.B. | 1 | Devon, Rt. Hon. Earl of | 1 |
| Bowyer, Sir. Geo., Bart. | 1 | Drummond, H. E., Esq. | 1 |

# NAMES OF TRUSTEES AND DIRECTORS.

| Name. | No. of Trusts to which each belongs. | Name. | No. of Trusts to which each belongs. |
|---|---|---|---|
| Dyer, C. K., Esq., J.P. | 2 | Macpherson, D., Esq. | 1 |
| Elder, Geo., Esq. | 1 | Maitland, G. G., Esq. | 1 |
| Elibank, Rt. Hon. Lord | 1 | Mar, Rt. Hon. Earl of | 1 |
| Elliott, Sir G., Bart., M.P. | 1 | Martin, R. B., Esq. | 2 |
| Evens, J. H., Esq. | 1 | Massey, Rt. Hon. W. N., M.P. | 1 |
| Field, Cyrus W., Esq. | 1 | Moring, Thos., Esq. | 1 |
| Fitzwilliam, Hon. C. W. W., M.P. | 2 | Monck, Rt. Hon. Viscount | 1 |
| Fitzgerald, Rt. Hon. Sir S., G.C.S.I. | 1 | Mulkern, E. C., Esq. | 1 |
| Ford, W., Esq. | 1 | Mundella, A. J., Esq., M.P. | 1 |
| Fowler, F. H., Esq. | 1 | Murray, Sir John, Bart. | 1 |
| Fowler, R. N., Esq., M.P. | 2 | Otway, A., Esq., M.P. | 1 |
| Friend, Hy. Saml., Esq. | 1 | Paget, Rt. Hon. Lord Alfred | 1 |
| Fremantle, Hon. Thomas F. | 1 | Palliser, Major Sir W., C.B. | 1 |
| Gibbons, Sir S. J., Bart. | 4 | Patterson, John, Esq. | 1 |
| Giffard, J. C., Esq. | 1 | Pelly, Capt. R. W., R.N. | 2 |
| Goodricke, Sir H. II., Bart. | 1 | Pender, John, Esq., M.P. | 4 |
| Goodson, James, Esq. | 2 | Pré-Grenfell, P. Du | 1 |
| Gooch, Sir Daniel, Bart., M.P. | 1 | Raikes, Henry Cecil, Esq. | 1 |
| Grey, Sir William, K.C.S.I. | 1 | Ravenscroft, H. Esq. | 1 |
| Grosvenor, Geo., Esq. | 1 | Rawson, Philip, Esq. | 1 |
| Guild, John, Esq. | 1 | Rayner R., Esq. | 1 |
| Habicht, C. E., Esq. | 1 | Riddell, Francis, Esq. | 1 |
| Harrison, R. P., Esq., C.S.I. | 1 | Rolls, Edward J., Esq. | 1 |
| Harvey, E. A., Esq. | 1 | Rose, Sir Philip, Bart. | 4 |
| Hartley, J., Esq. | 1 | Ross, Edwd., Esq. | 1 |
| Hawes, Wm., Esq., F.G.S. | 1 | Runtz, John, Esq. | 1 |
| Hay, Rt. Hon. Lord W. M. | 2 | Ryder, Granville R., Esq., M.P. | 1 |
| Hay, Lord John | 1 | Sandford, G. M. W., Esq., M.P. | 2 |
| Headlam. Rt. Hon. T. E., M.P. | 1 | Sebay, Joseph, Esq. | 1 |
| Hester, John Cooke, Esq. | 1 | Sharp, John, Esq. | 1 |
| Heyworth, Major L. | 2 | Shields, F. W., Esq., M.I.C.E. | 1 |
| Hind, Henry Chas., Esq. | 1 | Smith, Thos., Esq. | 1 |
| Hornby, Admiral W. W. | 1 | Surtees, C. F. Esq. | 1 |
| Isbister, A. K., Esq. | 1 | Talbot, J. G., Esq., M.P. | 1 |
| Johnston, A., Esq., M.P. | 2 | Taylor, Wm. L., Esq. | 1 |
| Jones, Wm., Esq. | 1 | Thwaites, Wm., Esq. | 1 |
| Jeune, Francis, Esq. | 1 | Trewhella, H. E., Esq., M.D. | 1 |
| Kennedy, Matthew, Esq. | 1 | Trotter, W., Esq. | 1 |
| Kinnaird, Hon. A., M.P. | 3 | Vaughan, General, C.B. | 1 |
| Laing, M. A., Esq. | 3 | Walker, Wm., Esq. | 1 |
| Laing, S., Esq., M.P. | 2 | Walpole, Hon. F., M.P. | 1 |
| Leeman, Geo., Esq., M.P. | 2 | Watkin, Sir E. W., M.P. | 2 |
| Leggatt, Daniel, Esq., LL.D. | 1 | Wetherill, Chas., Esq. | 1 |
| Lewis, C. E., Esq., M.P. | 3 | Wilbraham, R. W., Esq. | 1 |
| Lloyd, John H., Esq. | 4 | Wood, Alex., Esq. | 1 |
| Lord, Walter J., Esq. | 1 | Wythes, G. E., Esq. | 2 |
| Mackenzie, R., Esq. | 1 | | |

*Names and particulars of existing Trusts.*

I.—June, 1871.—The Submarine Cables Trust, capital £1,000,000 in shares of £100 issued at £90.

---

II.—Jan. 1872.—The Government Stock Investment Company (Limited).

1st Issue. Capital £1,000,000 in Shares of £100, bearing 6 per cent. interest, issued at par.

June, 1872.—The Government Stock Investment Company (Limited.)

2nd Issue. Capital £1,000,000 in Shares of £20, bearing 6 per cent. interest, issued at par.

Jan. 1873.—The Government Stock Investment Company (Limited).

3rd Issue of 7,137 Shares (being the remainder of 25,000 Shares) of £20 each, bearing 6 per cent. interest, issued at par.

The amount of preliminary expenses are fixed by contract, under which every expense is guaranteed, including advertising, printing, brokerage, *ad valorem* and other stamps, legal and all and every expense up to the date of allotment of the Shares of the Company, and also all expenses which the Company may incur in purchasing and transferring the Stocks or guaranteed undertakings on which the capital is to be invested at a commission of £2 per cent. on the nominal amount of Stocks purchased.

At the general meeting of the shareholders, held in March, 1875, the chairman called attention to the continuously prosperous condition of the Company last year which had resulted in a net balance in favour of £46,837 2s. 4d., which enabled them to pay the dividend of 6 per cent. for the year, amounting to £34,139 17s. From the balance remaining the directors had placed £3,000 to the reserve fund, raising it to £10,000, and carrying forward £8,834.

---

III.—Feb. 1872.—The Share Investment Trust.

Capital £500,000 to £2,000,000 (£560,000 subscribed) in Shares of £100, bearing 6 per cent. interest, issued at par, and redeemable at £110. Formation expenses, limited to 2 per cent. on the price of Securities purchased or taken over, and management expenses to £2,500 per annum.

It is stated of this Trust, "that the original cost of the Securities held by the Trust, at March 1874, was £558,290 8s. 2d.; of this total it is estimated the amount not yielding revenue is £31,363 3s. 2d; leaving as present amount of productive capital £526,927 5s. The present selling price of the Certificate is as follows :—5,525 Preferred Certificates (75 having been drawn and paid off at 68, £375,700; 5,600 Deferred Certificates at 7, £39,200; total £414,900—that is to say, the selling price of the whole of the Preferred and Deferred Certificates at the present time is £414,900, while the estimated amount of the productive capital held by the Trust is £526,927, showing an apparent depreciation of value in the securities held by the Trust to the extent of £112,027." To pay the 6 per cent. interest on the Preference Certificates, it is reported that the value should be, " Preferred Certificates £76 2s.; Deferred Certificates, £19 0s. 6d." The paying off of the Preference Certificates from revenue increases value of the Deferred; the Preferred Certificates, at the market price, pay an investor 9 per cent., added to the chance of a drawing at the price of £110 per Certificate.

The report of the Trustees to the fourth yearly meeting of Certificate-holders, 10th May, 1875, stated—"No dividend has been received on four of the original investments.

"The revenue received up to March 15 was £38,722 8s. 3d., from which is deducted £2,300 for expenses of the Trust, and £33,150 for the 6 per cent. interest on the Preference Certificates, leaving £3,190 for the redemption of 29 Certificates at £110 each, which, with the 75 already redeemed, make a total of 104 Certificates cancelled."

Mr. Abbott states that the Share Investment Trust Preferred Certificates at £76 pay 8 per cent., while the usual drawing at £110 takes place in April, also, that a careful examination of the property of the Trust gives a clear value of £83 per Preferred Certificate, and about £12 for the Deferred, quoted at £10.

---

## IV.—June 1872.—The Governments and Guaranteed Securities Permanent Trust.

1st Issue. Capital £1,000,000, in Shares of £100, bearing 6 per cent. interest, issued at £94.

April 1874.—2nd Issue. Capital £1,000,000, in Shares of £10, £50, £100, £500, issued at the rate of £84 for each £100 Share, and bearing Interest at the rate of £5 19s. per cent.

"The working expenses of the Trust are restricted to an annual sum not exceeding in any one year one-half per cent. of the nominal amount of the Fund subscribed. The Trustees have signed a contract under which all preliminary expenses, inclusive of brokerage on the original purchases, stamps, advertisements, legal expenses, and all charges are undertaken for 1½ per cent. on the nominal amount of the Stocks and Securities purchased."

### V.—February 1873.—The Scottish American Investment Trust.

1st issue. Capital £300,000, in shares of £100, bearing 6 per cent. interest, issued at par.

Sept. 1873.—2nd issue. Capital £400,000, in shares of £100, bearing 6 per cent. interest, issued at par. Management expenses are limited to a sum not exceeding £1,400 per annum.

### VI.—March 1873.—The Mortgage Debenture and Government Securities Trust.

Capital £1,000,000, in Shares of £20 issued at par. Formation expenses are estimated not to exceed 1 per cent. on the nominal capital.

### VII.—March 1873.—The American Investment Trust.

Capital £750,000, in Shares of £100, bearing 6 per cent. Interest, issued at £95, and redeemable at £105.

Preliminary expenses £2 per cent. on the nominal amount of Stocks purchased, and working expenses limited to £2,500 per annum.

The following extract from the report of the trustees shows the position of the trust in 1875 :—

"The revenue of the past year has suffered in consequence of no interest having been received upon the bonds of the Detroit and Milwaukee, the Gilman, Clinton, and Springfield, Missouri, Kansas, and Texas, and Mobile and Montgomery railroads, and upon the shares of the Michigan Central railroad company, and from only one half-year's interest having been received upon the Canada Southern, Toledo, Peoria, and Warsaw, and Toledo, Wabash, and Western railroad companies; but, notwithstanding these defaults, the interest which has been received during the year ended on March 15, 1875, has been sufficient to pay the interest on the certificates of the Trust and expenses, and to leave a surplus of £2,368 8s. 7d., which, added to the amount of £623 6s. 8d., received from bonds drawn, and £40 1s. 10d. interest uninvested from last year, makes a total surplus of £3,031 17s. 1d., as shown in the revenue account, and which, in pursuance of clause 17 of the trust-deed, will be invested by the trustees under the advice of the committee of certificate-holders, to be held by the trustees upon the Trusts of the reserved fund. After the 15th of March, 1876, the surplus revenue of each year will be available for the redemption of Trust certificates, at the price of £105."

The Chairman, in moving the adoption of the report, said that almost simultaneously with the completion of the investment of the Trust, business in the United States of America entered upon a period of depression almost unequalled in their recollection, and circumstances occurred most seriously detrimental to the traffic of many railways in which the money of this Trust was invested. He thought that, on the whole, they might *congratulate themselves upon the soundness of the scheme in which they had embarked*, for, notwithstanding the serious defaults alluded to in the report, they were able to divide the full dividend upon the certificates, in addition to putting a considerable amount to reserve.

## VIII.—March 1873.—The Anglo-American Railroad Mortgage Trust.

Capital £1,000,000, in Shares of £100, bearing 6 per cent. Interest, issued at £85. Preliminary expenses 2 per cent. on nominal amount of capital subscribed, and ordinary working and management expenses fixed at ½ per cent. on nominal amount of capital.

## IX.—March 1873.— The Railway Debenture Trust Company (Limited).

Capital £3,000,200, in Shares of £20, bearing 6 per cent. Interest.—1st issue.—£1,000,000 at par, and 200 Founders' Shares of £1. Directors' allowance £2,000 per annum, and 5 per cent. extra on net profits of any year in which a Dividend of not less than 6 per cent. is paid.; Founders undertaking to pay all preliminary and other expenses, up to and including allotment and issue of the Shares in consideration of receiving 10 per cent. on the net profits in every year in which not less than 6 per cent. is declared on the whole of the paid up capital, and after providing for the Directors' allowance.

July 1873.—2nd issue.—£500,000 5 per cent. Debentures at £95, and redeemable at £110.

May 1874.—3rd issue.—£500,000 5 per cent. Debentures at £97, redeemable by Annual Drawings in 51 years, at £110 by a cumulative Sinking fund of ⅛ per cent. per annum.

The 1874 Prospectus states:

"By the Articles of Association, all moneys raised by the issue of Debentures are to be invested in Mortgages, Debentures, or Obligations of Railways (or to an extent not exceeding one-fourth in the Debentures of other undertakings, such as Docks, Waterworks, Gas, Telegraphs, &c.). These Investments are selected with peculiar care, and under the condition that no more than one-tenth of the Capital raised is ever to be invested in any one security.

"In addition to this, the £1,000,000 of Share Capital, half of which is paid up and invested, and half remaining to be called, will constitute a Guarantee Fund for the Debentures. All Capital raised by this and other issues of the Company's Debentures (which are limited by the Articles of Association to £5,000,000 for each £1,000,000 of Share Capital) will rank *pari passu* as a common preferential charge on all the securities, as well as on the entire Share Capital.

"From the investment of the £500,000 of paid-up Share Capital, and the £500,000 Debenture Capital already issued, the Directors were able at the first Annual General Meeting held in February, 1874, to declare a dividend at the rate of 7 per cent. per annum, carrying forward the sum of £14,323 6s. 2d.

"It may safely be said, therefore, that the Debentures of this Company practically represent an investment in a careful selection of good Railway and other Debentures, with a margin so large as to make it a security which may be fairly classed with that of the Debenture Stocks of the leading British Railways, the return on which barely yields 4 per cent. per annum, while that of the Debentures now offered, at the price of issue is above 5 per cent., without taking into consideration the premium on the amortisation amounting to 13 per cent."

---

## X.—April 1873.—The Railway Share Trust Company (Limited).

Capital £2,000,200, in Shares of £20, £1,000,000 in "A" or Ordinary Shares, and £1,000,000 in "B" or Preference Shares.

1st issue.—£1,000,000 "A" Shares at par, and 200 Founders' Shares of £1 (to be fully paid up at once).

1. The "*B*" *Shares are to be fully paid up* and will bear a fixed Preferential Interest. They will *never* exceed the number of "*A*" *Shares* for the time *being issued*, and on which one half will have been paid up.

2. The "A" Shares will thus give a practical guarantee for the punctual payment of the interest on the "B" Shares.

3. The investment of all capital is limited to approved Shares or securities of Railway Companies, or, to an extent not exceeding one-fourth of the whole, of other undertakings, but no more than one-tenth of the amount raised is ever to be invested in any one security.

4. The *remuneration of the Directors* is made mainly contingent on profits, the fixed allowance being limited to £2,000 a year, in *addition to which* they are to receive 5 per cent. upon the *net profits* (after deducting preference interest) of any year in which *a dividend* of not less than 7 *per cent.* is paid to the "A" Shareholders on the paid-up Share Capital.

5. The *Founders guarantee the subscription of* £700,000 out of the first issue of £1,000,000 "*A*" *Share Capital.* They *further undertake to pay all preliminary and other expenses* up to and including the allotment and issue of the shares in *consideration* of *receiving* 10 *per cent. of the net profits (after deducting preference interest),* in *every year* in which not less *than 7 per cent. dividend is paid* to the "*A*" *Shareholder* on the paid up share capital, *and after providing for the Directors* percentage. This arrangement, by which the Founders undertake such large immediate liabilities for a share of prospective profits—payable only after a remunerative dividend has been earned—proves their entire confidence in the success of the undertaking, and gives the advantage to the Company of commencing with its Share Capital intact.

Feb. 1874.—2nd issue.—£500,000 in "B" Shares of £20, bearing six per cent. interest, issued at par.

The reports and accounts (January, 1875) of the Railway Share Trust Company and the Railway Debenture Trust Company (Limited) are interesting, especially from the fact that both Trusts possess the same directorate, and work for each other. Between them they made a profit of £166,609, the larger half of which, £89,000, falls to the Share Trust Company, which holds over £300,000 less investments than the Debenture Company. A paragraph in the report explains matters. The Share Trust Company made the larger part of its profits from "commissions and other business," and not merely from investing the funds intrusted to it. The Share Company pays 8 per cent. and the Debenture 7 per cent. for the year.

---

### XI.—July 1873.—The Globe Telegraph and Trust.

Original Capital £3,000,000, divided into 150,000 6 per cent. preference shares of £10 each (interest payable quarterly), and 150,000 ordinary shares of £10 each (interim dividends contingent on profits payable quarterly).

May 1875.—The Shareholders sanctioned an increase of the Capital (thereby raising it to £5,000,000), by the issue of 100,000 new ordinary shares of £10 each, and 100,000 new preference shares of £10 each, to rank equal to, and be entitled to the like privileges as attached to the existing ordinary and preferred shares.

Mr. W. Abbott (who undoubtedly possesses great knowledge of the subject) points out that in July, 1873, the holders of £849,354 Anglo-American Telegraph Stock transferred it to the Globe Telegraph and Trust Company, against which they received equal amounts of 6 per cent. preferred and ordinary shares, the latter, in Stock, is now worth £60, and the former £102¼ averaging 81¼, whereas those who did not join the Globe now see their property selling for £64—a reduction of 17¼ per cent., or as much as 21 per cent. on the money value. Applied to the whole of the £7,000,000 of capital of the Anglo-American Company, the comparison would give an increased value to that stock, if in the Globe, of no less than £1,207,500, and, including the Eastern and Eastern Extension, the formidable total of £1,652,106 is attained as the result of the increased security afforded by means of the Globe Telegraph and Trust Company. The importance of such a combination as the Globe Company as affecting telegraph property may be also shown by the following statement:—"The investments in Eastern, Eastern Extension, German Union, Indo-European, and Submarine Cables Trust, give an average yield of 6 per cent. The holding of Anglo-American, amounting to £849,354, has, however, owing to an exceptionally large amount having been carried to renewal account in the past year, only brought in 5 per cent. to the Trust, thus showing, in respect of this investment, a deficiency of 1 per cent., or £8,493. Against this, however, is to be set the dividend on the 4,647 shares in the Telegraph Construction Company, which cost £167,761 ; 6 per cent. upon this amount would be £10,065, whereas it has yielded to the Trust during the past year £25,094, and deducting the 6 per cent. there remains £15,029 to meet the £8,493 deficiency on the Anglo-American investment, thus leaving a surplus of £6,536, after allowing for 6 per cent. dividend on both preference and ordinary shares. Another favourable feature in connection with the Globe Company is the fact that the directors have exchanged with the Telegraph Construction Company £250,000 of the ordinary shares for an equal amount of Brazilian Submarine Shares, and, according to the market quotations, that operation gives an enhanced value in favour of the Globe Company of £31,250, besides which there is the further advantage that there has been no fresh issue of preference shares against this ordinary capital. Such facts as the foregoing make the Globe ordinary shares rank as the cheapest Telegraph Stock in the market."

The prospectus of 1875 stated that: —
" The preference shares have attracted to telegraphic property a new class of investors, whilst the combined market values of the preference and ordinary shares of this company have been uniformly in excess of the market values of the shares taken in exchange. The *preference dividend is cumulative;* that is, if a deficiency should occur in any year it will be made up out of the profits of subsequent years."

### XII.—November 1873.—The Gas and Water Debenture Trust Company (Limited).

Capital £2,000,200, in shares of £20 (and 200 Founders' shares of £1 each, to be paid up in full).

1st issue.—£1,000,000 in shares of £20 each at par.

No promotion money is to be paid; and the founders of the Company undertake to pay all preliminary and other expenses of its establishment, and to guarantee the subscription of two-thirds of the present issue (being the amount required by the rules of the Stock Exchange for obtaining an official quotation) in consideration of receiving 10 per cent. of the net profits in every year in which not less than 7 per cent. Dividend is paid on the entire paid-up Share Capital. This arrangement not only assures the successful foundation of the Company, but enables it to start with its Share Capital intact.

The remuneration of the Directors is made mainly contingent on profits, the fixed allowance being limited to £2,000 a year, in addition to which they are to receive 5 per cent. upon the net profits of any year in which a Dividend of of not less than 7 per cent. is paid to the Shareholders.

### XIII.—December 1873.—The Municipal Trust.

Capital £1,000,000 in " A" Certificates of £50 and £100, bearing 7 per cent. interest, with which will be issued a " B" Certificate of £25 and £50 respectively, entitling the holder to payment of both certificates at par on drawing of the " A " Certificate.

The ordinary yearly expenses of offices and management have been fixed at ½ per cent. on the amount of capital. The remuneration of the Trustees, Committee, and Auditors is fixed by the Trust deed, and no other expenses will be incurred without the vote of a general meeting of the certificate-holders. The preliminary expenses, including *ad valorem* stamp, are limited to a charge of 1½ per cent. on the amount of capital.

One-third of the original amount of capital will be redeemed, by drawings, at par, out of the surplus interest and profits. With each " A " certificate the

PARTICULARS OF EXISTING TRUSTS. 31

corresponding "B" certificate will be redeemed. When one-third of the "A" and "B" certificates shall have thus been paid off, the Securities representing the amount of the original capital will be realized and applied to the immediate redemption of the remaining "A" and "B" certificates, and the Trust finally closed.

By this arrangement all the certificate holders will in like manner participate in the advantages of the Trust; *i. e.*, they will receive, besides 7 per cent. interest per annum, a bonus (as represented by the "B" certificates) of 50 per cent. on the invested capital.

The constitution of this Trust will provide for the investment of not more than 5 per cent. of the capital in any one security.

The prospectus stated that:

" The bonds of corporations and public bodies in this country, such as those of the city of London and the Metropolitan Board of Works, are well known and command a high value in the market. In America, each separate Municipality raises the necessary funds for public purposes, such as improving streets and constructing roads, bridges, school-houses, court-houses, city halls and markets, by the issue of bonds for fixed periods, repayable by a sinking fund, and secured upon the taxable property of the district. The Municipalities are legally empowered to issue bonds to the extent of from 5 to 10 per cent. upon the *assessed* value of all real and personal property, which assessed value, in America, does not usually exceed one-third of the salable value.

" The Municipalities are bound by law to levy taxes upon the real and personal property of the whole district for payment of the interest and principal of bonds issued by them.

" These bonds are as secure as mortgages or ground rents. They are not affected by changes of government, are not of a fluctuating nature, and consequently have become a favourite security for family settlements, savings banks, insurance companies, and other trusts.

" The savings banks of New York State alone, *according to the last Government report*, hold an aggregate sum of over seventy-eight millions of dollars in Municipal bonds; this being about one-fourth of their total assets.

" The object of this Trust is to acquire bonds of the nature described, and thus to secure to investors a safe and steady interest by judicious employment of the funds of the Trust. A provisional contract has been entered into and advantage taken of the recent depressed state of the American markets, for the purchase of bonds of various Municipalities, at prices which will secure to the Trust an average interest of at least 9½ per cent., exclusive of the profit which will be derived from the periodical payment of the bonds at par, from time to time, over an average period of say fifteen years. By this contract these bonds are guaranteed to be in conformity with law, and to be subsisting debts against the several Municipalities issuing the same; and, further, that the entire indebtedness in no case exceeds 10 per cent. *of the assessed value of the property liable for the loan.* In ordinary times such Securities are almost entirely absorbed in America, where the advantages they offer of high interest, combined with undoubted security, are fully understood. The present is, therefore, an exceptionally favourable opportunity for the formation of this Trust."

### XIV.—January 1874.—The Government Securities Debenture Company (Limited).

Capital £2,000,000, 1st issue £500,000 in shares of £20 at par. Expenses not to exceed 2½ per cent. on nominal capital up to £1,500,000.

### XV.—January 1874.—The Omnium Stock Trust.

Capital £1,000,000, in shares of £50, bearing interest at 5 per cent., issued at £40 and redeemable at par.

The Omnium Stock Trust, in its prospectus, invited subscriptions for Certificates of £50 each, to be issued at £40. The leading features are:—

1. The interest is 5 per cent. on the £50, which upon £40 paid equals £6 5s. per cent., and is payable half yearly by Coupons attached to the Certificate.

2. After payment of the interest and expenses, which together amount to 6¾ per cent., the surplus income will be appropriated to paying off the Certificates at par. This will be accomplished by annual drawings, and the holders of Certificates thus drawn will receive £50 per Certificate, and will retain a Coupon which entitles them to a share of the final distribution of the Trust.

3. At the end of 20 years the entire Capital of the Trust will be sold, and after paying off those Certificates that may not have been drawn, the balance remaining will be divided equally among the holders of remaining Coupons.

4. The expenses of the Trust are limited to ½ per cent. on the subscription. This must not exceed £2,500, even although the ½ per cent. should amount to more than that sum. [Some modification of this clause was introduced in 1875.]

### XVI.—February 1874.—The Birkbeck Property Investment Trust.

Capital £500,000, in shares of £25, £50, and £100, bearing 5 per cent. interest, issued at the rate of £88 for each £100 share.

"The Trust will be under the management of the Directors of the old-established Birkbeck Building Society, together with a Council of Certificate-holders, whose duties it will be to audit the accounts of the Trust. In terms of the Deed of Trust it is provided that the members of the Board shall receive no remuneration for their services until the annual produce arising from the Trust properties shall reach £25,000, being 5 per cent. on the amount to be raised. It is further provided that the expenses of management shall be limited to 1 per cent. on the amount to be raised under the Trust, while the preliminary expenses, including the stamp duty payable under the Act, are fixed at 1¼ per cent. Any further expenses will be borne by the promoters of the Trust."

XVII.—February 1874.—The North British Foreign and Colonial Investment Trust.

Capital £500,000 in shares of £100, bearing 6 per cent. interest, issued at £95. Working expenses limited to £1,400 per annum; preliminary expenses limited to 1½ per cent. on amount of Stocks purchased.

XVIII.—March 1874.—The Investors' Trust Company (Limited).

Capital £100,000, in Shares of £10 each (issued at par), and 20 fully paid Founders' Shares of £1.

Directors' allowance £150 per annum and 1 per cent. extra as soon as a profit of 11 per cent. has been realized. Founders will receive 3 per cent. on all Capital subscribed, which sum is to include all legal and other expenses, and also to receive a bonus of 1 per cent. as soon as a profit of 10 per cent. has been realized, and a further bonus of 1 per cent. as soon as a further profit of 12 per cent. has been realized. Half the above bonuses will be retained for three years to provide against the contingency of the declared profits proving less than anticipated.

## Section 2.—*Rate of Profit reported.*

ART. 21.—There are other excellent Trusts which we have not included, as they are more in the nature of small savings associations for investment in general securities, and in principles of working are similar to building societies.

It will be observed that most of the existing Trusts have distinctive features. Some are for investment in foreign and colonial government stocks of all kinds, others are for guaranteed securities, others purchase English and Foreign railway shares, and herein probably lies the secret of success.

Their managers recognize that it is better for each Trust to endeavour to lay its funds out in a well selected but not too large variety of some particular species of stocks, the merits of which can be better gauged, and a more accurate knowledge obtained than by indiscriminate purchases. To this cause may be attributed the rate of profit reported in some of these Trusts.

Mr. Samuel Laing, M.P., stated at the first meeting of the Railway Share Trust Company, Limited, that "the whole of the ordinary share capital of £1,000,000 had been subscribed, and the amount intended to be called up, viz., £500,000, had all been paid :—

"The investment of this money has been so far completed that the directors are able to give the following approximate statement of the results, which they consider very favourable. The number of investments is about 36, making the average of each about £12,400. In order to form a solid basis for the Company's Preferred Shares, which will shortly be issued, a large proportion of these investments has been made in Debentures and Preferred Stocks, giving a high fixed rate of interest, with good security, and prospect of improvement. Other investments have been made in the Shares of Companies paying high Dividends, or holding out prospects of a considerable rise. The original prospectus of the Company stated that the investments would probably be made to realise an average rate of from 7 to 8 per cent. per annum. The rate of return on the whole capital actually invested will, as nearly as can be estimated, average about £7 9s. 4d. per cent. per annum, in addition to profits already earned from commissions and other sources."

In 1874, the next Report stated that—
"The net profits, after deducting current expenses, directors' and founders' percentages, and income-tax, amount to £29,638, being at the rate of 10 per cent. per annum on the paid up Share Capital. . . . . . . Considering that the Company is yet in its infancy, and that it is desirable that its course should be one of constant progress to higher Dividends, the directors consider that it will be more prudent to declare a Dividend at the rate of only 8 per cent. per annum . . . . . . A review of the present position of the Company, with the experience acquired, enables the directors to repeat the confident assurance that the principles upon which it is based are sound, and that it has a great future before it, both in convenience to the investing public and in profit to the Shareholders."

22.—At the annual general meeting of the Railway Share Trust Company, held in February, 1875, the chairman stated that—
"The net profits for the year, after deducting current expenses, interest on the Preference Shares, directors' and founders' percentages, and income-tax, amounted to £54,753. This, with the balance of £6,305 brought from the last account, made the total amount at the credit of revenue account £61,058. The directors recommended that a Dividend be declared at the rate of 8 per cent. per annum. This left a balance of £21,058 to be carried forward to next year as undivided profit. An issue of £500,000 of the £1,000,000 of 6 per cent. Preference Stock, authorized by the articles, was made during the past year, of which £373,280 had been placed. The report concluded by congratulating the Shareholders on the position which the Company had attained at such an early period of its existence, notwithstanding the general depression of trade, &c. The chairman, in moving the adoption of the report, apologized for their only declaring an £8 per cent. Dividend when it was evident they might have proposed a larger one. They thought, however, that the permanent interests of the Shareholders would be best consulted by carrying forward a large balance. He wished them particularly to understand that the nature of the business done by the Company was not at all speculative. They had no business which in the ordinary sense of the word was speculative. Their great object was to obtain a name for offering good securities to the public, and he thought they had done something toward this end during the past half-year, for he might

say with confidence that these stood at a high market value. As regarded the accounts, he thought, as far as this Company was concerned, they should make a valuation of their securities at the end of the year—that was the opinion of their auditors—and where there were any depreciations write off a proper amount from them. They had obtained a profit of £82,000 for the year, and he hoped the result would be considered satisfactory. With respect to the question about a reserve fund, he thought if they carried over £21,000 undivided profits, it was practically a reserve fund; and, as this was on the first year's operations, he thought they were in the right way for the £100,000 referred to." A Shareholder then moved the following resolution :—" That the directors be requested to endeavour, and are hereby authorized to commute the founders' Shares which exist in this Company on the best terms they can, not exceeding the payment of £250 in this Company's ' B ' 6 per cent. Preference Shares for each one founder's Share."

23.—The Report in 1874, of the Railway Debenture Trust Company (Limited), stated that—

" The net profits, after deducting current expenses, interest on the Company's own Debentures, directors' and founders' percentages, and income-tax, amount to £37,656 being at the rate of 11¼ per cent. per annum on the paid up Share Capital . . . . . As the Company has no liabilities except upon its own Debentures, whose repayment is provided for by a sinking fund, no necessity exists at present for the creation of a further special reserve. Considering, however, that the Company is yet in its infancy, that it is desirable that its course should be one of constant progress to higher Dividends, and that, with a large issue of the Company's own Debentures in prospect, it is important to maintain its credit at the highest point the directors consider that it will be more prudent to declare a Dividend at the rate of only 7 per cent. per annum."

Mr. Laing, the chairman, informed the meeting—

" That the principle which they went upon was issuing Debentures from time to time, and investing the proceeds at a rate of interest much higher than that paid on the Debentures. The first step had been successfully taken, as they had placed £500,000 of Debenture Capital, and they had no doubt that they would shortly proceed to issue another £500,000. He considered that generally they might reckon that every £500,000 ought to add 1¼ to 2 per cent. additional dividend on the Share Capital. That being the case, it was evidently of importance to get a name for stability, and a reputation for prudent and careful management. There was another reason why they should carry forward a large balance, and that was the enhanced value of their securities. Of course it was satisfactory for them to know that though they were in their infancy, and had had applied a very severe test by the panic in the United States, that the securities stood on that day at a considerably higher figure, if they were realised at the present, than when they were purchased. At the same time he thought that they should not treat profit resulting from the enhanced price quite as if it were cash realised. He did not think their dividends ought to depend upon the mere temporary fluctuations of the money market. He stated that it was desirable that the progress of the Company should be one of progress towards higher Dividend" . . . . . . "He had only to say that their prosperity depended considerably upon the issue of their own Debenture Stock. He certainly considered that that Stock offered an advantageous opening for investments by persons—clergymen, retired officers, and others—who required a safe investment, paying 5 or 6 per cent. interest. They were all aware that good Preference Stocks only paid 4 to 4½ per cent., while this Stock which was really secured upon Preference Stocks of high class, paid considerably more."

24.—At the annual general meeting of the same Trust, held in February, 1875, the chairman remarked that—

"The securities held by the company were now worth £12,454 more than than their actual cash cost, and £3,621 more than the cost at which they stood in the company's books by the valuation of the 15th of January, 1874. The net profits for the year, after deducting current expenses, interest on the company's own debentures, directors' and founders' percentages, and income-tax, amounted to £36,268. Of this, £5,866 had been applied during the year as a Sinking fund on the company's own debentures, which amounted to a reserve fund of that amount taken from profits. There remained £30,402, which, with the balance of £14,323 brought forward from last year, made the total amount at the credit of revenue account £44,725. The directors recommended a dividend at the rate of 7 per cent. per annum, leaving £9,725 to be carried forward to next year, making, with £6,250 which had been applied as Sinking fund, a total reserve of £15,975 from profits. The chairman, in moving the adoption of the report, congratulated the proprietors on the position of the company. Great care had been taken in making the investments, as a considerable amount was held in American Mortgage Bonds. The panic in America last year had affected nearly every kind of security in that country except only the soundest and best securities. The only security they had that was at all affected was the Detroit and Milwaukee Railway Bonds. The line was worked by the Great Western of Canada Company, and as Mr.

Childers, the chairman of the latter company, was now in London the over-due coupons would be met by some satisfactory arrangement. If the United States Government should resume specie payments, the securities held by the company would be further increased in value. As regarded the Sinking fund, they had carried over a moderate amount, and if continued for 30 years it would extinguish a large amount of debentures entirely out of profits. They now had a reserve of £15,975, which would be sufficient to pay 3 per cent. on the share capital. They now proposed to limit the borrowed capital to twice the amount of the paid-up capital. The prospects of the company were very good. Every increase of £500,000 in the borrowed money at 5 per cent. interest, and ½ per cent. for Sinking fund, would add 1¼ per cent. dividend to the share capital, so that with a borrowed capital of £2,000,000 they would be able to pay a steady dividend of 10 per cent. on the share capital, which would not interfere with commissions, and the shares would be worth a considerable premium. That was a state of things they wished to arrive at as early as possible. They could buy wholesale at a reduced price and sell retail at a higher price. They had bought in one case valuable securities at 93, and had been offered 102¾ for them in New York. The larger the business they could do the better would be the class of securities they would get. He might say they had never done any speculative business. By acting on those principles they could utilize a large debenture capital."

A question arose on the founders' share of the profits which a proprietor proposed to commute by offering them debentures to the amount of £50,000 at 5 per cent. interest, which would yield them £2,500 à year. At present a dividend of 6 per cent. would yield the founders of the company £3,000 a year, the 7 per cent. £3,500 a year, and a dividend of 10 per cent. £5,000 a year. The chairman said he could not bind the founders to accept the offer, but would do his best. A resolution to that effect was adopted by the meeting and carried unanimously. A resolution was also adopted to the effect " that it be a rule of the company that the amount of debenture capital should never at any one time exceed twice the amount of share capital which at that time had been subscribed, and on which not less than 50 per cent. had been paid up, and that Article 22 be altered in accordance therewith."

## CHAPTER III.

OF SOME DEFECTS IN EXISTING TRUST ASSOCIATIONS.

Section 1.—*Objections to a Premature System of Drawings.*

ART. 25.—Those Trust Associations, which were founded in the years 1871 and 1872, had to start with purchases made at high prices. They did not anticipate the great fall which occurred in the two years 1873 and 1874 and the unfavourable* fluctuations since, nor the number of Foreign States whose dividend payments would fall into arrear. For a time some of the Trusts appeared at a considerable nominal loss. It was nominal, however, because not being compelled to realize, they simply waited and were relieved by a recovery of full value on some of their Stocks, much of which took place in the buoyant season represented by the first six months of 1875.

The fluctuations in stock securities render evident the fact that the system of annual or periodic drawings (by which the members of the Trusts are repaid their money with Bonuses) should not be exercised too early. In some of the existing Trusts, members have been paid off at a time when certain stocks were valued at high prices, which now present a depreciation. The declaration of dividends half-yearly, out of average profits earned, is reasonable enough; but it is clear, from the way stocks fall and rise in value, and from the contingencies of social convulsions and wars, that it would be more prudent to make the drawings or return of money not more frequently than once in three years. Time would thus be obtained, not only for averaging

---

[* Further on will be found an additional account of the fluctuations, with a comparison of prices.]

the operations of the Trust, but for appreciating the character of those public events by which the investments are likely to be influenced.

## Section 2.—*Of Reserve Funds and Contingencies of Loss.*

ART. 26.—One of the first requirements of a Trust is a *reserve fund* for equalizing payments, since at any valuation of the securities a loss may appear sufficient to affect the Dividends. A trust formed of foreign stocks or other stock exchange securities is, in its essence, a speculative investment, although, if carried out on a proper basis the probability of loss is small.

The properties, as a whole, may return a large rate of interest, but the excess over $4\frac{1}{2}$ or 5 per cent. (in addition to all receipts from Government drawings) should be reinvested as a reserve fund, to be applied only at periodic divisions.

27.—The contingencies of Loss to be provided for are illustrated by the experience of one of the leading Trusts, which is known to be under excellent management, viz., the Share Investment Trust.

The Report of the Trustees to the third yearly meeting of Certificate-holders, held April, 1874, said:—

"The trustees present to the certificate-holders the balance-sheet and revenue account of the Trust for the year ending March 15th, 1874. The *revenue of* the past year has suffered in consequence of *no dividend* having been received upon the Western of Canada Oil Lands and Works Company's Debentures, the Shares of the Glasgow Tramway and Omnibus Company, the West India and Panama Telegraph Company, the New Sombrero Phosphate Company, and from the dividend on the Anglo-American Telegraph Company's Stock being only 6 per cent.

"The revenue received up to March 15th was £37,757 16s. 5d., to which being added £33 2s. 10d., the balance of last year's Sinking fund, makes £37,790 19s. 3d.; from this must be deducted £2,300 for expenses of the Trust, leaving for appropriation to the 6 per cent. interest on the preference certificates the sum of £33,456, and £2,034 19s. 3d. to the Sinking fund. This last amount, together with £3,575 0s. 9d. from the balance of profits on sales of securities, making together a total of £5,610, will be applied at the meeting in redemption of 51 preference certificates to be drawn by lot at £110 each.

"The trustees, considering that the amounts held by them in the various Submarine Telegraph companies were relatively too great, resolved to lessen their holdings in those companies, and have accordingly reduced the amounts held in the Anglo-American Telegraph company, limited, to £132,355 stock; in the Eastern Telegraph company, limited, to 1,109 shares; and in the Eastern Extension, Australasia, and China Telegraph company, limited, to 4,611 shares. They have also disposed of the following securities:—100 shares Palmer's Shipbuilding and Iron company, limited; 1,200 shares in Ransome's Patent Stone company, limited; 100 shares in London Tramway company, limited; 100 shares in the North German Telegraph company; 10 debentures in the Western of Canada Oil Lands and Works company, limited; and £2,000 Stock Midland Railway of Canada.

"The result of all these sales has been a balance of profit over the amount originally invested of £6,391 18s. 7d. to the Trust. The amount of original investment has, with the sanction of the committee of certificate-holders, been already re-invested in securities, which are included in the schedule hereto."

28.—The accuracy of this* view is shown in the Report of July, 1874, of the Foreign and Colonial Government Trust (Third Issue), wherein it is stated that :—

"During the past year the interest on the following securities has not been received :—Alabama Eight per Cent. State Bonds, one year, £3,220 16s. 8d.; Alabama Six per Cent., one year, £252 4s. 6d.; Central Argentine Railway, one year, £1,365; City of Mobile Alabama Eight per Cent. Bonds, one year, £550 19s. 2d.; Spanish Three per Cent., one year, £2,524 10s.; total, £7,913 10s. 4d.; and the Georgia Seven per Cent. Coupons and the Louisiana Six per Cent. Coupons have only lately been sent to America for collection. The Trustees have been obliged to carry over the sum of £5,540 8s. 8d., which represents the bonds drawn in April last in the Spanish Six per Cent National Lands."

---

[* At the meeting of the certificate-holders of the American Investment Trust, 1874, the report presented was adopted. It showed that there had been a loss of interest amounting to £2,928 from defaults, but a part of this was in a fair way of being recovered. It was stated that the dividends due on Canada Southern Railway Bonds, held by the Trust, had been discharged.]

Section 3.—*Of the Unequal effect of Drawings when of fixed amounts.*

ART. 29.—Apart from the previous considerations, there is a certain disproportionate effect in the drawings system when not properly arranged. This is exemplified by a Trust of high reputation, where 10s. a year is set aside to constitute a fund that in 51 years shall, with £5 a year for interest, liquidate* by annual drawings the debentures by payments of £110 in return for £95 received.

On each debenture drawn in the first year a Bonus of £15 is to be paid; so also on each one drawn in the last or 51st year a like Bonus will be allotted. But the present worth of the latter £15 discounted for 50 years at 5 per cent. is only £1. 6s. The early recipient gains, however, more than the money value of his full Bonus for he also escapes the uncertainty of the future. No one can measure the chance of a Trust being able—in such far distant years—to return to all its debenture holders £110 out of a saving of 10s. a year from its profits.

30.—If a system of Drawings be retained, then, as compensation to those who run much risk in waiting, a plan of periodic increasing Bonuses, payable with the Drawings (themselves modified in nature and amount), might be adopted. Three years is a reasonable time in which to average a Trust's yearly experience, and then it would be convenient to estimate the Bonuses.

---

[* *Indeed as a mere question of figures this Trust would not be able to liquidate its drawings of £110 out of the £5 10s. a-year per debenture, as we shall explain in a subsequent part.*

*This point is of some weight, where from the form of the contract a specific fund of limited amount (as £55,000 a-year to liquidate a million of debentures) is all that is available for the drawings. In such case, at the end of the 51st year (the term fixed for extinction) instead of the debentures being extinguished as contemplated, there will be a deficiency exceeding £135,000.*]

## UNEQUAL EFFECT OF DRAWINGS. 43

Without some such compensation, an investor—who might be quite willing to put his money into the actual debentures of a Railway Company for 50 years—would hesitate to do so in those of a Trust Association, even for the higher interest and contingent Bonus. This is further illustrated in another Trust of which the prospectus of the second issue of certificates (28th April, 1874) stated that :—

"The principles of the present issue embrace the permanent maintenance of the fund in its entirety ; provisions for reserve ; payment of a fixed minimum interest ; the further immediate distribution of a percentage of each year's realised profit as bonuses in cash to the whole body of certificate-holders : and, as far as possible, the redemption of certificates out of profits remaining after paying the annual bonus.

"The Trust funds will be invested in carefully selected governments and guaranteed Securities, such as Stocks, Obligations and Bonds of Home, Foreign, or Colonial Governments, States and Municipalities, and guaranteed or subsidised Stocks, Shares, and Obligations of Railways and Public Works, or Mortgages or Debentures on similar undertakings. Whenever any of the capital originally invested is set free by the operation of Sinking funds or otherwise, it will be immediately re-invested in the same or similar security.

"An investor in this issue would receive as interest £5 per certificate, or £5 19s. per cent., and an annual cash bonus not exceeding 10s. (equal to 11s. 11d. per cent), making together £6 10s. 11d. per cent. per annum on each £100 invested by him; and further, in the event of his certificate being drawn, *he would have a cash bonus of* £41 over and above the price paid (£84) for the same.

"It is anticipated that at the end of twenty years a considerable proportion of certificates will have been paid off out of surplus profits, at the rate of £125 for each £100 certificate."

31.—As the Issue proposed in this Trust was £1,000,000 in 10,000 Certificates of £100 at price £84, the cash received would be £840,000 (subject to a deduction for expenses attending such Issue).

The Bonuses of £41 each on the 10,000 certificates would cost £410,000 ; so that the Trust would have to make sufficient *surplus profits* on an investment capital of £840,000 to return (after dividends to be paid at £6. 10s. 11d. per cent. per annum on that capital and expenses) a bonus of £410,000.

Here, moreover, the inequality is apparent of the money value of the £41 bonus to the recipient, according as he receives it in the earlier or in the later years of this Trust. Hence the necessity of large reserves to protect those whose debentures remain undrawn until the later years of the Trust; otherwise it is not unlikely that from political and financial contingencies, there will be a deficiency hereafter caused by the payment of these Bonuses.

This case illustrates how much better it would be to give a Reversionary coupon, payable at the end of the term, for whatever surplus may be then found divisible, instead of prematurely distributing Bonuses.

## Section 4.—*Of the Wide Field for "Trust" Operations.*

ART. 32.—These Trusts will have had a most mischievous effect, if they should foster an imprudent desire to obtain large dividends without regard to security of investment.

If 4 per cent. be taken as the average standard rate obtainable by *individuals* with safety, through their own independent action, then 4½ per cent. or 5 per cent. may be considered as a sufficiently high rate for *Associations* to promise.

That security is the real attraction to investors is shown by the fact that the many millions, placed in the Savings Banks, receive only rates of interest ranging from, nominally, £2 10s. to less than £3 per cent. per annum.

At this time the amount so invested is nearly* £66,000,000, having increased £27,000,000 since we published our Treatise on Savings Banks in 1859.

[* In 1859, when there were no Post Office Banks, the money due to the Savings Banks was under £39,000,000. In May, 1875, the two systems together had nearly £66,000,000.]

33.—With these facts before them, Trusts may well keep in mind the speculative nature of the investments they have to select, and content themselves with offering 4½ or 5 per cent. for the first five or seven years. They can augment the benefits to their subscribers by periodic Bonuses out of such surplus profits, as they may, in due time, find they have made. Above all they should, as we have before pointed out, remember the necessity of building up a reserve, to secure the just rights of all the members, and avoid frittering away, in premature drawings to a few, the profits they appear in the earlier years to be making. In the words of a writer we have already quoted:—

"Considering the utility of these Trusts, and the important rank which they occupy amongst investments, it is very desirable that their present character for safety should be maintained, and that their position with investors should not be disturbed, for were anything to bring them into discredit, the result would be deplorable, as money would be withdrawn from them, and to a large extent reinvested in more risky Securities. As long as the fresh schemes are carefully planned and conducted by able men, they can be welcomed as adding to the number of sound investments. The original or first Trust was formed on certain well-established facts, as an investment offering certain advantages, but the uncertain or speculative element, was as much as possible kept out of the scheme. In some recent issues of Trust schemes, the speculative element has not been sufficiently excluded to caution investors against the attractive appearance of schemes in which the dividends are to depend upon some uncertain result." It is to be hoped that such will not be introduced in the form of Trusts.

34.—The success that has attended existing Trusts, and the probability that each year's experience will, by inducing much caution, increase their stability — are circumstances likely to encourage the formation of new ones.

In the provincial towns of the United Kingdom, where effective and prudent supervision can be obtained, there would be no disadvantage, but the converse, in local Trusts being established.

That there is room for such is attested by the fact that the united *nominal* Capital of the existing Associations of the kind is but a small percentage on the many millions of * Securities, held by the general public in this country as individuals, a large portion of which it would be safer for them to hold as members of an Average Investment Trust.

---

[* 1. The figures of the various Securities will be found at Part I, sect. 3.

2. At the Geneva meeting in September, 1874, the chairman of the Foreign Bondholder's Protection Committee, Mr. Isidore Gerstenberg stated, that in London alone £1,000,000,000 sterling of paying securities were held.

3. The number of Joint Stock Companies, registered during the past ten years, has exceeded 7,500. The gross amount of share capital nominally created was £1,070,000,000 sterling. In the year 1865, 897 companies were registered, representing a total nominal capital of £198,000,000, but the number of enterprises since brought forward has fluctuated very considerably. In 1870 it had fallen to 517, with only £40,000,000 of nominal capital.

4. In his Report, 1874, M. Leon Say estimates that the annual value of the Coupons for Dividends on Foreign Securities held in France was from 600,000,000 francs to 700,000,000 francs. He adds, also, that in the three years after the war a great sale, abroad, of Foreign Securities (previously held in France), took place. An exportation of Bonds or Titles was carried out on a large scale. Two examples prove the extent of those sales of Securities. On the 1st of July, 1869, the half-yearly Coupons of Italian Rente paid in Paris amounted to over 40,000,000 francs; while on the 1st of January, 1874, it was only 25,000,000. During the interval France had consequently sold abroad Italian Rente for a sum of 30,000,000 francs per annum, representing a capital of from 400,000,000 to 500,000,000 francs. The Turkish Coupons paid in France also decreased from 3,265,612 francs in January, 1870, to 728,181 francs in July, 1873.

M. Say computes the sum expended in France by foreigners at from 200,000,000 to 300,000,000 francs annually.

Even allowing for the diminution in the number of strangers since the war, he estimates that about 500,000,000 francs were nevertheless obtained from that source in the three years.

5. The Paris correspondent of the *Economist*, October, 1874, observed that,

"The issues of new Securities on the Paris market are now rare and of little importance, but to judge from the facility with which they are covered more considerable native Stocks would be placed with little difficulty now that so many of the foreign funds excite mistrust. The Vosges Railway Company recently invited subscriptions for 10,000 obligations, and received applications for 196,000; and the Lille to Valenciennes, which had 24,000 to issue, received demands for 401,000. These successes are the more remarkable that the interest of the bonds is not guaranteed by the State like those of the great Companies, and the bonds of few of the local railway companies have maintained their original price; many have, indeed, suffered a very great depreciation."

6. On the question of the total amount of the debts of America held abroad, Mr. Edward Young, the chief of the Government Bureau of Statistics at Washington, has in an unofficial paper lately published a calculation. The total so held before the commencement of the civil war in 1862 was, he considers, £10,000,000, and he now arrives at the conclusion that £230,000,000 has since been added, making an aggregate of £240,000,000, represented mainly by National State, municipal and railway, and other corporation bonds. The data on which the calculation is based are, however, admittedly imperfect.]

PART II.

# THE PRINCIPLES OF NEW TRUST ASSOCIATIONS.

---

#### CONTENTS.

CHAPTER I.—*Plan of a " Trust" Company with Shares.*

,, II.—*Of new Trusts (continued):—Of Subscription Trusts and special kinds of Trusts.*

,, III.—*Of new Trusts (continued):—Of the kind of Share Capital; Preferred and Deferred Shares.*

# OF THE PRINCIPLES OF NEW TRUST ASSOCIATIONS.

## CHAPTER I.

PLAN OF A "TRUST" COMPANY WITH SHARES.

ART. 1.—As an illustration of the features adopted, we gave in Part I., Chapter I., a copy of the original prospectus of the first Trust founded in 1868, under a Trust Deed, and we now add a copy of a more recent one, which stands in the first rank, from being one of the best of the new Trusts formed under most experienced management; it was established with a proprietary capital in shares, under the Companies Acts.

The statements carry weight from being the opinions on the capabilities of such a Trust advanced by men of the highest financial standing and experience, one of whom (the Chairman) is a distinguished political economist, to whom India is indebted for many fiscal measures of great value :—

*The ———— Debenture Trust Company (Limited).*

"Incorporated with limited liability, under the "Companies Acts, 1862 and 1867," limiting the liability of Shareholders to the amount of their Shares.

CAPITAL £3,000,200.

"In 150,000 Shares of £20 each. To be issued in three Series of 50,000 Shares each, and 200 Founders' Shares of £1 each, to be paid up in full.

"First Issue 50,000 Shares of £20 each, at par, on which £10 per Share is intended to be called up, payable as follows :—

£1 per Share, payable on Application.
£3 „ „ Allotment.
£3 „ „
£3 „ „
——
£10

"Option being reserved to Allottees to pay up the whole £10 in one payment on Allotment, under discount at 5 per cent. per annum."

## Observations.

"I.—The ————— Debenture Trust Company (Limited) is founded to place within reach of every member of the community the means of investing any amount of Capital, small or large, on the security of first-class Railway and other Debentures, with the further security of a Guarantee Fund furnished by a large Share Capital.

"This will be attained by the principle on which the Trust Company is established, of issuing its own Debentures to an extent limited to five times the amount of the subscribed Share Capital, the proceeds being invested in Railway and other Debentures.

"The price of British Railway Debentures has now risen to a point which makes the average return on the Capital invested in this description of security barely 4 per cent. per annum; and the tendency is towards still higher prices, as the Capital seeking safe investment constantly increases, while the supply of fresh first-class British Railway Debentures is practically very limited.

"II.—Under these circumstances, a large and increasing amount of Capital is forced to seek investment in Foreign Loans and speculative undertakings.

"There are many Investors, however, who would prefer the solid security of Railway Debentures to loans of foreign countries, subject to political vicissitudes, if such securities could be brought within their reach in a convenient form, whilst practically having a security equal to that of English Railway Debentures.

"The Debentures of the leading Railways of France, Germany, Austria, Russia, the United States, Canada, and other parts of British North America, and other countries and colonies, give an immense choice of such investments, yielding on the average a return of 6 per cent. per annum and upwards, with a security not really inferior to that of the best English Railways.

"It may be confidently asserted that, for the last 20 years, there has been no instance of default in any of such cases where experience, combined with prudence, has been used in avoiding hazardous securities, where a high rate of interest rather than safety was the primary consideration.

"III.—There are, however, several reasons which make it difficult for the general public to find such investments, viz. :—

"1. They have no special knowledge on the subject, and no means of distinguishing good from hazardous investments, or of watching the progress and obtaining information of the undertakings in which their money is invested.

2. The fluctuations of exchange, and difficulty of collecting coupons payable abroad in francs, dollars, and other foreign coin, deter a large class of Investors.

"3. In the case of isolated investments the difficulty of realising is often great, and the margin between the buying and selling price excessive, so that a holder who may have occasion to realize often, without his security having become deteriorated, loses 5 per cent. or more, from the mere fact that it is not well known and largely dealt in on the London Market.

" The ——————— Debenture Trust Company (Limited), will effectually meet these wants, being founded on the principle of seeking safety rather than speculatively high interest on its investments.

"The leading principle is that of distributing the investments over a large number of well selected securities.

" IV.—Each Debenture of this Company will thus be represented by an equal amount of Debentures of various Companies, guaranteed by their own Share Capital respectively, and supplemented by the large Share Capital of this Company, which will form a special Guarantee Fund, to be always maintained, at a sum never less than one-fifth of the amount of the Debentures of this Company, represented half by the paid-up capital invested in similar Debentures, and the other half by the uncalled capital.

"The Debentures will be issued from time to time at such prices as the Directors may decide, on the basis of £5,000,000 Debentures for each £1,000,000 Share Capital subscribed.

" Thus each £5,000,000 of Debentures issued will be secured:—

"1. By the proceeds thereof invested in Railway and other Debentures of various Companies.

" 2. By £500,000 of paid up Share Capital invested in similar securities as a Guarantee Fund.

" 3. By £500,000 uncalled Share Capital.

"It is obvious that Debentures thus secured, and issued of such uniform denomination, as to facilitate quotation on the Stock Exchange, thus affording a large and ready market for them, will enable holders to realize with facility, and with due care in the selection of sound investments, may be considered practically quite as safe and desirable for Investors as that of the very best British Railways.

" V.—As regards the essential point, that of safe investment, every possible safeguard, dictated by combined and practical experience, will be provided; amongst the leading features of which are the following :—

"1. The first and fixed principle will be, that of absolutely avoiding speculative securities, and there is no inducement to depart from this principle, as the profits of the Shareholders, resulting in a great part, from the margin between the rate of interest paid on the Debentures of the Trust Company, and that received on the securities in which the proceeds are invested, will be best promoted by whatever inspires thorough confidence, and enables the Debentures to be issued at the best price possible.

"2. The investment of the Capital raised by shares or Debentures is limited to Railway Debentures, Mortgages, or Obligations, or to an extent not exceeding one-fourth of the whole in similar Debentures, Mortgages, or Obligations of other undertakings, such as Docks, Waterworks, Gas, Telegraphs, or other undertakings, but not more than one-tenth of the amount raised by Debentures is ever to be invested in any one security.

"3. No investment can be made or varied unless approved by a majority of at least three-fourths of the Directors present, including the Chairman or acting Chairman.

"4. The qualification of the Board is fixed unusually high, viz., that of the Chairman at £20,000, and of each Director at £5,000, thereby giving the most solid guarantee for their identification with the success of the undertaking.

"5. The remuneration of the Directors is made mainly contingent on profits, the fixed allowance being limited to £2,000 a year in addition to which they are to receive 5 per cent. upon the net profits of any year in which a dividend of not less than 6 per cent. is paid to the Shareholders.

"The Founders guarantee the subscription of £700,000 out of the first issue of £1,000,000 Share Capital, being the minimum amount required by the regulations of the Stock Exchange for obtaining the official quotation. They further undertake to pay all preliminary and other expenses up to and including the allotment and issue of the shares, in consideration of receiving 10 per cent. of the net profits in every year in which not less than 6 per cent. dividend is paid on the entire paid-up capital, and after providing for the Directors' per centage. This arrangement, by which the Founders undertake such large immediate liabilities for a share of prospective profits—payable only after a remunerative dividend has been earned—proves their entire confidence in the success of the undertaking, and gives the advantage of the Company commencing with the Share Capital intact.

"VI.—The following is a summary of the results which may be anticipated from the operations of this Company :—

"The Share Capital being in the first instance invested in securities as before mentioned, may be taken as giving an average return of 6 per cent. per annum, or upwards.

"As Debentures are issued, they will furnish further Capital for investment, at a rate which, as the solid security of the Debentures comes to be known, may be expected to approximate to that of the best British Railway Debentures, and thus afford a large margin of profit on the Share Capital.

"Considerable profit may also be expected to accrue from *drawings* and *sinking funds*, as well as from judicious realizations and changes of investment into other similar securities, as favourable opportunities occur.

"Profits may often be further realized without incurring any risk or liability from Commissions on the purchase of large parcels of Debentures for investment, and by acting simply as agent for the issue or sale of securities for account of Railway and other Companies, for which its position will afford unusual advantages.

"Supposing the paid-up Capital to be invested at 6 per cent.—that each £1,000,000 of Debentures issued gives an average profit of 1 per cent. per annum from the difference of interest paid on it, and that received from the securities in which it is invested—and that the profit from commissions, sales, and reinvestments, and all other sources, averages 1 per cent. per annum, which appears a moderate estimate, the results would be, approximately, as follows, after deducting Directors' and Founders' percentages, and an ample allowance for expenses :—

|  £ | Dividend per ann. on paid-up Share Capital. |
|---|---|
| With 1,000,000 Share Capital | 6 p.c. on the amount called up. |
| „ 1,000,000 of Debentures issued | - 8 „ „ „ |
| „ 2,000,000 „ „ | - 11 „ „ „ |
| „ 3,000,000 „ „ | - 14 „ „ „ |
| „ 4,000,000 „ „ | - 17 „ „ „ |
| „ 5,000,000 „ „ | - 20 „ „ „ |

"From the experience of the Board of Directors, they feel justified in stating their belief that seldom has an institution been founded so free from risk, and yet possessing elements that hold out so good a prospect of a highly remunerative return to the Shareholders."

## CHAPTER II.

## OF NEW TRUSTS (*continued*).

*Section* 1.—*Subscription Trusts with, or without, Share Capital.*

ART. 2.—In a previous chapter we adverted to the fact that some of the existing Societies have nothing in common with Trusts but the name; for they are merely Mutual Loan Associations, the plan being to give every certificate-holder the right to an advance out of the subscriptions contributed, which are usually monthly, at a small rate, such as 2s. 6d. or 5s. a month per certificate.

The certificates are sometimes of no definite amount, and occasionally fixed at £25 or £30. Much looseness in respect to the legal considerations affecting this point seems to prevail; nor is provision always made to define the liability of the certificate-holders. Some of these Subscription Trusts profess to have a share capital; others have none, adopting the principles of self-relying mutuality.

3.—To give a sort of lottery attraction to the Trust, one loan or appropriation in every four (or rather £100 out of every £400 it has ready to lend out of the subscriptions) is advanced by ballot, for a term not exceeding 22 years, without any charge for interest.

The other three advances are made to the highest bidder of a premium on each £100 to be lent; such premium being in place of the charge for interest which would otherwise be required.

The loan with the premium is then repaid in full by gradual * subscription, over a term of years selected. One

---

[* Among the tables, which will be found appended to this division, is one that shows what the subscription of £100 by instalments, in various terms of years, would amount to at 4 per cent. interest, and the equivalent present values].

objection to this premium system is that, although ample security is stated to be required by the committee, the necessitous member, with the least sound security to offer, may be the one to tender the highest premium in order to induce the committee to grant him the loan.

4.—The one loan out of four, which is granted without charge for interest or premium, is undoubtedly an artificial cause of the popularity of this kind of society. The attraction is increased by the privilege accorded to the lucky drawer of disposing of his appropriation at a profit to any other person, who may desire the advance, and offer to pay him a good price for it.

The prospect of this profit being made is dressed up in glowing words in the examples set forth in the prospectuses.

Its effect, however, is to cause a higher premium to be necessary on every £300 out of £400 advanced, in order that the society may make the average profit all round which it wants for its money.

By way of illustration, in one society, 5 per cent. is required for interest which the society proffers to those members who are investors or depositors, and 1 per cent. for expenses and contingencies. Together, these make 6 per cent.

Now, to obtain 6 per cent. profit all round on the society's funds, 8 per cent. must be charged on the £300.

It is matter for regret that the general excellence of the principles involved in these subscription Trusts should be qualified by the gratuitous appropriation system. Where larger payments are required from the majority of members, in order that a lucky few may have their loans without interest, it is time to admit that all real mutuality, as a fact, is destroyed, however much it may be asserted.

Some of these Loan Trusts are in such respectable hands, that one may well wonder at the foolish feature not having been abandoned earlier. They are exceedingly popular, and in many cases would be of undoubted prosperity if placed on a sounder footing as to the principles adopted.

5.—We append an example from another existing Trust, which is curious as illustrating the ideas that prevail on the subject:—

EXAMPLE.—"L. M. is desirous of becoming a borrower of £400, and takes four certificates (entitling him to loans of that amount) at a monthly payment of £1 thereon. The directors having given notice of a Loan Meeting, L. M. fills up a form of tender (provided by the Association), sends it to the head office, and (at his option) attends the meeting. The tenders are then opened, and L. M.'s offer of a premium (say) £60 for each £100 loan, payable with the loan itself by instalments of £10 13s. 4d. quarterly in 15 years, being the highest, is accepted, and having provided approved security, he receives the money. Apparently L. M. has paid a high rate for the advance, seeing that loans on good security may usually be obtained at £5 per cent.; but then the rate depends upon the fluctuating value of money, and the loans are made for short periods only, or are liable to be called in on short notice; moreover, both principal and interest have to be paid in lump sums. L. M. in the meantime has paid up his 4 certificates (£100) and has received interest at £5 per cent. per annum on his subscriptions as paid, together with £48 per cent. of the profits of the 'Fund' triennially, and is entitled to four equal shares of the reserve, distributable at the close of the 'Fund.' If L. M. applied his profits to the repayment of his loan, he would materially lessen its cost, because by anticipating the period of its redemption, the premium payable for such period would be extinguished."

6.—In the above example, for a cash advance of £400 the borrower has to pay up in 15 years four times £160, or £640 by instalments of £10 13s. 4d. a quarter, which is equivalent to paying interest at from 6½ to under 7 per cent. per annum, according as the interest is reckoned at yearly, half-yearly, or quarterly rests. The mean rate of interest even at 7 per cent. is but 5¼ per cent., as only three out of four of the loans carry interest. If the society continue to lend its money at this low rate of interest loss must follow, considering the miscellaneous nature of the securities on which advances are made, unless the number of years for which the member makes the above quarterly payment of £10 13s. 4d. are extended, or unless the premium be increased.

## Section 2.—*Of the rate of Premium charged in place of interest and of Valuations.*

ART. 7.—The premium charged in place of interest by Subscription Trusts varies. In some, as above, it is only £60 per £100 loan. In one of the largest and best societies of the kind it is fixed at not less than £70, which with the £100 cash advanced, making £170, is, however, only to be returned by instalments (monthly or quarterly) at the rate of £8 10s. a year in 20 years. If this were the highest premium obtained, the interest realized would be scarcely sufficient, for it is* under 6 per cent. per annum; even reckoning interest as made quarterly.

This is shown by the following rates of repayment per annum for a loan of £100 in 20 years, according as the subscriptions (with interest at 6 per cent. per annum) are calculated as—

| | | | |
|---|---|---|---|
| Compounded annually, viz., | - | - | £8 14 4 |
| ,, half-yearly ,, | - | - | 8 13 0 |
| ,, quarterly ,, | - | - | 8 12 5 |

8.—When the affairs of a society of the kind are being valued, error will be made if in estimating the *present worth* of the repayments (receivable on existing loans over unexpired terms of years) deduction is not made for the fact that, as such repayments come in, only three-fourths of them are capable of being

---

[* As 6 per cent. on £300 would be only £4 10s. on the £400, the average rate on its funds obtained by a Society lending at £70 premium would be only 4½ per cent. In practice, however, the premium actually bid is frequently much more than the minimum £70—sometimes it is as much as £100—so that for 20 years, in return for a loan of £100 the borrower pays £10 a year in quarterly instalments. The rate of interest he then pays is about 8 per cent. This 8 per cent. or £100 premium is, therefore, what the society must charge which desires an average profit of 6 per cent., since 4 times 6 equal 3 times 8].

re-invested at interest, since a quarter of the appropriations is to be made without any premium or interest being charged.

The necessity for this provision arises, also, from the fact that 5 per cent. interest per annum is by the rules to be credited continuously in future years on the subscription moneys, which constitute the liability side of the account. Hence the amount set down in the assets side must be obtained by valuing at not less than £6 13s. 4d. per cent. per annum discount, since 5 per cent. can only be credited on £400 in future by providing in the form of discount £6 13s. 4d. on three-fourths of the assets discounted.

This may be met indirectly by making a large reserve off the assets, when valued at a lower rate of discount, such as 6 per cent. The reserve will, also, have to be considerable from the very miscellaneous nature of the securities accepted by these Subscription Trusts, which are exposed to loss not only from the security not turning out "good," but from legal defects not detected, and from chance of fraud when its bonds are 'payable to bearer.'

It may be incidentally mentioned that if the repayments are receivable quarterly, the valuation should be by a table at half-yearly not quarterly compounding of interest, as frequently money, in order to be securely invested, has to lie unproductive for a time.

---

*Section 3.—Regulations of Subscription Trusts.*

ART. 9.—The following are the principal Regulations adopted by a Trust which has collaterally a Share Capital :—

### I.—DEBENTURE FUNDS.

"Funds" are formed for the purpose of receiving sums of money from Subscribers on Certificates, and for lending them to Subscribers *only*, in the manner hereinafter described.

## II.—Certificates.

The Association issues Certificates of £25 each, which are subscribed for by instalments at the rate of 5s. per month. All instalments bear interest from date of payment. Subscriptions may be paid in advance.

A "Fund" is * closed when all the holders of Certificates therein, requiring an advance, shall have exercised that right.

The following advantages attach to each Certificate as an investment:—

1st.—The return of all Subscriptions is *guaranteed* by the Capital † of the Association.

2nd.—Interest at —— per cent. per annum, payable on the 1st of January and 1st of July is also guaranteed on the amount of Subscriptions received.

3rd.—*Eighty* per cent. of the net *yearly profits* of the "Fund" are paid to Subscribers as follows:—

£48 per cent. thereof is paid *in cash* at the end of each *third* year, and the remaining £32 per cent. is carried to a Reserve Fund to be divided ratably amongst the holders of existing Certificates at the close of the Fund.

4th.—*Each* Certificate entitles the holder to an *advance* of £100, repayable by instalments, spread over a term not exceeding 22 years.

5th.—Holders can at any time sell or transfer their Certificates.

6th.—After a Certificate has been two years in force, the Subscriptions and interest may, upon notice, be withdrawn.

7th.—Any number of Certificates can be subscribed for, in the same or in different "Funds."

8th.—Failure to pay Subscriptions *does not entail fines,* but Certificates will not bear interest while in arrear.

---

[* This provision is unnecessary and impedes the development of the Trust].

[† The actual Capital *subscribed* should be stated in the Prospectus and not the *nominal* amounts *registered*, otherwise the Directors and Officials may incur personal liability (see also note, p. 79). In some Subscription Trusts, termed "Mutual," no Share Capital is issued, and the Funds consist solely of the Members' payments on their Certificates or Loans].

The Holders of Certificates can obtain advances from the "Fund" to which they subscribe, repayable by instalments as shall be agreed, extending over a period not exceeding 22 years, with the following advantages:—

1st.—The right to a loan of £100 attaches to each Certificate.

2nd.—*One-fourth* of the Subscriptions received on Certificates are advanced to Subscribers *free of Interest, Premium, or Bonus*. Priority to Loans is determined by Ballot. All Certificates in respect to which Loans have not been made are eligible to Ballot.

3rd.—*Three-fourths* of the Subscriptions received on Certificates are advanced to Subscribers on tender of premium, but otherwise free of Interest, Bonus, or Discount.

4th.—Each Subscriber can tender in writing for an advance, and the highest Premium offered will be accepted.

5th.—*Premiums are paid by instalments,* pro rata *with the repayment of the advance.*

6th.—Subscribers are entitled to be present at the Ballots.

7th.—Subscribers, who obtain through the Ballot the right to a free advance, may sell such right, or may transfer the same to the Association on liberal terms.

8th.—Subscribers securing an advance by * Ballot are required to continue subscribing on their Certificates, without receiving interest, but participating in the profits of the "Fund."

9th.—Subscribers receiving an advance by tender of Premium may, by agreement, discontinue their subscriptions, otherwise they will receive interest half-yearly on the amount paid, and will participate in the profits of the "Fund."

10th.—Every description of sound security may be given by Borrowers.

11th.—Securities held by the Association may be redeemed, exchanged, varied, or reduced.

---

[* It will be observed that the Society requires that a Ballot Borrower of £100 should keep in force at the same time a Certificate for each £100 on which (with regard to the subscription he pays) he draws no interest half-yearly.

This is but a small gain to the Trust, for the prospectus states that his money is returned to him (when the Loan term is expired) with his share in the surplus profits; but it operates as a reserve against contingencies of loss.]

12th.—Under certain contingencies—such as sickness, &c.—repayments of advances may be temporarily suspended.

### III.—Security to Subscribers.

"No liability of any kind is incurred by Subscribers or Borrowers.

"Auditors are appointed to examine periodically the books, accounts, and securities of each 'Fund.'

"Each 'Fund' with interest is guaranteed by the Subscribed Capital of the Association.

"£32 per cent. of the net profits form a constantly augmenting Reserve Fund."

### IV.—Formation of Funds.

Certificates issued prior to the date named for the closing of a "Fund" to Subscribers, form a distinct and complete "Fund," and no new Subscribers are admitted thereto.

As soon as the right and option to a loan of £100 (which attaches to each Certificate) shall have been exercised, the "Fund" shall be closed; and the Directors will, as the Loan Instalments are received, divide them among the Subscribers, together with the "Reserve" and all other assets appertaining to such "Fund."

### V.—Securities.

The following Securities are accepted as security for advances, subject only to adequate value and title in each case, viz. :—Freehold, Leasehold, and Copyhold premises and Land, Ground Rents, Life Interests, Reversions, Annuities, Life Policies, Warrants, Delivery Orders, Home, Foreign, and Colonial Stocks, Funds, and Bonds, and Colonial Bank or Railway Debenture Shares and Obligations, and Shares in any Public Undertaking in the United Kingdom, and the *Debenture and Tontine Certificates of the Association.*

*Bills of Sale,* * *Bills of Exchange, Promissory Notes, or simple personal security will not be accepted.*

---

[* These Subscription Trusts make Advances and Investments not only on Stock Exchange Securities, but in Real and Leasehold and Miscellaneous property, excluding only such as are enumerated above.]

## VI.—REMARKS.

" From the foregoing, it will be seen—

" 1st.—That Subscribers are *not* required to contribute towards *Management Expenses*.

" 2nd.—That they are *not* required to pay *Entrance Fees* or *Fines*.

" 3rd.—That they *receive* their *half-yearly* interest and declared profits *in Cash*.

" 4th.—That the premium *tendered* by Subscribers for Loans is the *Sole charge* thereon.

" 5th.—That Instalments on Loans are *not* payable *in advance*.

" 6th.—That Subscribers *receive interest* on their *subscriptions* until they obtain a Loan by *Ballot* ;—*they* also *participate in every triennial division of profits during the currency of the Loan* and in the *final division of assets* at the *closing of the Fund*.

" 7th.—Subscriptions on Certificates commence from the *date of entering a " Fund ;"* hence there are no *back payments*.

" 8th.—That *every* Subscriber participates in the *advantages* afforded by this Association on a footing of *absolute equality*."

## Section 4.—*Other provisions of Subscription Trusts.*

ART. 10. The following is from a Society without Share Capital and illustrates the sanguine views entertained :—

" The ―― Society, whilst promoting saving habits in the ' Young,' provides a mode of Investment for the ' Old ' when Life Insurance is no longer available.

"To suit the convenience of all classes of society, subscriptions are received monthly, for any period desired.

"Interest at the rate of 5 per cent. per annum is allowed on all subscriptions upon unappropriated certificates, and is paid every quarter on application."

### " ADVANCES AND INVESTMENTS.

| "CLASS I. | "CLASS II. |
|---|---|
| "Cash Bonus and 5 per cent. interest. Five shillings per month (twopence per day, | "Tontine Bonus and 5 per cent. interest. Five shillings per month (twopence per day), |
| *Each Appropriation Certificate,* | *Each Appropriation Certificate,* |
| "Entitling the holder to an advance, on approved security, of £100 either by ballot or tender for twenty years repayable quarterly. A ballot advance, being free of interest or premium, can be sold for over £30 cash. | "Entitling the holder to an advance of £100, either by ballot or tender (as Class I). Interest as above stated, is payable on Subscriptions; but instead of taking a Cash Bonus each year, the Members form a Tontine, and those whose Nominees survive will begin to participate in the accumulated profits in about fifteen years after the commencement of the Fund. It is expected that as much as £150 per Certificate will thus become payable. Elderly persons can nominate young people, thus making a provision for them which they cannot do by insuring their own lives, the premium being too high at advanced age." |
| "Interest as above stated, is payable on the Subscriptions as well as an Annual Cash Bonus, the latter varying according to the profits of the Society." | |

## "INVESTMENTS ONLY.

| "Class III. | "Class IV. |
|---|---|
| "Cash Bonus and 5 per cent. Interest. Half-a-crown a month (one penny a day), | "Tontine Bonus and 5 per cent, Interest. Half-a-crown a month (one penny a day), |
| *Each Bonus Certificate,* | *Each Bonus Certificate,* |
| "Entitling the holder to Cash Bonus and Interest (same as Class I.), but without the advance." | "Entitling the holder to Tontine Bonus and 5 per cent. Interest (same as Class II.), but without the advance." |

"Every fourth advance is by ballot, free of all interest or premium, and repayable by quarterly instalments spreading over twenty years. The intermediate advances are made to members who have given the highest written tender.

"There is no bidding or sale by auction for any of the Society's moneys, so that the country members enjoy the same facilities as those in London, and the ballots are drawn in the presence of a notary public, whose certificate of the successful members is advertised in the public journals."

*The following are a few of the other Principal Clauses:—*

### I.—Members.

Every person shall be deemed a member of the Society, who shall have signed an application for a Certificate, who shall have been approved by the directors, and whose name is entered in the register of members.

Every person shall cease to be a member in respect of any Certificate immediately such Certificate shall have been cancelled or forfeited, or upon his receiving from the Society a return of the Subscriptions paid by him in respect of such Certificate, in accordance with the regulations hereinafter contained.

An Appropriation-Certificate shall be a document issued to every such member on his entering the Society, and shall certify his title to receive an advance of £100 out of the funds of the Society as soon as he shall have paid £3 in respect of such Certificate, as well as to participate in the profits, pursuant to the conditions and regulations hereinafter contained.

## II.—FUNDS.

Any two or more Funds may be at any time united into one Fund, upon such union being resolved on by the Board of Directors, and sanctioned in writing by three-fourths in number of the Members of each Fund to be thus consolidated.

Provided such three-fourths represent at least one-half of the value of each of the Funds proposed to be united.

## III.—LOANS.

A Deed of Mortgage charge or security, prepared in such forms as the Directors may from time to time prescribe, shall be duly executed by every borrowing member at the time the advance to him or her is made.

Every member applying for an advance on the security of any property other than Certificates of the Society, shall upon such application pay a Report Fee of 5s. per cent. on the amount applied for, in order to enable the Directors to procure a proper report as to the nature and sufficiency of such security, provided that such Report Fee shall be in addition and without prejudice to the payments of any travelling expenses and professional charges incurred in examining the security (which last-mentioned payments, expenses, and charges may be deducted out of the sum advanced), and shall not be returnable in the event of the proposed security being declined.

If any member is desirous of paying off the balance of any

loan or loans due from him, he may receive credit for any balance of * subscriptions due to him by the Society;—the withdrawal fee, and such a fine (if any) as the Actuary may recommend, and the Directors approve, being first deducted, anything in Article — to the contrary notwithstanding.

### IV.—Profits.

At the close of the year 18—, and at the close of every fifth year thereafter, the Actuary shall report to the Directors the exact state of each Fund, specifying the amount of profits earned in respect thereof, and shall recommend such a sum to be allotted in Bonuses to the Subscribers thereto, as in his judgment will be prudent and expedient.

### V.—Transfers.

The person appearing in the Register of Members, for the time being, to be the holder of any Certificate shall be entitled (subject to the regulations hereinafter contained) in manner therein expressed, to sell and transfer such certificate to any person not being an infant, lunatic, married woman, or under any legal disability; but the Directors shall have power to refuse to allow any transfer, without stating any reason for such refusal.

It shall be incumbent upon the Directors in the case of a Transfer of any Certificate (deposited as security and subject thereto) to any

---

[* There is some confusion of idea in the prospectuses of these Subscription Trusts, that, through a member continuing simultaneously with his loan to pay on a corresponding number of Investing Certificates, he is thereby reducing the cost of his loan. In fact, however, there is no connection between the two payments, as he is to be credited with 5 per cent. per annum for his subscriptions and a share in the surplus profits. His rights as an Investor belong to him as such, whether he seek for a Loan and pay a premium for it, or not. Many investors never become borrowers].

Society, Public Company, or the Trustee or Trustees of any Society, or Public Company, to demand in the case of such Societies or Companies as have no uncalled Capital or Reserve Fund, a margin of not less than double the amount required from any other borrowing member or mortgagee.

### VI.—WITHDRAWALS.

Any member who, after the expiration of three calendar months from his entry, may wish to withdraw from the Society, and the legal representatives of any member who shall have died, shall be entitled to have the total amount of the subscriptions which shall have been paid upon each Certificate held by such withdrawing or deceased member, returned to him or them;—a Withdrawal fee of 10s. per Certificate being first deducted in the case of Appropriation Certificates, and of 5s. in the case of Bonus Certificates.

Provided nevertheless, that such payments shall be made solely out of moneys existing at the time in any Fund, and composed exclusively of sums which shall have been paid as premiums upon or received in respect of, repayment of Appropriations. Provided that in all cases payment shall be only made in rotation, according to the date of the receipt of the notice from such withdrawing members or representatives of such deceased members.

But in the event of any such member giving notice to withdraw a portion of the certificates held by him, and directing the amount so withdrawn to be applied in payment of subscriptions on other certificates held by him, the Board may, upon the recommendation of the Consulting Actuary, and payment of the usual withdrawal fees, agree to such withdrawal and forthwith proceed to give effect to such mentioned notice, notwithstanding anything hereinbefore contained to the contrary.

### VII.—VOTES.

No member shall be entitled to vote in respect of any certificate, unless at the time of voting he shall have been the registered holder of such certificate for at least six calendar months.

No member shall be entitled to vote in respect of any certificate unless all subscriptions thereon due a month prior to the meeting shall have been paid, but he shall be entitled to vote in respect of certificates which shall have been so paid up, notwithstanding that he may hold other certificates on which payments are in arrear.

No member shall be allowed to vote at all if his repayments of Appropriations are in arrear beyond the twenty-one days' grace allowed by these Articles.

At every meeting where a poll has been demanded, two or more scrutineers may be appointed by such meeting, or, failing such appointment, by the Directors;—but not more than one-half of the number of scrutineers shall be Directors or Officers of the Society.

## VIII.—OFFICERS.

The Officers of the Society shall consist of Directors, Auditors, Consulting Actuary, Surveyor, Solicitor, Secretary, General Manager, and such other Officers as the Directors may at any time deem expedient. No Officer of the Society shall under any circumstances be entitled to any claim upon the Funds thereof for loss of office, in consequence of his dismissal therefrom, or of his ceasing to hold such office.

## IX. DIRECTORS.

The number of Directors shall not be less than five or more than seven. But in case the Directors shall at any time by casual vacancies be less in number than five, it shall be lawful for them to continue to transact all such business as they might have transacted had their number not been less than five, until such time as such vacancy or vacancies shall be filled up as hereinafter provided.

The qualification of each Director shall be the holding of 50 Appropriation or 100 Bonus Certificates, with at least two years' subscriptions paid thereon, or an aggregate investment of £300; exclusive of moneys borrowed from the Society.

If he shall become a Director of another Company, having objects similar to the objects of this Society, or, if he shall accept any office of profit in the Society, he shall *ipso facto* cease to be a Director of the Society, but he shall be eligible for re-election by a General Meeting.

No Director shall be present during the discussion of, or vote upon any subject in which he is interested, either personally or as Director, or Trustee of any Company having dealings with the Society.

The remuneration of the Directors shall from and after the first day of ——, 18—, consist of such sum or allowance as the Members may from time to time determine at any ordinary General Meeting. [In one Trust these words follow :—"such amount not to exceed the sum of £2,100"].

## X.—Accounts.

The accounts of the Society shall be examined and the correctness of the Balance Sheet ascertained every quarter by Auditors appointed annually.

All moneys received at the Registered Office of the Society shall be paid to the Society's account at their Bankers the same day, provided the same shall exceed the sum of £10, and shall have been received before 3 p.m.

## Section 5.—*Future Subscription Trusts.*

Art. 11.—The following modifications seem desirable for a Trust of the Subscription class :—

(*a*) *The certificates always to be fixed at some definite amount.*

(*b*) *The amount, such as £25 or £30, to be paid up in one sum.*

(*c*) *Or, if preferred, the amount to be paid up by* 10s. *a month, so as to define the time taken for paying it up.*

(*d*) *The Trust to consist of Triennial Series, each lasting fifteen or twenty years.*

(*e*) 4 *or* 4½ *per cent. only to be credited at the close of each financial half year, for interest on the subscriptions, out of the profits, but not to be guaranteed.*

(*f*) *Subscriptions to be withdrawable—after notice and in rotation—but only out of the loan repayments. Unless the Committee think proper to direct otherwise, no sale of Stock to be made to meet withdrawals; the interest on the withdrawals to be only up to the end of the last expired half year.*

(*g*) *When the certificate is paid up, then, instead of only* 4 *or* 4½ *per cent. being credited, the certificate to receive Dividends at the rate realized, and a coupon of Reversion to be then given to the holder entitling him to participate in the surplus profits at the expiration of his series in the Trust. Each coupon to consist of as many Units of Reversion as may be proportionate to the number of years the certificate has been paid up before the series expires.*

## Section 6.—*Of Tontine Bonuses and Subscription Shares.*

Art. 12.—In addition to the regulations, quoted in previous sections, some of these Subscription Trusts adopt what is termed the * " Tontine ". system of paying bonuses from the profits and even some of the shares themselves, at dates depending on lives surviving some number of years, such as 20.

The following paragraphs from the prospectus of a Tontine Subscription Trust illustrate the application of the Tontine principle:

I.—" The 'Tontine' consists of the Deposit by several persons of an equal sum, or of sums varying in amount according to the ages of the lives nominated, in a common purse; the whole, with compounded profits, to be paid at the expiration of a previously agreed period to the survivors.

"The distinguishing feature of the ' Tontine ' is that by its means a small disbursement will secure, at a future fixed period, a larger return. The cause of the increase, apart from † compound interest, which takes place on the original Deposits, is the acquisition by the survivors of the shares of deceased members or of those for whom the payments are made. The loss of the deposit by the death of the life nominated by the Depositor, unconnected with other considerations, would deprive the Deposit of the character of an investment; but it is obvious that, in many cases, Deposits will be made, not as a pure investment, but in the name and for the benefit of children, or other persons, whom the Depositor is desirous of serving at a future fixed period, but whose decease before the

---

[* A full account of the nature and principles of Tontines is furnished in the earlier editions of our *Treatise on Building and Land Societies.*]

[† In the draft prospectus of an " Average Investment Trust " appended to this publication will be found a table for " Doubling Accumulative Bonds," showing how, from and after the end of ten years, £200 is returnable for £100 invested. If the Tontine principle were adopted of paying only to the lives surviving each year in which the drawings take place, a considerable increase on the £200 returned would occur as the term of the drawings runs out.]

L

arrival of the period of distribution would render the loss to him of little or no importance. In this point of view, the 'Tontine' may afford to the provident, without any of the evils of speculation and gambling, the *maximum* of advantage with the *minimum* of expense."

" II.—The 'Tontine' principle is as capable of beneficial application to the most important social purposes as Life Assurance, the fundamental difference between the two systems is, that in the case of Life Assurance the common fund is apportioned amongst the representatives of the subscribers *as they die*, while in the case of a 'Tontine,' it is divided amongst the subscribers themselves who survive.

" The Deposit once made, if so desired, may become a final and irrevocable gift not liable to be affected by any reverse of circumstances affecting the Depositor.

" No enquiry is necessary as to the health of the lives nominated.

" 'Funds' may be opened to enable persons of every age, class, and condition, by subscribing to secure the following benefits :—

i. *A provision for the education, apprenticeship, or advancement in life of children attaining specified ages.*

ii. *A provision may also be made against the incapacities of old age.*

iii. *Employers can make provision for old and faithful servants.*

iv. *Prospective liabilities and contingencies can be provided against.*"

" III.—The certificates issued entitle the subscriber, if surviving at the final distribution, to participate in the division of the moneys of the ' Funds,' or his rights may be vested in another person. The life selected for nomination may be his own, or that of another person of any age, according to the conditions of the ' Fund.'

" *Proof of Birth.*—Satisfactory evidence of the age of the life nominated must be furnished to the Association before the final distribution of the ' Fund ' is made.

" *Subscriptions.*—The *single payment* value for one certificate is given in the tables, but subscriptions can be paid by instalments.

" *Forfeiture of Subscriptions.*—The death of the life nominated in the certificate at any period from the date of subscription to the final closing of the 'Fund' cancels all claim to participate in the distribution."

## Section 7.—*Of some special kinds of Trusts that may be formed with advantage.*

ART. 13.—(i.) *Real and Leasehold\* Property Investment Trusts.*—Trust Associations of this kind lay out their Capital and Funds in houses or land in the United Kingdom, and in such other selected securities and investments as may from time to time be deemed expedient. Land, however, is usually only purchased "when desirable for building purposes, or likely, from its situation, to advance in value, while the principal operations of the Trust are made in such houses and shops, with their fixtures, fittings, &c., as would produce safely good rentals, in settled and improving localities." This affords an immediate return on the money invested.

The experience of the past twenty-five years has shown that in many parts of London, as well as in the large provincial towns, houses and shops have much increased in rental value.

The causes which have led to this augmentation are still active and continuous, and it is evident that, for a Trust Association, property of this character, when dealt with on a sufficiently large scale, affords a safe and reasonably profitable investment.

(ii.) *Annuity Trusts*† to grant annuities on lives, and for terms of years certain, increasing periodically out of the divisions of profit.

(iii.) *Deferred Securities Trusts* to invest in Securities not at present fully developed, but from which increase in value is likely to arise in future years.

---

[\* See hereon the *Treatise on Building and Land Societies*, 4th edition, revised, 5s. Laytons, 150, Fleet Street.]

[† Respecting "*Life Assurance Trusts*" see our *Treatise on Life Contingencies and Reversions.* Revised edition, 7s. 6d., Laytons.]

## CHAPTER III.

### Of New Trusts (*continued*).

*Section 1.—Of the kind of Share Capital for Trusts, of Preferred and Deferred Shares, and of Trusts Limited by Guarantee.*

Art. 14.—The question of whether shares or certificates alone should be issued, or both, is one to be settled according to the requirements of the locality or special connection for which a Trust is founded.

In constituting a new Trust with a Share Capital, or indeed any Association under the Companies' Acts, it is sometimes of advantage to divide the Capital into* Preferred and Deferred Shares.

This plan, originally adopted with success in certain railways, has of late years become very popular; especially as the division of ordinary Railway Shares into Preferred and Deferred is found to increase the aggregate market value of the Stock.

In companies a portion of the shares are frequently issued as Preference Shares, carrying some definite rate of dividend (such as 5 or 6 per cent.) if the profits will allow it; and the remainder are made ordinary shares upon which, after paying the Preferences, the net profit revenues of the Company are divisible.

---

[* In a recent conversion of a private business into a Joint Stock Company, the shares were classed "A" and "B," the former being held by the late partners, while the latter of £100 each were offered to the *employés* and intimate connexions of the firm. It is provided that a holder of "B" Shares wishing to realise his holding shall not dispose of it to an outsider at its estimated value, but shall be paid its *par* value by the Company. In the same way, any "B" Share unallotted is to be tendered for by the holders of the "A" Shares, and any addition to the *par* value arising from the tenders is to be added to the revenue of the Company.]

If Debentures are also issued, which are a first charge preceding even the Preference Shares, they are taken up by one set of capitalists; the Preference Shares, which pay a rather better interest, attracting another set; and finally the ordinary shares, which take all the risk of the business, suiting the more speculative Investor.

15.—*Of Trusts limited by Guarantee.* — The liability of the members of a Trust may, under the provisions of the Companies Acts, be limited to such amount as the members may respectively undertake to contribute to the assets of the Trust in the event of its being wound up.

In the case of a Trust with liability so limited, the memorandum of association must contain the following *things :—

(i.) The name of the proposed Trust, with the addition of the word "Limited" as the "last word," in such name:

(ii.) The part of the United Kingdom, whether England, Scotland, or Ireland, in which the registered office of the Trust is proposed to be situate:

(iii.) The objects for which the proposed Trust is to be established:

(iv.) A declaration that each member undertakes to contribute to the assets of the Trust, in the event of the same being wound up during the time that he is a member, or within one year afterwards, for payment of the debts and liabilities of the Trust contracted before the time at which he ceases to be a member, and of the costs, charges, and expenses of winding up the Trust, and for the adjustment of the rights of the contributories amongst themselves, such amount as may be required, not exceeding a specified amount.

During the continuance of the guarantee, the guarantors may legally receive a bonus yearly, or dividend out of the profits, as compensation for the risk they undertake.

[* "Things" is the statutory expression.]

That plan was advantageously tried in the earlier years of a now very prosperous and large * Mutual Life Assurance Society which, being formed without capital, required in its earlier years a guarantee for the policy-holders.

16.—*Share Capital Redemptions.*—Where only one kind of Share is issued, it has been suggested that the surplus profits might be applied to the payment of Bonuses equivalent to a return of a portion, or even the entirety, of the money paid up on the Shares, instead of augmenting the periodic Dividends beyond 5 per cent. per annum. Supposing a Trust with a Capital of £100,000 in 1,000 Shares of £100 each, makes on the average 8 per cent. per annum (half yearly), clear of expenses, but pays only 5 per cent. in Dividends, then it could by drawings of 50 Shares each half year, in a term of 20½ years return during the last 10 years the whole of the Capital out of the 3 per cent. surplus profits, and yet leave the Capital intact at the end of the term, with a surplus of £849 5s. (even after allowing for a small loss between the decimal fractions and the actual cash payments). The first drawing not taking place till the end of the 11th year, and the last at the close of 20½ years.

In this example all the Shares, whether drawn or not, would continue to receive the Dividends at 5 per cent. half yearly; for the return of Capital, being made by drawings out of the surplus profits only, leaves in a legal sense the Capital, originally paid up, intact for the continuance of future Dividends at whatever rate,

---

[* The prospectuses of some of the existing Subscription Trusts, which have a liability limited to the amount unpaid on the Shares, state that their Debentures and Certificates are secured and guaranteed by the Capital of the Trust, leaving open the inference that it is the *nominal* Capital stated in the memorandum of association. This is frequently a large figure exceeding the number and amount of the Shares actually taken up. The statute of 1862 contains an express provision, designed to prevent any misleading which might arise from this practice. On this point see the legal portion of this book further on.]

whether 5 per cent. or more, which the Society can subsequently afford to pay.

If it were desired to multiply the chances in the drawings the tickets might be made for parts only of the money paid up on the Shares. Thus, on a £10 Share, five tickets of £2 each might be given at each drawing to those who had not yet drawn any portion out.

To those, who have been partially repaid, a proportionately reduced number of tickets would be issued at the subsequent drawings.

*Section 2.—Of the Privileges of Founders and Expenses of Management.*

ART. 17.—Of late years, instead of paying promotion money to Founders, an attempt has been made to meet their claims for labour and ability in establishing successful associations by giving them certain shares, which are to participate in the surplus profits after a certain per centage on the ordinary Capital has been paid.

Thus in * one important Trust the Directors' allowance is

---

[* "No promotion money is to be paid ; and the Founders of the Company undertake to pay all preliminary and other expenses of its establishment and to guarantee the subscription of two-thirds of the present issue (being the amount required by the rules of the Stock Exchange for obtaining an official quotation) in' consideration of receiving 10 per cent. of the net profits in every year in which not less than 7 per cent. dividend is paid on the entire paid-up Share Capital. This arrangement not only assures the successful foundation of the Company, but enables it to start with its Share Capital intact.

"The remuneration of the Directors is made mainly contingent on profits, the fixed allowance being limited to £2,000 a year, in addition to which they are to receive 5 per cent. upon the net profits of any year in which a dividend of not less than 7 per cent. is paid to the Shareholders."]

£2,000 per annum, and 5 per cent. additional on the net profits of any year in which a dividend of not less than 6 per cent. is paid.

The Founders receive on their* shares a tenth part of the net profits in every year, in which not less than 6 per cent. dividend is declared on the whole of the paid-up Capital, and after providing for the Directors' allowance.

In some other Trusts the Directors and Founders receive the same privileges, but only when not less than 7 per cent. dividend is paid on the entire paid-up Share Capital.

---

*Section 3.—Of Erroneous Dividends and Deposits.*

ART. 18.—The gravity of the error committed, when large dividends are declared without setting aside a sufficient Reserve or Equalisation Fund, was amply shown by the condition of certain London Credit and Finance Societies in the year 1866 before their transmutation and present management. To avoid invidious reference to any one of these, it will be sufficient to advert to the history of the Crédit Mobilier of France, the parent institution of the kind, which might have served as a warning to those of this country, but for the evil influence exercised upon them by the Stock Exchange. Up to the close of 1855, that society met with uninterrupted success. Its profits that year were estimated at 50 per cent. upon the paid-up capital, and an actual division took place at about that rate. Succeeding years, however, showed a diminution of the factitious prosperity. The profit announced at the close of 1856 was barely more than half that of 1855, and the profit at the close of 1857 was scarcely more than a third of the profit of 1856; so that in that year the society found itself com-

---

[* The Founders' shares in this case were 200 of £1 each, and the ordinary shares £20 each.]

pelled to forego the declaration of any dividend—1857 being one of the decennial years of panic. The avidity of the shareholders for dividends, which led them to accept one year the whole 50 per cent. as profit actually made, was thus the cause that no dividend at all could be declared two years afterwards; a Reserve fund of only one-third would have allowed of a dividend exceeding 30 per cent., and yet have very sensibly mitigated the subsequent fall.

One fertile cause of improvident declarations of profit and dividends has been the provision by which Directors are entitled to a percentage on the profits declared, while they themselves are vested with authority to declare the amount made;—thus they are liable to the temptation to exaggerate the profits earned. It is a sound principle to make the remuneration of Directors dependent on the profits, but only when the profits are ascertained and determined by independent persons.

---

[* *Public Securities Investment Companies and their Profits.*—The *Economist* lately took exception to a portion of the last report of the ——— Company, on the ground that it adopts and defends what that journal deems an unsafe method of reckoning profits. The securities of the company, it is stated in the report, are reckoned according to a fair valuation, based on the market value at a given date; and although this method would not be considered expedient for a mere investment company, it is considered to be so for a concern which has other business, and makes a profit by its commissions as well. It is a good rule of safe stock-taking, even in private business, that articles purchased should not be valued at more than what they cost, however much they may have risen in market value in the interval, although a market depreciation would always be allowed for by a prudent business man. And the reason of the rule is obvious. It is unwise to exaggerate profits, and the fluctuations of business are such that it is time enough to take credit for a profit when the commodity has been actually sold, or the operation otherwise completed. When the business is not a private one, and the accounts are made up for a Joint Stock Company for the purpose of distributing a dividend earned among a miscellaneous body of proprietors, what is simply an act of prudence in private business may be pronounced an absolute necessity. The profit shown in the accounts, whatever it is, is meant for the most part to be paid away, and how is it to be paid if it has not been "encashed" by means of an actual sale? For this purpose, of course, securities

19.—*Of Deposits.*—From the special nature of the securities purchased by these Trusts and the uncertainty which would always attend their realization without loss in times of pressure, it is strongly to be recommended that the directors should not attempt to receive deposits after the banking system, nor unless they be on the security of debentures.

---

are only a species of commodity, to which, therefore, the same rule applies, with perhaps the more reason that the market price of a particular security at a given moment is frequently the result of accidents, and the profit proportionally unstable. A very similar point, we may observe, came up some years ago in the affairs of the Crédit Foncier, when it was discovered that large dividends had been paid out of so-called "Commissions," which had not been received by the company in cash, but in securities of various kinds which ultimately did *not* realize their full nominal amount. It was justly remarked that such dividends ought not to have been paid, and several of the directors who had been paid by a percentage on these supposed profits returned in whole or in part what they had so received. It is manifest that the directors of any company, which treats a rise in market price as a profit, run the risk of afterwards discovering that the profit should never have been paid away, and that the transaction eventually resulted in a loss ; and if they have received a per centage on any such profits they are placed in a most invidious position. There is good reason, therefore, to recommend a very sober method of valuation to companies which have securities to deal with in their balance-sheets.

The Valuation of securities was ably discussed by the directors of the Railway Debenture Trust Company (limited), at the close (January, 1875) of the first complete year of the company's operations, in a statement of the principle upon which the balance-sheet and profit and loss accounts were made out,—

(i.) They pointed out that the securities might either be taken at a Fluctuating valuation, based on their market value, at the close of each year, or at a Fixed valuation, based on their actual cost, which would only be altered when any security was actually realised, in which case the profit or loss would become part of the revenue account of the year; or, in case of any continued default in payment of interest, or other permanent cause of depreciation, when a proper amount would be written off :—"The latter is evidently the proper course to adopt for a company whose main object is investment. It would be unreasonable, and would introduce a speculative element altogether foreign to the nature of this company, that in one year the shareholders should apparently

## VALUATIONS OF SECURITIES.

With regard to the notices to be required before repayment it is well to keep in view possible political and social fluctuations, and the impossibility of a Trust safely undertaking to return deposits at any particular dates.

---

earn a double dividend, and in another no dividend at all, owing to some temporary fluctuation in the state of the money market, or in the rates of gold and exchange, while in reality the cash income and permanent value of the securities had remained the same. The directors have accordingly no hesitation in recommending the shareholders to adopt the principle of a Fixed valuation, and the accounts are framed on this principle, taking the last valuation on the 15th January, 1874, as the basis.

"The present is a good opportunity for establishing this principle, as it fortunately happens that the company has no securities upon which any permanent default is apprehended; and the result of a careful valuation taken on the other principle of the actual market value of each security on the 15th January, 1875, shows that the securities held by the company are now worth £12,454 more than their actual cash cost, and £3,621 more than the cost at which they stand in the company's books by the valuation of the 15th January, 1874. It cannot, therefore, be supposed that the principle of a fixed valuation is adopted from any wish to assist the present dividend. The accounts, framed on this principle of a Fixed valuation, show that the net profits for the year, after deducting current expenses, interest on the company's own Debentures, directors' and founders' percentages, and income-tax, amount to £36,268.

(ii.) "The first establishment of a company of this description, 'while experience has to be acquired and connections formed,' is always a period of difficulty, and in the present instance it has been exposed to a severe trial by the general dulness of most European money markets, and the occurrence of a panic of unexampled severity in the United States. Large profits also were never anticipated until a larger amount of Debenture capital had been placed. Notwithstanding these unfavourable circumstances, the company finds itself, at the end of the first complete year of its existence, with its Capital intact, a large portion of it immediately realisable, and paying a dividend of 7 per cent. per annum, with a balance of undivided profit more than equal to another 3 per cent. on its paid-up capital. The elements of further success seem now to be securely established, and the question of attaining higher dividends mainly reduced to that of placing more Debenture capital. Upon this point, the directors think that, with a view to arriving sooner at a position where the company might fairly be expected to pay 10 per cent., it will be advisable

Casual deposits of small and varying amounts, received from day to day, also open the way to a temptation to fraud.

It is this which makes the system preferable of Debentures, repayable by periodic drawings as the funds come in from the investments of a Trust. [*See Tables at the end.*]

---

to limit the amount of debenture capital that may be issued against the present share capital. The Articles of association provide for the possible issue of £5,000,000 of debenture capital, against the present Share capital of £1,000,000 half paid up. With this amount issued, no doubt the company might look forward to paying dividends of 20 per cent. or upwards, and the security of the debentures would be intrinsically excellent. But with this proportion between Debenture and Share capital, a long time must elapse before anything like that amount could be placed.

(iii.) "If, on the other hand, the debenture capital were limited to £2,000,000, the first-rate nature of the security would at once strike everyone. The £110,000 a year, which would be the maximum amount that could be required for interest and sinking fund, would be secured. 1. By the investment of the £2,000,000 in first-class securities, producing an income of from £120,000 to £140,000 a year. 2. By the £500,000 of paid-up share capital invested in similar securities, and earning a dividend of at least £35,000, and probably £50,000 per annum. 3. By the £500,000 of share capital remaining to be called up in case of need. It is evident that the security thus afforded for the Debentures would be such that under no conceivable state of things could their safety be affected. It seems to the directors to be better for the shareholders to arrive soon at a position when they could reckon on a secure dividend of 10 per cent. per annum, rather than wait for a possible 20 per cent. in some remote future.

"For the present the object is to arrive as quickly as possible at the point when a sufficient amount of Debenture capital is placed to insure a high rate of dividend on the shares, without relying on Commissions or other profits, and without any temptation to take any but the very best and soundest investments.

(iv.) Accordingly it was Resolved "that the amount of Debenture capital shall never, at any one time, exceed twice the amount of Share capital which at that time has been subscribed, and on which not less than one-half or fifty per cent. has been paid up."

(v.) In conclusion, the directors congratulated the shareholders on the position of the Trust, and expressed their confidence in its continued success.]

PART III.

# THE DEBTS OF NATIONS.

---

### CONTENTS.

CHAPTER I.—*The Debts of Nations, their Amount and Progress, and the Foreign Loans in Default.*

,,   II.—*Particulars of the Debts, etc., of each Country.*

# CHAPTER I.

## THE DEBTS OF NATIONS.

*Section 1.—Their Amount and recent Progress.*

ART. 1.—National Debts have been incurred by every civilized nation, and have received during the last quarter of a century an immense extension. The late Mr. Baxter, in an elaborate work, pointed out that a new series of National Debts dates from 1848. All before that belonged to the old regime. They were contracted in the days of sailing ships, post roads and semaphores, and were the result of the first great outburst of democracy that swept over America and Europe a little less than a century ago, which in Europe was merged into military despotism, and finally extinguished by the resuscitated monarchies. The new debts began with the second struggle of democracy and military empire, in an era of steamships, railroads, electric telegraphs, and accumulations of wealth.

2.—According to the figures furnished by the *Economist* and other authorities, the aggregate of the National Debts of the world, including *Home* debts, may be placed at £4,576,527,877, which is in excess of the amounts that have been quoted in recent publications. A large portion of this has accrued in the last two or three years. New countries and old countries vie with each other in the money markets of Europe, and even China has lately commenced a National Debt. We give further on the details of the Debts of various countries, of which the following is a summary. The charges for these Debts exceed the rates of interest, as they involve annuity repayments in some cases.

## 88 SUMMARY OF TOTAL INDEBTEDNESS OF VARIOUS COUNTRIES.

| | Name. | Amount. |
|---|---|---:|
| | | £ |
| 1. | United Kingdom | 779,283,245 |
| 2. | Antigua | 52,350 |
| 3. | Argentine Confederation | 16,500,000 |
| 4. | Australasia | 47,014,761 |
| 5. | Austria | 350,000,000 |
| 6. | Belgium | 36,000,000 |
| 7. | Bolivia | 2,250,000 |
| 8. | Brazil | 62,000,000 |
| 9. | British Columbia | 322,328 |
| 10. | Buenos Ayres | 3,020,100 |
| 11. | Canada | 30,000,000 |
| 12. | Cape of Good Hope | 2,093,400 |
| 13. | Ceylon | 640,000 |
| 14. | Chili | 10,300,000 |
| 15. | Colombia | 4,300,000 |
| 16. | Costa Rica | 3,400,000 |
| 17. | Cuba | 277,600 |
| 18. | Danubian Principalities | 6,444,188 |
| 19. | Denmark | 12,747,500 |
| 20. | Egypt | 75,000,000 |
| 21. | Entre-Rios | 211,600 |
| 22. | Equador | 1,824,000 |
| 23. | France | 900,000,000 |
| 24. | Greece | 8,000,000 |
| 25. | Guatemala | 551,600 |
| 26. | Holland | 80,511,443 |
| 27. | Honduras | 3,224,450 |
| 28. | Hungary | 32,000,000 |
| 29. | India | 130,000,000 |
| 30. | Italy | 390,024,528 |
| 31. | Jamaica | 1,000,000 |
| 32. | Japan | 8,644,940 |

## DEBTS OF NATIONS.

### Summary of total Indebtedness—*continued*.

| | Name. | Amount. |
|---|---|---:|
| | | £ |
| 33. | Liberia | 100,000 |
| 34. | Mauritius | 1,095,500 |
| 35. | Mexico | 63,470,000 |
| 36. | Morocco | 226,500 |
| 37. | Natal | 334,400 |
| 38. | Paraguay | 2,915,700 |
| 39. | Peru | 37,000,000 |
| 40. | Portugal | 69,211,584 |
| 41. | Russia | 340,000,000 |
| 42. | San Domingo | 728,500 |
| 43. | Santa Fé | 296,300 |
| 44. | Sardinia | 2,665,360 |
| 45. | Spain | 375,000,000 |
| 46. | Sweden | 6,700,000 |
| 47. | Trinidad | 100,000 |
| 48. | Turkey | 135,000,000 |
| 49. | United States (General Debt) | 441,050,000 |
| 50. | United States (Separate States Debt) | 78,000,000 |
| 51. | Uruguay | 8,296,000 |
| 52. | Venezuela | 16,700,000 |

*Section 2.—Foreign Loans on which Default has been made.*

ART. 3.—During the Session of 1875 in the House of Commons a Select Committee inquired into the circumstances attending the making of contracts for Loans with certain Foreign States, and the causes which have led to the non-payment of the principal moneys and interests due on such loans. The following may be considered to be a complete list of the Foreign Loans brought out from time to time in the English market, upon which default has been made, with the date of such default. Not the least significant feature in it is that the names of some of the great city firms appear as the agents for one or more defaulting loans.

4.—On this point the *Financier* justly remarks that, no matter how propitious may seem the circumstances of the moment when a new Foreign Loan is brought out, and no matter how eminent may be the position and character of the issuing firm, Foreign Loans, as a class, have special risks of their own. They must always be regarded as more or less *speculative* investments, and should never exercise so attractive an influence over the English investor as to induce him to put the whole of his capital into any one Foreign Stock however good it may appear to be :—

| Name of State. | Date of Default. | Capital Debt in Default. |
|---|---|---:|
| | | £ |
| 1. Bolivia | — | 1,700,000 |
| 2. Costa Rica | April 1, 1874 | 2,362,800 |
| 3. Equador | Nov. 1, 1867 | 1,824,000 |
| 4. Greece | On £800,000, July 1, 1826; on £2,000,000, July 1, 1827; on the balance since its issue in 1833 | 5,143,750 |
| 5. Honduras | Jan. 1, 1873 | 4,972,000 |
| 6. Liberia | Aug. 1, 1874 | 100,000 |

| Name of State. | Date of Default. | Capital Debt in Default. |
|---|---|---|
| | | £ |
| 7. Mexico | — | 16,375,756 |
| 8. Paraguay | April 1, 1874 | 2,903,700 |
| 9. Nicaragua | — | 27,000 |
| 10. San Domingo | Jan. 1, 1873 | 714,300 |
| 11. Spain | June, 1873 | 160,749,670 |
| 12. Venezuela | On £4,411,900 July, 1864; on £917,900 Nov., 1864; on balance April, 1867 | 6,616,800 |
| 13. Confederate States of America | November, 1865 | 2,796,000 |
| 14. Alabama | July, 1871 | 3,750,000 |
| 15. Arkansas | April, 1873 | 2,190,000 |
| 16. Florida | — | 950,000 |
| 17. Georgia | December, 1871 | 4,750,000 |
| 18. Louisiana | Jan. 1, 1874 | 4,725,000 |
| 19. Minnesota | — | 460,000 |
| 20. Mississippi | July, 1839 | 1,600,000 |
| 21. North Carolina | — | 6,100,000 |
| 22. South Carolina | — | 4,225,000 |
| 23. Virginia | — | 5,250,000 |

5.—The total amount of Foreign State or National Debt on which there is at present default, is, in round numbers, £240,000,000; but this has to be regarded relatively, that is to say, what proportion it bears to the total Foreign *Stock* Indebtedness of all countries.

The aggregate (excluding *Home* Debts) is £2,388,032,586, so that the £240,000,000 in default are a little over 10 per cent. This percentage is somewhat in excess, for the figures represent the nominal amounts of the public debts in default, on which but a small price in money was paid in some cases.

## CHAPTER II.

### Particulars of the Debts, &c., of each Country.

### I. UNITED KINGDOM.

Population in 1871 (including Army and Navy), 31,817,108, showing 2,500,000 increase in the decade. Area, 121,000 square miles. Five millions of taxation were repealed in April, 1874, making a *net* forty millions of taxes repealed in less than thirty years. Imports in 1860, £210,530,873; in 1870, £303,296,082; in 1873, £371,287,372. Exports in 1860, £164,521,351; in 1870, £244,080,577; in 1873, £310,994,765.

Mr. John Noble in his able work on National Finance (Longmans, Green and Co., 1875) states that when Mr. Gladstone accepted office, in 1859, the total value of the imports and exports was £304,366,611, or £10 14s. 5d. per head of the population; when he retired, in 1866, the total was £534,195,956, or £17 15s. 2d. per head. The increase in the internal trade of the kingdom is shown by the rapid growth of railway communication; the length of Railways opened increased from 9,542 miles in 1858 to 13,854 miles in 1866; the capital paid up from £325,375,507 to £481,872,184; and the total Traffic receipts from £23,956,749 to £38,164,354.

In the following table the debt includes estimated "Capital" of annuity liabilities; debt per head £24 10s., and annual charge per head, 16s. 8d :—

| Year. | Revenue. Gross. £ | Less Collection. £ | Expenditure. £ | Debt. £ | Charge. £ | Year. |
|---|---|---|---|---|---|---|
| 1820 | — | 54,282,058 | 54,457,247 | 850,000,000 | 31,354,749 | 1820 |
| 1830 | — | 50,056,616 | 49,078,108 | 830,000,000 | 29,067,658 | 1830 |
| 1840 | — | 47,567,565 | 49,161,536 | 820,000,000 | 29,285,451 | 1840 |
| 1850 | 57,323,983 | 53,057,053 | 50,507,599 | 810,000,000 | 28,025,523 | 1850 |
| 1860 | 70,283,074 | 65,796,226 | 68,304,611 | 821,936,564 | 26,335,114 | 1860 |
| 1865 | 67,812,392 | 63,210,255 | 61,312,420 | 811,919,165 | 26,233,288 | 1865 |
| 1870 | 69,945,220 | 64,636,818 | 64,240,137 | 795,370,122 | 26,826,437 | 1870 |
| 1872 | 76,608,770 | 70,538,572 | 64,644,250 | 784,972,003 | 26,615,345 | 1872 |

On the 31st March, 1874—

|   |   |
|---|---|
|   | £ |
| The Funded Debt was | 723,514,005 |
| „ Unfunded „ | 4,479,600 |
| „ Terminable Annuities (value) .. | 51,289,640 |
| Total amount of National Debt was | £779,283,245 |

Sir Stafford Northcote in his budget speech, 1874, stated that the National Debt had been reduced since 1842, in the thirty-two years, to the extent of £70,195,000, and that the Terminable annuities now in operation would strike off a further £50,000,000 in the next eleven years, making over £120,000,000 of debt reduction in forty-three years; besides which there will be the further reduction year by year from the use of part of the surplus revenue to cancel Consols.

Together with this important reduction in the National Debt, immense sums in the aggregate have, in the last thirty-two years, been left to "fructify" in the pockets of the people in the shape of remission of taxation.

The statute of 1875, devised by Sir Stafford Northcote, provides for a large definite interest and Sinking Fund of 28 millions a year, which, if steadily set aside, will have a material effect in further diminishing the National Debt.

*The following is a brief Summary of the Fluctuations in the Price of 3 per cent. Consols from 1730 to 1875.*

1. From 1730 to 1745 the 3 per cent. Consols ruled not under 89; in fact, in June, 1737, they went up to 107.
2. In 1745 (year of rebellion) they fell in price to 76. In 1749 they went up again to 100.
3. In 1763 (year of the peace of Paris), until the commencement of the American war, the 3 per cents. averaged 80 to 90; by the close of the war they were down at 54.

4. By 1792 they had risen to 96. 20th September, 1797, owing to French success, they fell to 47⅜.

5. In August, 1798, in spite of the battle of the Nile, they again fell to 47¼, the lowest price known.

6. In 1802, the Consols, though already down at 79, fell to 66¼, by fear of Buonaparte.

7. In 1814-15 the Consols fluctuated from 72 to 62; in 1815-1816, from 65 to 53⅞.

8. In 1819 (the year of cash payments resumption by the Bank of England), they fell from 79 to 64⅞ because Mr. Robert Peel's Currency Bill was passed, declaring the *Bank Note* to be convertible once more on demand into gold, and the fundholders became alarmed at the prospect.

9. In 1825 (year of Bank failures and Bubble Companies) Consols fell from 94 to 75. The glut of money in 1824 and early in 1825 had caused private bankers to make advances on Securities not easily realizable. 79 banks failed, with 500 branches and liabilities at £14,000,000.

10. In 1847 (railway crisis), Consols fell from 94 to 78¼. In 1852 they reached 101¾.

11. In 1854 they fell to 85. In 1859 (Stock Exchange Italian panic, which continued to April) 100 members of the Stock Exchange were said to have failed. Consols fell from 95 to 88.

12. In 1866 they ranged from 86⅔ to 88½.

13. In July 1875 they were at 94¼.

## II. ANTIGUA.

Population in 1871, 35,157. Area, 183 square miles. *Debt in* 1872, £52,350. Revenue in 1872, £38,817. Expenditure, £39,870. Exports in 1871, £247,630; in 1872, £153,195.

## III. ARGENTINE CONFEDERATION.

Population in 1866, 1,465,000; in 1870, 1,737,000. Area, 550,000 square miles. Population per square mile, 3. *Public debt in* 1873 *(including Buenos Ayres old loans, but excluding railway guarantees), about* £16,500,000. Annual charge, including redemption, £1,500,000. Debt per head £9, expended on works of improvement and Paraguayan war. Annual charge per head, 16s. Revenue in 1863, £1,295,000; in 1870, £2,966,781; in 1872, £3,634,400; in 1873, £4,120,000. Expenditure, owing to war, rebellions, and yellow fever, somewhat in excess. Trade rapidly increasing, the exports being about £4,000,000 in 1862 and £10,000,000 in 1872. The duty-paying imports in 1872 were £11,460,110; total imports, £12,045,827. The railway guarantees are of moderate extent, but the lines are fairly profitable. *The Buenos Ayres new loans,* besides the *Entre-Rios* and *Santa Fé debts,* are *not liabilities* of the Confederated Government.

At the opening of Congress, in 1875, President Avellaneda described the effect of the War and the crisis of the previous year on the finances of the Republic, by which a very large deficit was caused.

|  | $ | £ |
|---|---|---|
| The total expenditure was | 29,784,000 | 5,957,000 |
| And the receipts were | 16,527,000 | 3,305,000 |
| Deficit | 13,257,000 | 2,652,000 |

The expenditure included an item of £1,786,000 on account of special loans, which is additional, apparently, to the War expenditure of the year, estimated at £780,000. The ordinary budget showed an expenditure of £3,936,000, being a deficit of about £600,000 compared with the above receipts. This deficit arose mainly from a reduction of customs duties. The estimated receipts from imports in 1873 were 16,516,000 dols., and the actual yield was only 12,540,000 dols., a difference of 3,976,000 dols., or £795,000. In previous years the estimates of the Government have frequently been exceeded in the result. The change now observed is significant of the depression which the raw material-producing countries have been passing through. The President stated that the falling off in the imports themselves amounts to £4,337,000, although the exports had only diminished 2,857,000 dols., or £571,000. A comparison was drawn between the expense of suppressing the late revolt and the previous ones. The first revolt in Entre-Rios cost £1,500,000; the second, £920,000; but the one of September, 1874, is reported to have only cost £780,000; this diminution of the cost of suppressing insurrections being cited by the President as an illustration of the increased power of the Central Government. The President remarked on the present position of the Treasury:—

"We have paid the war expenses and met the ordinary expenditure of the budget, in spite of a decline in revenue; we have also paid 4¼ millions of arrears to the War Office between January 1, 1874, and April 30, 1875. We have also paid for the arms and ships bought in Europe, and for which no funds had been set apart. All this has been done without injury to our credit, or even having to negotiate the balance of the loan in London. The Finance Minister, even at the darkest moment, paid no higher for money than the National Bank rate.

"The Public Works of the 1871 loan proceed without interruption, and are defrayed out of the loan.

\* \* \* \* \* \* \* \*

"The Finance Minister jealously guards our credit in Europe. The money is already in London for payment of the July coupons of the 1824 and 1868 loans, besides a considerable sum remitted for the coupons due next September on the Public Works loan of 1871."

## IV. AUSTRALASIA.

NEW SOUTH WALES. Population in 1871, 519,182. Area, 323,437 square miles. Population per square mile, 1¾. *Debt in* 1874, £13,962,529. Annual charge at 6 per cent., including sinking fund, £830,000. Debt per head, £26; charge per head, 30s. Debt incurred upon railways and productive works. Revenue in 1872, £4,161,415, including £568,436 from loans. Expenditure, £3,638,623. Imports in 1871, £8,981,200; in 1872, £8,587,030. Exports in 1871, £7,784,766; in 1872, £8,005,571.

NEW ZEALAND. Population in 1871, 266,986. Area, 106,259 square miles. Population per square mile, 2½. Public debt in 1872, £9,985,386, including amalgamated provincial loans. *Present* debt, £11,250,000. The annual charge at 5½ per cent. is £620,000 including sinking fund. The debt per head is £40; and the annual charge per head £2¼. As in other Australasian colonies, debt mostly raised for reproductive purposes. Revenue in 1873-4, £2,459,014, including £1,038,798 land sales; revenue surplus, £207,461. Exports in 1871, £5,282,084; in 1872, £5,190,665. Gold export in 1871, £2,811,723; in 1872, £1,742,427. Imports in 1871, £4,078,193; in 1872, £5,142,951. The population in 1861 was only 98,971, and the colony has grown rapidly since the gold discoveries.

QUEENSLAND. Population in 1871, 125,146. Area, 678,000 square miles. *Debt in* 1872, £4,547,850; *now* £5,500,000. Debt per head, £40; charge per head, £2¼, at 5½ per cent. Revenue in 1872, £996,323; expenditure, £865,743. Exports, £2,635,026, including £660,553 gold. Imports, £2,175,590.

SOUTH AUSTRALIA. Population in 1871, 187,851. Area, 383,328 square miles. Population per square mile, ½. *Debt in* 1873, £2,325,900. Annual charge at 6 per cent., £140,000. Debt per head, £12¼; charge per head, 15s. Revenue in 1869-70, £878,124; in 1873-4, £974,628. Expenditure in 1873-4, £943,807. Exports in 1872, £3,738,623, chiefly wool and copper; in 1870, £2,419,488. Imports in 1872, £2,801,572; in 1870, £2,029,794.

TASMANIA. Population in 1870, 101,785. Area, 26,215 square miles. *Debt in* 1872, £1,455,900; charge at 6 per cent., £87,300. Revenue in 1872, £479,063. Exports in 1872, £910,663.

VICTORIA. Population in 1871, 752,445. Area, 86,831 square miles. Population per square mile, 8½. *Debt in* 1874, £12,520,432, excluding loan of October, 1874, £1,500,000. Annual charge at 5¾ per cent., £720,000. Debt per head, £16¾; charge per head, 19s. 6d. Debt incurred for railways (515 miles at work), waterworks, and docks. Revenue in 1873-4, £4,054,924. Expenditure,

£4,448,062. Imports in 1872, £13,691,322; exports, £13,871,195 including £5,884,011 gold. Gold export in 1856, £12,929,818.

## V. AUSTRIA.

Population, 36,000,000. Area, 227,230 square miles. Population per square mile, 158. *Debt, including £215,000,000 compulsorily converted, about £350,000,000;* annual charge (deducting income tax), £15,000,000; annual charge (say), 8s. 4d. per head. All these figures *include the debt of Hungary.*

The report of the commission for controlling the debt of Austria states that the amount of the irredeemable consolidated debt of the Empire (*exclusive* of the debt of *Hungary*) at the end of June, 1874, was £215,471,000. It had increased six millions since December, 1873, and nearly 8½ millions since June, 1873. The redeemable consolidated debt amounted, with arrears of interest, to 49 millions, and had decreased £287,000 since December, and £616,000 since June, 1874. The whole consolidated debt of Austria, consequently, stood at £264,530,000, and had, after deducting debt redeemed, grown about six millions in the course of the year. This increase is due chiefly to the eight million loan voted by the Reichsrath in the Sessions of 1873. The special floating debt amounted to £9,650,000, or more than double what it stood at a year before. The guaranteed debt stood at £21,500,000, a decrease of about £700,000 on the year. The amount payable in interest, &c., on the whole debt of the Austrian State is estimated at £10,600,000 in the paper currency of the country and £6,556,000 in gold. The general floating debt of the Empire stood at 32 millions.

## VI. BELGIUM.

Population in 1867, 5,000,000. Area, 11,313 square miles. *Public debt, including railway loan of* 1873, *not yet paid in full,* £36,000,000. Annual charge, £1,700,000; charge per head, 7s. 3d. Revenue £7½ millions; expenditure rather less.

## VII. BOLIVIA.

Population, 2,750,000. *Debt*, about £2,250,000; annual charge at 8 per cent., £180,000. A loan in 1872 was raised for rail and navigation purposes.

(i). *Improvement Loans for Foreign States.*—The decision of the Master of the Rolls in the suit in 1875, between the *National Bolivian Navigation Company* and the Public Works Construction Company, again draws attention to the danger of clauses in public loans, which lay stress on the fact that the money is required for *works of public improvement*. The Bolivian Government introduced a clause of this nature into the prospectus of the loan issued in 1872, and by way of additional security agreed to the creation of a Trust by which a sum of £600,000 was to be specifically applied in constructing a railway around the rapids of the Madera River. But this clause has created a difficulty for both the Government and the bondholders. The Public Works Construction Company, by which the railway was to be made, threw up the contract, and the money was so locked up as to prevent the Bolivian Government from using it for general purposes, or from returning it to the bondholders. In a suit between (1) the Navigation Company that held the concession for the railway, (2) the Public Works Construction Company, which was employed in the actual construction, and (3) the representatives of the bondholders, the Court held that the Navigation Company was entitled to a declaration that the money must be paid to them as the works proceed, and that the failure of the Public Works Construction Company does not concern them. The rights of the Bolivian Government, which did not appear in the suit were reserved, but as against all other parties the Navigation Company were held entitled to the fund. Thus the bondholders were unable to get back their money, although the public improvement, for which it was wanted, was thrown up as impracticable. The Bolivian Government failed to get possession of the fund, although it is liable for interest and drawings in respect of it, and has not got the public work by which its ability to pay the interest was to have been increased. All these mishaps would clearly have been avoided if Bolivia had borrowed only what those who knew it were willing to lend *on the faith of its own resources*, instead of a great loan by which the proposed advantage was to be obtained at immense cost. The lenders did not know anything about Bolivia, and were partly induced to subscribe by a doubtful security.

(ii). The Bolivian Loan of 1872 for £1,700,000, at 68 per cent., should have produced .. £1,156,000

| | |
|---|---:|
| The fund set apart for the proposed railway, respecting which the litigation arose was to meet a contract of £4,000 per mile for 150 miles .. .. .. .. .. .. | 600,000 |
| Agent's commission, stamps, printing, &c., consumed .. .. .. .. .. | 116,393 |
| Bolivian Government .. .. .. .. | 10,000 |
| Bolivian Navigation Company .. .. .. | 107,664 |
| The balance of the Loan applicable to dividends and drawings; of this, the amount consumed was about .. .. .. .. .. | 265,000 |
| Leaving a balance of about .. .. | 56,943 |
| | £1,156,000 |

## VIII. BRAZIL.

Population, 10,100,000, including 2,000,000 slaves and Indians. Area, 3,100,000 square miles. *Total debt*, including paper money and treasury bills, *about* £62,000,000 *of which* £15,000,000 *is foreign, and* £28,000,000 *home funded debt*. Annual charge at 5 per cent., £3,100,000. Debt per head, £6; charge per head, 6s. Revenue in 1865–6, £6,105,841; in 1870–71, £9,750,905; estimate for 1873–4, 12,360,707, showing a surplus. Imports in 1870, £16,824,369. Exports, £19,706,320. The Paraguayan war cost the country £45,000,000.

## IX. BRITISH COLUMBIA.

Population of Vancouver's Island, 23,000; mainland, 12,000. Areas, 13,000 and 200,000 square miles respectively. *Debt in* 1870, £322,328. This colony is absorbed in the Canadian Dominion, and a railway is to be constructed from Canada, through Manitoba (Red River), to British Columbia. Great Britain will guarantee interest on part of the outlay thereon.

## X. BUENOS AYRES.

*Debt in* 1874, £3,020,100.

## XI. CANADA.

Population of Dominion in 1871, 3,497,714; consisting—Canada, 2,812,367; New Brunswick, 285,594; Nova Scotia, 387,800; and Manitoba, 11,953; British Columbia in addition. Occupied area about 400,000 square miles; unoccupied (say), 2,500,000 square miles. Debt in 1872, £21,655,541, mostly expended productively. *Present debt nearly* £30,000,000, owing to railway extensions, with a view to construct the Canadian-Pacific line. Annual charge at 5 per cent., £1,500,000. Debt per head £8¼; charge per head, 8s. 3d. Population in 1861, 3,100,000. Revenue in 1872, £4,315,586; expenditure, £3,664,473. Imports in 1871, £18,355,037; ditto in 1872, £22,542,828, including £13,007,174 from the United Kingdom. Exports in 1871, £13,750,239; ditto in 1872, £14,940,173, including £5,254,955 to the United Kingdom. British Columbia, Manitoba, and Prince Edward Island (194,021 inhabitants) have now joined the Dominion; but Newfoundland (146,536 inhabitants) still holds aloof. The estimated expenditure for 1873-4 was £4,517,344, leaving a deficit on the revenue account, but this included £140,000 for the acquisition of Prince Edward Island.

### XII. CAPE OF GOOD HOPE.

Population in 1865, 566,158. Area 200,610 square miles. *Debt in* 1873, £2,093,400, *including Cape Railway Capital.* Annual charge at 5½ per cent., £115,000, or per head, 3s. 6d. Revenue in 1872, £1,161,548; expenditure, £922,568. Imports in 1870, £2,502,043; in 1872, £5,442,439. Exports in 1870, £2,603,211; in 1872, £4,829,589, chiefly to United Kingdom. In 1872, wool exported, £3,276,052; copper, £328,458; diamonds, £306,041; feathers, £158,904; skins, £331,352. Large Railway outlay recently sanctioned.

### XIII. CEYLON.

Population in 1871, 2,405,287. Area, 24,454 square miles. *Debt,* £640,000, incurred on railway, costing £1,250,000. Annual charge, £38,400; per head, 4d. Revenue in 1873, £1,290,918; expenditure, £1,176,258. Exports in 1872, £3,139,060.

### XIV. CHILI.

Population, 2,000,000. Area, 250,000 square miles. *Foreign debt, about* £7,400,000; *total debt, about* £10,300,000. Annual charge, £675,000. Debt per head, £5; charge per head, 6s. 9d. Chili has spent about £6,000,000 on railways, and the war with Spain increased the debt. Revenue in 1873, £6,500,000. Imports in 1870, £5,644,827; in 1873, £7,585,685. Exports in 1870, £5,395,163; in 1873, £7,762,054—£3,260,000 being mining produce, chiefly copper. Trade one-half with United Kingdom.

### XV. COLOMBIA.

*Debt after the conversion of New Granada bonds into* 4½ *per cent. Stock, about* £4,300,000. The Panama Railroad has, since the opening of the San Francisco route, not proved so remunerative a property, and the State has at times been in arrear with its payments. Since 1871, it is stated that the revenue, previously showing constant deficits, has exhibited a surplus. Estimated revenue for year 1874-5, £800,745.

### XVI. COSTA RICA.

*The whole of the debt of the Republic is estimated at £3,400,000.* It has been contracted to provide for the construction of roads and railways. Costa Rica is in default upon both of its loans, and the railway is said to require another £1,000,000 to complete it.

### XVII. CUBA.

*Debt in* 1874, £277,600. Population in 1867, 1,414,508, including 350,000 slaves, since which there has been some decrease, owing to the insurrection, &c. Area, 48,500 square miles.

### XVIII. DANUBIAN PRINCIPALITIES.

Population of the Roumania, 4,000,000. Area 45,500 square miles. *Debt, including railway loan (except Roumania Railway shares, which are a heavy liability), about* £6,444,188. This Railway debt was for some time repudiated, and new issues were consequently refused recognition on the Stock Exchange. At the end of 1871, however, a conversion of the repudiated 7½ per cent. bonds into 5 per cent. guaranteed shares was undertaken through the agency of the Anglo-Hungarian Bank. Revenue for 1873, £3,506,968; expenditure, £3,799,904. Trade chiefly in grain from the Danube.

### XIX. DENMARK.

Population, 1,785,000. Area, 14,550 square miles. *Debt in* 1867, £14,512,200; *in* 1872, £12,747,500; a portion spent on productive works. Annual charge at 5 per cent. would be £640,000, or per head, 7s. The original amount of the foreign loans was

£12,328,000, and the present amount about £3,200,000. This steady application of the sinking fund enables Denmark to command as high a market value for its debt as any other foreign State. The revenue in 1870-71 was £2,602,180. Exports in 1872-3, £5,650,000.

## XX. EGYPT.

Population in 1871, 5,250,000 of all races. Area, 200,000 square miles. Foreign debt about £50,000,000, exclusive of the Viceroy's Daira loans, which amount to £9,000,000. In addition to this £59,000,000, there is a floating debt of rather large amount, part of which is secured on the Daira estates. *Altogether the State and Daira indebtedness has been estimated at* £75,000,000. Including heavy redemptions, the annual charge has been stated at £7,500,000, including £705,000 tribute to Turkey. Debt per head, £14; charge per head, £1⅜. As special security for the 1868 loan, the Customs receipts, lock tolls, salt revenues, &c., are hypothecated, and for the 1873 loan, the railway revenue in Lower Egypt, the personal and indirect taxes, and "Moukabala." The government revenue in 1873-4 officially estimated at £10,000,000, and the surplus at £1,100,000. State Railways, 750 miles. Exports in 1868, £16,230,880; in 1871, £14,716,145.

## XXI. ENTRE-RIOS.

*Debt in* 1874, £211,600.

## XXII. EQUADOR.

*Debt in* 1874, £1,824,000. In May, 1869, the dividends for 1867 were announced, but the Finance Minister then confiscated the payment of the Customs dues to the bondholders to meet deficits. Interest has been in arrear since 1860.

## XXIII. FRANCE.

Population in 1872, 36,102,821, ex ceded territory. Area, 202,000 square miles. *Debt*, £900,000,000. Annual charge about £33,000,000. Debt per head, £25; charge, 18s. The war has added nearly £20,000,000 annually to the expenditure, and the war and indemnity have increased the debt by over £400,000,000. The two national loans for £200,000,000 in all, involved stock issues to the extent of £276,000,000. Commerce imports in 1873, £144,007,120; exports, £157,075,800. The debt of Paris amounted to £73,200,000 before the recent loan.

(i.)—M. Leroy Beaulieu, in an able article in the *Débats* on the Paris Loan, 1875, remarked that the certainty of 4½ per cent. interest and the chance every year of four *lots* of 100,000f. for each bond of 5,000f. were quite enough to tempt all the possesssors of small sums. The savings of former years have almost absorbed the National Loans, and recent savings had not found equally productive investments. The price of issue, 88, was indeed too low. The Administration, not liking to intrust the loan to a syndicate of bankers, who would have required a commission, fixed a low price.

(ii.)—Up to 1854 the French Government invited bankers to tender for public loans, and accepted the best offers, the bankers taking all risk of disposing of the bonds they had subscribed for *en masse*. All the great European houses competed, and the State was sure of obtaining the most favourable terms. Now, however, the State fixes the price, and, fearing a failure, which would be more serious politically than financially, it generally fixes it below the mark. In 1830 the house of Rothschild tendered for a Four per Cent. loan at 102f. 57c., and in 1844 for a Three per Cent. loan at 84f. 75c. The object of the new system was to enable the real *rentiers* to obtain bonds at first hand, and to secure better terms for the State by appealing to what was

P

called the "universal suffrage of capital." The first loan of the empire in 1854 for 250,000,000f. was nearly twice covered; the second, of double that amount, some months afterwards, was four times covered; in 1855, when 750,000,000f. was asked for, 3,652,000,000f. was offered; in 1859, for a loan of 520,000,000f., the applications amounted to 2,500,000,000f., in 1864, 315,000,000f. was applied for and 5,000,000,000f. offered; in 1868 a loan of 450,000,000f. was thirty-four times covered. On the other hand, the War Loan of 800,000,000f. in August, 1870, was barely covered, and the loan of two milliards in 1871 was not quite twice covered, speculators being timid and leaving real capitalists to absorb it; but with the Paris Loan of 1871 speculation revived, and for the loan of three milliards in 1872, 43 milliards were subscribed. It is, however, the great banks which subscribe the enormous sums. Their direct co-operation being refused, though it would guarantee the placing of the loan and might raise the price of issue, they co-operate indirectly, the only effect being to prevent the bonds from promptly coming into the hands of those who will keep them. The present system really shuts out small capitalists. When fifty times the desired amount has to be offered, and four or five times that amount has to be deposited in cash, prudent men see that the chance of gain is too small and the chance of loss too great. Their safest course they consider is to purchase the amount they desire on the Bourse at a slight premium either before, during, or after the issue.

(iii.)—The City of Paris new "Lottery" Loan of January, 1875, was an illustration of the popularity of this sort of Loan. It was for £10,000,000 nominal, or in 500,000 bonds of 500f. each, at the issue price of 440f. per bond, payable in four equal instalments. The bonds bear interest at 4 per cent., or 20f. per bond, and the loan to be redeemed in 75 years by quarterly drawings commencing on the 5th of May, 1875. At each of these drawings lottery prizes of 225,000f. will be given, in sums of from 100,000f. down to 1,000f. Despite the low rate of about $4\frac{2}{3}$ per cent. net interest, this loan will cost the City of Paris much money, but the debt of the city is already very large. A French writer observes that, "The great success of the City of Paris Loan is another testimony to the same financial strength. The issue of £10,000,000 has been 42½ times applied for, and although it is well known of course how speculation manipulates such affairs, and applications are multiplied because the allotment will be small, still the great eagerness of speculators to compete for the premium on such an issue is in itself a proof of the abundance of the money ready for investment by which the premium is ultimately supported."

(iv.)—It is becoming more and more clear now that when the Emperor Napoleon III. made use of the system of offering public loans to the masses, raising thereby some three milliards—in six loans, from 1854 to 1868—he merely opened up the surface of a mine of wealth. That France has six millions of freeholders explains much, but not all. It is asserted by some political economists, that France is the only country in Europe where property is *not* accumulating among the few.

(v.)—To what an extent the wealth of France is not only increasing, but spreading among the native population, is strikingly shown by a return published in 1875 from the *Journal Officiel*. The number is given of the holders of "Rentes," together with the amount of "Rentes," or interest of the National debt, at decennial periods from 1798 to 1870, and annually from 1870 to 1875 :—

| Years. January 1. | Number of holders of Rentes. | Amount of annual Rentes. Francs. |
|---|---|---|
| 1798 .. | 24,791 | 25,111,785 |
| 1810 .. | 145,663 | 56,730,583 |
| 1820 .. | 199,697 | 172,784,838 |
| 1830 .. | 195,370 | 204,696,459 |
| 1840 .. | 265,447 | 195,911,137 |
| 1850 .. | 846,330 | 229,608,758 |
| 1860 .. | 1,073,801 | 338,356,589 |

## THE DEBT OF FRANCE.

| Years. January 1. | Number of holders of Rentes. | Amount of annual Rentes. Francs. |
|---|---|---|
| 1870 | 1,254,040 | 358,087,510 |
| 1871 | 1.269,730 | 386,222,343 |
| 1872 | 2,147.130 | 502,126,256 |
| 1873 | 3,473,475 | 626,120,206 |
| 1874 | 4,130,040 | 693,013,493 |
| 1875 | 4,380,933 | 748,404,971 |

Since the war the number of fundholders has become about three and a-half times as many. It will be observed, also, that while the annual interest of the debt, or the "Rentes," has multiplied not quite thirtyfold since 1798, the number of holders of the debt —"Rentiers," as they and all possessors of capital are called— have multiplied 182 times. The number of holders of "Rentes" at the present time is about equal to the number of freeholders of the soil. The wide and even distribution of wealth in France exceeds that of other countries of Europe.

### XXIV. GERMAN EMPIRE.

*Debt* not publicly known.

### XXV. GREECE.

Population in 1861, 1,332,500; in 1871, 1,457,894. Area, 20,000 square miles. *Debt, say* £8,000,000; *foreign debt repudiated.* Revenue, about £1,250,000; expenditure in excess, notwithstanding repudiation. Imports about £2,200,000; exports, £1,500,000.

### XXVI. GUATEMALA.

*Debt in* 1874, £551,600. Population about 1,200,000, including Indians. Revenue in 1871, £159,563; deficit, £42,429. Revenue now increasing. The President in 1872 "questioned" the legality of the 1869 loan, which has since been recognized.

THE DEBT OF INDIA. 109

### XXVII. HOLLAND.

Population (exclusive of Luxembourg) in 1870, 3,618,452. Area, 12,400 square miles. Debt in 1864, £80,792,421; in 1872, £80,511,443. Annual charge, £2,248,439; or per head, 12s. 6d. The revenue was in 1870, £7,377,236; and the expenditure, £8,019,076. Estimated revenue in 1873, £7,601,065; expenditure £8,041,919. Imports in 1870, £51,084,898; exports, £43,497,540, exclusive of bullion.

### XXVIII. HONDURAS.

*Debt in* 1874, £3,224,450. The object of the loans of this state was said to be the construction of a railway between the Atlantic and the Pacific, with which some progress has been made. For several years the Government has been in default, and a proposal has been adopted to convert the railway into a company, and relieve the Government of its liability.

### XXIX. HUNGARY.

*Debt (separate from Austrian)*, £32,000,000; to a large extent expended on railways and other reproductive works. Estimated revenue for 1875, £22,281,691; expenditure, £25,030,289; deficit to be covered by sale of railway shares, raising price of tobaccos &c. Population, 15,509,455.

### XXX. INDIA.

Population over 190,600,000; has rapidly increased of late. Area, 1,000,000 square miles. Debt, £126,500,000, of which some £50,000,000 is held in England. This was inclusive of £6,000,000 E. I. Co.'s 10½ per cent. stock, redeemed last year at 200 per cent. Including 4 per cent. issue for this purpose, famine loan, and other debts and deposits, *the debt* may be set down at £130,000,000, bearing £5,900,000 annual interest. Debt per head, 14s.; charge 7½d. But this does not include the guaranteed 5 per cent. on railways and canals, the capital of which exceeds £95,000,000, and is increasing. The railways are productive to the extent of about three per cent.; but the guarantee increases the sum to be provided as interest to about £7,400,000 per annum; or, per head, 10d. Revenue in 1872, £50,110,215; expenditure, £48,614,512, including public works. Imports in 1872, £42,657,560, including bullion, £11,573,813; exports, £64,661,940, including bullion, £2,476,093. Principal exports—cotton, opium, dyes, rice, jute, silk, hides, seeds, and coffee. 5,872 miles of railway open.

## XXXI. ITALY.

Population, 27,000,000. Area, 115,000 square miles (including islands). Debt in 1873, £390,024,528; annual interest, £15,341,148; debt per head £14¼; charge per head, 11s. 6d. Inclusive of pensions, redemptions, railway guarantees, &c., the irreducible expenditure amounts to about £29,500,000, and this would be greater but for the imposition of a 13¼ per cent. income tax on coupons. Ordinary revenue in 1872, £46,333,105; total expenditure, £54,679,077. Ordinary revenue in 1873, £47,225,837; gross expenditure, £55,384,872. Imports in 1870, £33,710,948; in 1873, £47,378,565; exports in 1870, £22,916,840; in 1873, £43,339,920.

## XXXII. JAMAICA.

Population in 1871, 506,154. Area, 6,400 square miles. Revenue in 1872, £494,564. Expenditure, £454,774. Debt under £1,000,000. Exports, £1,418,444; imports, £1,559,602.

## XXXIII. JAPAN.

Since the resumption of power by the Mikado, the State of Japan has become more settled. *The total debt* of Japan is stated to be £8,644,940. Ordinary revenue estimated at £9,401,362. Imports in 1870, £6,224,128; exports in 1872, about £4,858,906; in 1873, about £4,132,188. 38 miles of Government railway open.

### XXXIV. LIBERIA.

*Debt in* 1874, £100,000. This is the first public loan, the money being required for works of improvement, and to liquidate Treasury Bonds.

### XXXV. MAURITIUS.

Population in 1871, 318,584. Area, 708 square miles. Population, 450 per square mile. *Debt*, £1,095,500, a large portion expended on railways. Revenue in 1872, £703,159. Expenditure, £650,328. Imports in 1871, £2,044,246; in 1872 £2,677,973. Exports in 1871, £3,120,529; in 1872, £3,243,101, —¾ of which were sugar.

### XXXVI. MEXICO.

Population in 1869, 8,567,000 of mixed races. Area, 1,030,000 square miles. The *foreign and internal debt in* 1865 was £63,470,000; annual charge, £3,945,100. The debt has been repudiated at various times since 1827, and since the revolution payments have again ceased. The Republic repudiates "Imperial loans," leaving £30,106,000 to be recognised, besides unpaid coupons.

### XXXVII. MOROCCO.

*Debt in* 1874, £226,500. Population said to be 8,000,000. Imports in 1872, £850,776 and £348,916 specie. Exports, £1,228,577; average of previous ten years, £800,000. Trade chiefly with England.

### XXXVIII. NATAL.

Population, 289,773. Area, 16,145 square miles. Population, chiefly natives. *Debt in* 1872, £334,400. Revenue in 1872,

£198,421. Expenditure, £149,694. Imports in 1871, £472,444. Exports, £403,308. Chief exports—sugar and wool. Imports in 1872, £852,252. Exports, £622,797.

### XXXIX. NEW GRANADA.

Population of Confederation, 2¾ to 3 millions. *Debt converted* —*see " Colombia."*

### XL. PARAGUAY.

*Debt in* 1874, £2,915,700. This comprises the only loans of Paraguay, raised to complete railway and roads, and to establish a bank, commercial routes, and immigration. Hypothecations— State lands, buildings, railway, &c. Paraguay is now a defaulter.

### XLI. PERU.

Population, 3,000,000. Area, 500,000 square miles. *Debt*, *including the railway loans*, £37,000,000. Annual charge, with sinking fund, £2,590,000, or 17*s*. 3*d*. per head. The Government are carrying out railways and many works of improvement. The chief item of revenue is derived from guano sales.

### XLII. PORTUGAL.

Population, 4,363,000, including Azores and Madeira. Area, 37,500 square miles. *Debt* £69,211,584, *in* 3 *per cent. stock.* Annual charge, £2,150,000; or per head, 9*s*. 10*d*. Revenue in 1871-2, £4,103,421; estimate, 1873-4, £4,966,836. Exports, £5,000,000.

### XLIII. RUSSIA.

Population, 82,200,000. Area, 7,750,000 square miles; of which in Europe 2,000,000 square miles. The trade of Russia has rapidly expanded of late, a fact largely attributable to the opening of her railways, of which some 9,200 miles were in operation in 1873. Imports in 1866, £25,453,000; ditto in 1871, £55,501,000. Exports in 1866, £27,834,000; ditto in 1871, £52,753,000. Principal exports to United Kingdom. These figures include Finland, whose imports in 1870 were £1,742,000; and exports, £1,846,000.

| Year. | Revenue. £ | Expenditure. £ | Debt. £ | Interest. £ |
|---|---|---|---|---|
| 1850 | 35,945,000 | 45,949,800 | 100,000,000 | 4,000,000 |
| 1855 | 42,259,104 | 84,155,152 | 175,000,000 | 7,000,000 |
| 1860 | 58,000,000 | 65,000,000 | 250,000,000 | 9,600,000 |
| 1865 | 53,828,000 | 59,437,000 | 270,000,000 | 10,700,000 |
| 1870 | 63,651,261 | 69,354,583 | 300,000,000 | 12,000,000 |
| 1872 | 68,109,285 | 68,056,609 | 330,000,000 | 13,000,000 |
| 1874 | 77,121,665 | 76,669,120 | 340,000,000 | 13,450,000 |

The revenue and expenditure for 1874 are estimates. The 1872 Budget showed the first surplus during a period of 40 years. The expenditure includes outlay on some reproductive works. The railway guarantees form another item of debt, subject to the net revenue from which covers a large portion of the guarantee. £35,000,000 has been subscribed in foreign markets alone towards these guarantees.

(i.)—*Railway Guarantees.*—An able foreign writer observes, that much satisfaction was felt in Russia at the success of the last Railway loan. In 1869 the Russian Government thought it expedient to adopt a new method of dealing with Guaranteed railway Stock. Up to that date, companies enjoying the prized advantage of a Government guarantee were allowed to take their Scrip to some Russian or foreign market, and realize it there as best they could; but from the beginning of 1870, the Government, when according guarantees, has invariably made it a condition that the Stock be disposed of by themselves, at the place and on the terms settled by the Finance Minister. The power thus conferred upon this official is more easily imagined than described; and as the practice soon arose of combining the Stock of several companies into a single loan, the details of the transaction were entirely withdrawn from public cognizance. Russian Government Stock commands a ready sale in every part of the world, and the Guaranteed Railway Debentures being virtually as good as a

Government loan, there is reason why they should rank with the latter in prices. The £12,000,000 sterling loan issued in January, 1870, and the loan of February, 1872, the first time at 79¼, and the second time at 81½, were at once taken up. The third and fourth issues of £15,000,000 each, in April, 1872, and November, 1873, though offered at the comparatively high prices of 89 and 93, were likewise well received. Owing to the gradual improvement in the rate of exchange, this Russian Security has since risen considerably in the market, and at Berlin, commands prices from 102 to 105. Such a marked success, of course, encouraged repetition, and in April, 1875, a fifth Guaranteed railway loan was issued at 92. Although the rate of interest was only 4½ per cent., against the 5 per cent. of the preceding four issues, yet six times the amount demanded was subscribed. The money is said to be designed for the Caucasian, Siberian, and other Eastern lines, which cannot be remunerative for years to come. Hence the 15,000,000 roubles annually expended by the Russian Exchequer on railway guarantees are likely to require a proportionate increase in consequence of the new transaction. From a mere railway point of view there is no reason why this operation should not be repeated many times while the Government think it profitable to pledge themselves for the deficit incurred. As yet Russia has only 0.55 kilometres of railway to the geographical square mile, figures, the insignificance of which is seen by comparing them with the 1·018 of Sweden, 3·8 of Prussia, 4·2 of America, 5·8 of England, and 6 of Belgium.

(ii.)—*Russian Finance and Commerce.*—The question, whether Russia is entitled to appeal to foreign markets to the extent she does, depends upon the state of her Finances and Commerce. A few words will supply the leading facts upon the subject.

In 1873, the total of the Russian income and expenditure amounted to 517,000,000 roubles, against 276,000,000 roubles in 1852. Of the total expenditure in 1852, 33,000,000 roubles were devoted to the interest on the public debt, the like purpose requiring 91,000,000 roubles in 1873. Thus, while both income and expenditure have not been doubled in the last 20 years, the National Debt has been nearly trebled. In other words, considerable as the increase of the productive forces has been, the public wants have been growing more rapidly than the public resources. If this had been mainly owing to the money consumed in creating railway communication, the outlay incurred might be regarded as a profitable investment in the long run; *but as* 15,000,000 *roubles a year pay the whole of the Railway interest*, the inference is that the greater part of the new loans have been applied to very different and less lucrative purposes than the laying down of metals in a formerly pathless Empire. Indeed, there is no difficulty in ascertaining into what channels the money has been flowing. The Army and Navy expenses were marked at 190,000,000 roubles in 1873, as against 96,000,000 roubles in 1852. Schools, on the other hand, which required about 8,000,000 roubles 20 years ago, are now accorded 12,000,000 roubles; so that comparing this small increase with the sums absorbed by the War Office, the balance is largely on the side of the unproductive instead of the productive investment.

(iii.)--A more favourable view is presented by Russian Commerce. Russia, which in 1851 exported to Europe goods to the amount of only 84,000,000 roubles, in 1871 exported to the amount of 353,000,000 roubles; the imports in these years being respectively 87,000,000 roubles and 345,000,000 roubles. Accordingly, both imports and exports, speaking in round numbers, have quadrupled, and the principle articles of export being corn, flax, and hemp, sent to England and Germany, there is a *primâ-facie* probability that the trade will continue and even increase as these two countries become more industrial and less agricultural, Germany, more especially, requiring every year a larger amount of Russian rye and wheat, promises to remain quite as good a customer for raw produce as she is in return a liberal purveyor of manufactured goods. The nearly 9,000,000 bushels of grain representing the excess of imports over exports in Germany in 1872 mostly came from Russia; the 162,000,000 roubles, which were the amount of Germany's exports to Russia in 1871, are on the other hand almost one half of the whole Russian imports that year. Considering that Germany, a *corn-exporting* country a very few years ago, has almost suddenly been converted into an importing one, it is easy to foresee that Russia may count upon her as a permanent customer, though American wheat proves a more and more dangerous rival to Russian grain in England. This conclusion is the more justifiable when it is taken into account that the natural tendency of commerce must make it advisable for Germany to buy where she sells so largely. German imports to Russia, only one-fifth of the total imports in 1851, were about one-half in 1871; whereas Russian imports to Germany, one-eighth of the total imports in 1851, have since risen to one-fifth. The full meaning of these figures will be understood when it is considered that German imports into Russia have increased by 329 per cent. in the last 10 years; English imports to that country having in the same period been augmented by only 103 per cent.

(iv.)—If this looks promising for the Russian agricultural interest, and the National Exchequer too, it has to be borne in mind that the sums, thus accruing to the country, are realized for raw produce only, and in consequence may be diminished by a rival development in other primitive lands. Agricultural progress in Hungary and the Danubian Principalities, for instance, might in a very few years deprive the Russian Empire of a considerable portion of what may be styled its foreign income. Of the 350,000,000 roubles of exports, 150,000,000 roubles are in corn, 40,000,000 roubles are in flax, 20,000,000 roubles in hemp, 23,000,000 roubles in timber, 10,000,000 roubles in cattle, 3,000,000 roubles in rape and linseed, 3,000,000 roubles in hides, 2,000,000 roubles in spirituous liquors, 1,000,000 roubles in butter, &c. The small sum of 2,000,000 roubles is the whole that is realized by manufactured exports. Such being the case, one cannot but perceive that the power of exporting, and with it the ability to pay taxes, is to no small extent dependent in Russia upon her remaining the principal granary of Western Europe. Her manufacturers have so long enjoyed the doubtful advantage of a prohibitive tariff, that even if a different policy were adopted—which is sure not to be unless at the last extremity—they would be unable for many years to come to compete with foreign goods.

### XLIV. SAN DOMINGO.

*Debt in* 1874, £728,500. This loan was raised for the purpose of constructing roads and railways. The country is now in default.

### XLV. SANTA FÉ.

*Debt in* 1874, £296,300.

### XLVI. SARDINIA.

*Debt in* 1874, £2,665,360; see Italy.

### XLVII. SPAIN.

Population in 1869, 16,673,481. Area, 182,750 square miles. *Debt*, £375,000,000, having increased from £160,000,000 in 1863. Annual charge, £11,000,000; or per head, 13s. Revenue in 1866, £21,500,000; expenditure, £27,473,000. Revenue in 1871-2, £19,000,000; expenditure, £26,250,000, showing a deficit of over £7,000,000. The internal debt sustained an income tax of 5 per cent. for some time, but the last three coupons of both internal and external debt remain altogether unpaid.

(i.)—The helpless condition of isolated investors in Foreign Stocks is shown by the way in which they have been treated by the successive Governments of Spain. For several half-years no Dividends have been paid, whilst several compromises have been offered and greedily accepted by bondholders at meetings in a manner that showed their weak financial condition.

The *third* compromise offered at the close of 1874 was a modification for the worse of a previous one. The indebtedness having grown and the Republican Minister having only got the Rio Tinto obligations to pledge he made a proposal,—(1) that the obligations should be put in Trust, the amount thus to be realised to the bondholder being estimated at one-third nominally, but about one-fourth according to estimated selling price, of his three overdue coupons; and (2) that for the remaining two-thirds of the nominal amount of the coupons the creditors should receive at the rate of £250 per £100 in new 3 per cent. Stock, which would probably realise about 25 per cent. more of the whole amount due. In other words, the new proposal was to give the creditor about *one-fourth of what is overdue to him in money* or its equivalent, and *another fourth in new paper*, which would be no real equivalent, as the creation, according to a fair reckoning, would *pro tanto* depreciate the selling price of what the creditor held. Spain being insolvent, the multiplication of its paper could do its creditors, in the aggregate, no good; the most they could hope for was a dividend.

The new compromise was thus, in fact, no better than a sacrifice by the creditors of the whole of their past due coupons for a payment of five shillings in the pound. But this compromise, too—notwithstanding the failure by the Spanish Government in regard to its previous offers—was accepted with alacrity by the creditors of Spain with the express sanction of the Council of Foreign Bondholders.

(ii).—The *Economist*, which furnished these details, then adds: "When the first proposal was made the civil war had not broken out, and at the time of the second all resources immediately available had not been so completely exhausted as they are now.

But the question is not whether Spain has offered from time to time to do as much as she could, but whether the creditors are to cancel their titles in full for only part payment, leaving them nothing to show for a period of future settlement, when a quiet and stable Government will permit the resources of the country to be developed. If the creditors will surrender their "titles" for a fraction of what is nominally due, the Spanish Government has not yet hit upon a fraction so small as to provoke a refusal. There could be no clearer revelation of the weakness of the mass of foreign bondholders. Their disposition always is to be passive, to take what is offered, and on the terms offered, if the dividend is an appreciable one at all, and to submit to the most ignominious treatment from their defaulting debtor. Too many of them, unfortunately, can hardly help themselves. Belonging to a class which ought not to have meddled with doubtful Securities, and having been tempted by the desire for income, any offer of something in the shape of income is irresistible to them. Thus a compromise which is recommended actively or passively by any species of authority, is readily accepted by the mass of bondholders; and the few who might be justified in taking the risk of lending to a country like Spain, and who could afford to wait and deal vigorously with their debtor, are overruled."

(iii).—"Such is the *first lesson* from the history narrated; but the *second* lesson—the little reliance to be placed on the special agencies created to protect the bondholders' interests, and the danger that these agencies may be converted, unless great care is taken, into a new cause of loss—is also a most important one. The Council of Foreign Bondholders, has undoubtedly on more than one occasion done good service to its constituents. The perversity and financial poverty of Spain, and the weakness of many of their own constituents, were fatal obstacles in their path. So far as a body, like the Council of Foreign Bondholders, does no real good, its existence must be reckoned prejudicial and has been utilised by the Spanish Government in its own interest. The zeal of the council in arranging the last two compromises, instead of holding off or insisting on much more, appears to have been more pronounced than it ought to be, if the interests of its clients are to be vigilantly guarded. If the council or any similar body is to be as serviceable in the future as it has formerly been, the bondholders in turn must supervise their action carefully and must rather be distrustful than otherwise of the compromises recommended, as probably sacrificing too much to the defaulting Government.

"It is impossible to say that any greater success would have been possible in the present case, but a series of such successes would soon ruin the foreign bondholder."

(iv.)—The story is not improved if we carry it back a year or two earlier. In 1873, the late Lord Westbury stated, that,—"The announcement made by the Spanish Minister of Finance of his intention to propose to the Cortes an income tax of 18 per cent. on the coupons of Spanish 3 per cent. bonds in the hands of foreigners, as well as of Spanish subjects, is so serious a thing that it demands prompt attention and action on the part of the holders of Spanish Stock in England. \*   \*   \*

"There is no doubt of the proposed measure being most illegal, and contrary to the understanding and practice that have always prevailed on the subject of an income-tax. The Spanish bond is payable to bearer, and is, therefore, transmissible from hand to hand. The coupons for interest attached to the bonds do not require that they should be presented for payment in Spain. They may be collected in foreign countries. No registration is required in Spain of the holders of the bonds from time to time. The difference between the holders of Spanish bonds and the owners of English Government Stock is palpable.

"The dividends on Consols are payable at and by the Bank of England alone. The contract, therefore, in respect of English Consols is purely a home or English contract. The *locus contractus* and the *locus solutionis* are in England. The English

Government, therefore, treats the owners of Consols as English subjects, and the dividends payable to them as part of their income, arising and payable in this country. It claims a right, therefore, to impose an income-tax.

"In the case of the Spanish bonds the contract is universal. It may be transferred anywhere, and not (as in the British funds) by an act in Spain alone. Spain contracts with the holder, whoever he may be, and if the holder owes no allegiance to Spain the debt due to him cannot be affected by Spanish legislation.

"If the Spanish Government ordered a steamship from an English builder it might as justly insist on the English builder paying a property-tax out of the money payable under the contract, as it can insist on retaining Spanish income-tax out of the dividends payable to the foreign holders of Spanish Stock."

(v).—On this matter it was also further urged, that,—" Every Government has authority to tax the property within its dominions, and that possessed by its own citizens, for the exigencies of the State, and when a debt is raised by a home subscription the right subsequently to tax the dividends payable to native holders of such debt has not been doubted."

But in those countries which possess an External as well as an Internal Debt the specific characteristic of the former is that the subscription is originally obtained abroad, and that it is assumed that a large proportion, at any rate, of the debt will be, in all probability, held abroad, and be in all times in the hands of foreign holders; that it is, consequently (within the State), simply a debt due, and can only be viewed as matter of property beyond the State's jurisdiction. Even apart, therefore, from any special stipulation it seems indisputable that an External debt must in its nature be free from taxation. To tax it as a debt would be simply a refusal of the Government to pay a portion of the amount in which it is indebted, and its character as an External debt precludes the Government from taxing it as property in the hands of holders who are beyond its jurisdiction.

R

But, quite apart from this, the prospectus of some of the loans contains a clear and positive statement that the issue will be free from Spanish taxes; and this under the authority of the Spanish Financial Commission, authorized by the Decree, and acting as its agents. This would clearly, as between individuals, constitute a binding contract, and is equally valid as between the Spanish Government and its creditors. The only difficulty is in the mode of enforcing it.

### XLVIII. SWEDEN.

Population in 1871 (without Norway), 4,204,177. Area, 168,042 square miles. *Debt*, £6,700,000. Annual charge, about £350,000; or per head, 1s. 6d. The sum expended on State railways has exceeded the National Debt. Exports in 1871, £8,471,432. NORWAY—Population, 1,738,000. Area, 121,000 square miles.

### XLIX. TRINIDAD.

*Debt in* 1874, £100,000. Population, 109,638. Area, 1,764 miles. Revenue in 1872, £296,060; expenditure, £285,384. Imports, £1,233,771; exports, £1,439,905.

### L. TURKEY.

Population—in Europe (less Roumania), 12,000,000; in Asia, 15,000,000; in Africa (less Egypt), 2,000,000. Area—in Europe, 150,000 square miles; in Asia, 600,000 square miles; in Africa (say), 500,000 square miles. *Public debt* in 1865, after the conversion of the internal debt, was £71,229,640, and in 1874 was, by the *Economist*, about £135,000,000. The annual charge for interest and considerable sinking funds was £9,500,000 (£700,000 being remitted from Egypt). In 1866 the Government fell into arrear in paying the interest of the general debt; but since the special hypothecation of revenues to the Ottoman Bank, this had

THE DEBT OF THE UNITED STATES.     123

not again occurred until 1875. Turkey has for years been in arrear with regard to the interest guaranteed on railways—the Ottoman, Varna, Cassaba, &c., but since the 1874 loan placed the Porte in funds, some considerable payments have been made in this respect. The revenue is reported to have risen from £14,500,000 in 1863 to £18,987,000 in 1873. The deficit of 1873 was £4,580,000. The Government then stated that they were endeavouring to carry out much needed financial reforms to reduce the deficit; and the guarantees given in the prospectus of the latest loan caused it to be a success and to materially raise Turkish credit, when the decree of 1875 appeared, announcing default in future payments, although the Budget for 1874 showed an estimated revenue of £22,327,000. The settlement of the Black Sea question and of disputes with Egypt had been regarded in a favourable light. In addition to the above debt, there is the Roumelia Railway Loan, with a guarantee of 3 per cent., the total of which is £31,000,000.

LI. UNITED STATES

Population in 1850, 23,191,876 (including 3,204,313 slaves); ditto in 1860, 31,445,889; ditto in 1870, 38,558,371 free. Area (excluding "Russian America," reported worthless), 2,820,000 square miles. Population per square mile, 13¾. *Public debt*, £15,905,900 in 1860; ditto in 1866, £574,000,000; annual charge, £26,400,000 gold; *debt in* 1874, £411,050,000; annual charge, £20,650,000 gold. Debt per head of population, £11; annual charge per head, 10s. 3d. This burden was raised during the four years' Civil War; and in addition there was a large *Confederate* debt, which has been repudiated. *Nearly every separate State has its debt, which, collected together, may be estimated at* £78,000,000; but a considerable portion has been spent on works reproductive. In 1860 the revenue was £12,385,000: and the expenditure, £15,905,000. In 1870-71 the revenue was £76,750,000 and the expenditure £58,500,000 the surplus going to debt reductions. Revenue in 1873-74, after reductions in taxes, £57,895,750; expenditure, £57,150,506. The debt interest is being considerably reduced by the operation of the Funded loan. Railroads open at the end of 1873, 66,237 miles. The foreign trade has rapidly increased, and in 1873 the imports were £119,172,250, including £5,600,000 bullion, and the exports were £138,629,610 including £12,000,000 bullion. Half this trade is with Great Britain and her colonies. Since the termination of the war the Southern States have greatly increased their debts, and some have been brought to a state of bankruptcy. The New York City net debt is £25,379,272.

The *Philadelphia Public Ledger* gives the following particulars regarding the debts of the various States of the Union:—

"The debts of all the States and Territories of the Union, it is estimated, do not much exceed 300,000,000 dols. A considerable amount of this sum was incurred by the loyal States to equip troops to aid in the suppression of the Confederacy. Of this 300,000,000 dols., the 11 Southern States owe one-half, or about 150,000,000 dols. And not a dollar of it is war debt. Much of it, indeed, was created by fraud since the war, but none for the support and maintenance of Confederate troops. All that was long ago repudiated, and now follows the lamentable fact that the condition of the debts of nearly all the Southern States is such as to excite the fears of those who desire to see American credit preserved abroad and justice done to innocent persons at home, who have made honest investments in Southern State bonds."

## LII. URUGUAY.

Population, 550,000. Area, 700,000 square miles. *Debt*, £8,296,000, *besides railway guarantees*. Principal source of revenue—Customs dues, which in 1862 were £354,000; in 1870, £907,700; and in 1873, £1,295,640. Imports in 1872, £3,771,945.

The amount of the "home debt" on which payment of interest has been suspended by the Republic of Uruguay is stated by an eminent writer to be about four millions and a quarter, or rather more than half the total funded debt of the State. This, at least, is the last obtainable official statement of the amount. "There is no repudiation of this debt, nor nominally even a suspension of payments, but the bondholders are to be compelled to take State paper money in lieu of cash. Supposing that paper money goes to a discount of 50 per cent. it will still be about equal in value to the Twelve per Cent. Bonds of the State, which have been selling at 56, should these be taken at par on payment. But nobody can tell what the new paper dollars will pass current for. If they are to be issued as a means of clearing off a heavy burden of debt, and with no other security to uphold them than that offered by a heavily over-burdened community, they may sink low enough to be almost worthless. At the same time it should be admitted that Uruguay is not yet anything like in the same position as its neighbour Paraguay, where 30,000 pesetas worth of Treasury bills were sold by auction lately for 1,200 paper pesetas, of what actual value is not stated."

## LIII. VENEZUELA.

*The foreign debt is about £6,700,000, while the home debt has been stated at £10,000,000.* Venezuela has at various times discontinued the payment of interest on loans, and has now done so since 1864. After a period of successive revolutions, a Government has been established, which in 1874 proposed a settlement of outstanding claims; but it has not come to anything.

# PART IV.

# OF THE TERMS ON WHICH FOREIGN DEBTS HAVE BEEN CONTRACTED, AND THE FINANCIAL PRINCIPLES INVOLVED.

## CONTENTS.

CHAPTER I.—*Of Sinking Funds, Loan-Repayments and Drawings.*
*Of Foreign Debts, with illustrations of the Cost thereof to the State borrowing.*
*As to Profit to Lenders.*
*Alternative Measures.*

,, II.—*Of the relative values of Dividends and Drawings on Foreign Stocks or other Investments.*
*As to Stocks at a premium which are redeemable at par.*
*On the effect of Surplus dividends, over a security rate of 4 per cent. per annum, in replacing Capital paid for Stocks.*

,, III.—*Memoria Technica Tables relating to the Doubling and Accumulating of money.*
*Of the present values of Decreasing and Increasing Annuities.*

# PART IV.

OF THE TERMS ON WHICH FOREIGN DEBTS HAVE BEEN CONTRACTED, AND THE FINANCIAL PRINCIPLES INVOLVED.

## CHAPTER I.

In another* publication which forms a division of this treatise we have explained in detail, for persons not familiar with the subject, the leading principles involved in the working of compound interest. It may be convenient here to recapitulate some of the elements, which enter into the working of Average Investment Trusts, and arise in the liquidation of public debts or loans.

*Section* 1.—*Of Sinking Funds, Loan-Repayments, and Drawings.*

ART. 1.—A Sinking Fund is the amount put by periodically (yearly, half-yearly, or otherwise), which, accumulated at compound interest, will amount to a definite sum. Thus, 1.0177 (£1 0s. 4¼d.) a year set aside in half-yearly accumulations would at 7 per cent. interest per annum amount to £100 by the end of 30 years.

2.—*Loan Repayments.*—When a loan is redeemed by equal annual or other payments, termed in some countries "*Amortization,*" the annuity required to be paid is merely the interest added to the sinking fund on the whole debt for the specified time. It is what is termed, with respect to a portion of the English debts, a terminable annuity.

---

[* See Chapter II. at the beginning of the *Building Society Treatise*, and for Mathematical readers, the Appendix at the end of that work.]

## OF SINKING FUNDS.

Thus, 8.0177 (£8 0s. 4¼d.) a year will repay or redeem in 30 years a loan of £100 carrying interest half-yearly at 7 per cent. per annum. Other rates are given by the following table:—

### SINKING FUND TABLE.

*Showing the annual Sinking Fund (set aside in equal parts at the end of each half-year) which will amount to £100 at various rates of interest.*

| In Years. | 4 per cent. | 5 per cent. | 6 per cent. | 7 per cent. | 8 per cent. | 9 per cent. | 10 per cent. |
|---|---|---|---|---|---|---|---|
| 1 | 99.0099 | 98.7654 | 98.5222 | 98.2801 | 98.0392 | 97.7995 | 97.5610 |
| 2 | 48.5248 | 48.1636 | 47.8054 | 47.4502 | 47.0980 | 46.7487 | 46.4024 |
| 3 | 31.7052 | 31.3100 | 30.9195 | 30.5336 | 30.1524 | 29.7757 | 29.4035 |
| 4 | 23.3020 | 22.8935 | 22.4913 | 22.0953 | 21.7056 | 21.3219 | 20.9444 |
| 5 | 18.2653 | 17.8518 | 17.4461 | 17.0483 | 16.6582 | 16.2758 | 15.9010 |
| 6 | 14.9119 | 14.4974 | 14.0924 | 13.6968 | 13.3104 | 12.9332 | 12.5651 |
| 7 | 12.5204 | 12.1073 | 11.7053 | 11.3141 | 10.9338 | 10.5641 | 10.2048 |
| 8 | 10.7300 | 10.3198 | 9.9222 | 9.5370 | 9.1640 | 8.8031 | 8.4540 |
| 9 | 9.3404 | 8.9340 | 8.5417 | 8.1634 | 7.7987 | 7.4474 | 7.1092 |
| 10 | 8.2313 | 7.8294 | 7.4432 | 7.0722 | 6.7164 | 6.3752 | 6.0485 |
| 11 | 7.3263 | 6.9293 | 6.5495 | 6.1864 | 5.8398 | 5.5091 | 5.1941 |
| 12 | 6.5742 | 6.1826 | 5.8095 | 5.4546 | 5.1174 | 4.7974 | 4.4942 |
| 13 | 5.9398 | 5.5538 | 5.1877 | 4.8411 | 4.5135 | 4.2043 | 3.9129 |
| 14 | 5.3979 | 5.0176 | 4.6587 | 4.3205 | 4.0026 | 3.7042 | 3.4245 |
| 15 | 4.9300 | 4.5555 | 4.2039 | 3.8743 | 3.5660 | 3.2783 | 3.0103 |
| 16 | 4.5221 | 4.1537 | 3.8093 | 3.4883 | 3.1897 | 2.9126 | 2.6561 |
| 17 | 4.1637 | 3.8014 | 3.4644 | 3.1519 | 2.8630 | 2.5964 | 2.3511 |
| 18 | 3.8466 | 3.4903 | 3.1608 | 2.8568 | 2.5774 | 2.3212 | 2.0869 |
| 19 | 3.5641 | 3.2140 | 2.8919 | 2.5964 | 2.3264 | 2.0803 | 1.8568 |
| 20 | 3.3112 | 2.9673 | 2.6525 | 2.3655 | 2.1047 | 1.8686 | 1.6556 |
| 21 | 3.0835 | 2.7458 | 2.4383 | 2.1597 | 1.9080 | 1.6817 | 1.4789 |
| 22 | 2.8776 | 2.5461 | 2.2460 | 1.9755 | 1.7329 | 1.5161 | 1.3233 |
| 23 | 2.6907 | 2.3654 | 2.0725 | 1.8102 | 1.5764 | 1.3689 | 1.1856 |
| 24 | 2.5204 | 2.2012 | 1.9156 | 1.6613 | 1.4361 | 1.2377 | 1.0637 |
| 25 | 2.3646 | 2.0516 | 1.7731 | 1.5267 | 1.3100 | 1.1204 | .9553 |
| 26 | 2.2218 | 1.9149 | 1.6434 | 1.4049 | 1.1964 | 1.0154 | .8589 |
| 27 | 2.0905 | 1.7896 | 1.5251 | 1.2942 | 1.0938 | .9210 | .7729 |
| 28 | 1.9693 | 1.6745 | 1.4169 | 1.1935 | 1.0010 | .8362 | .6960 |
| 29 | 1.8573 | 1.5685 | 1.3177 | 1.1016 | .9168 | .7598 | .6273 |
| 30 | 1.7536 | 1.4707 | 1.2266 | *1.0177 | .8404 | .6909 | .5656 |
| 31 | 1.6573 | 1.3803 | 1.1428 | .9410 | .7709 | .6286 | .5104 |
| 32 | 1.5677 | 1.2965 | 1.0656 | .8706 | .7076 | .5722 | .4607 |
| 33 | 1.4842 | 1.2188 | .9942 | .8061 | .6498 | .5212 | .4161 |
| 34 | 1.4064 | 1.1466 | .9283 | .7468 | .5972 | .4750 | .3760 |
| 35 | 1.3335 | 1.0794 | .8673 | .6922 | .5490 | .4330 | .3398 |
| 50 | .6406 | .4624 | .3293 | .2319 | .1616 | .1117 | .0766 |

# NEW RULES FOR CALCULATING SINKING FUNDS.

3.—In long terms of years a small sinking fund would suffice, with the interest, for the liquidation of a debt; and with an increase in the rate of interest the sinking fund is relatively less. Thus, while in a 30 years' term at 6 per cent. half-yearly the sinking fund is £1 4s. 6¼d. a year, at 7 per cent. half-yearly it is only £1 0s. 4¼d. a year.

On the other hand, the redemption annuity is smaller as the interest is less, being £8 0s. 4¼d. a year at 7 per cent., and £7 4s. 6¼d. at 6 per cent.

4.—£100 divided by the figures in the sinking fund table gives the amount of £1 a year in the time selected. Thus, £100 divided by 2·9673 or 33·7006 is the amount of £1 a year at 5 per cent. interest half-yearly in 20 years. In like manner £100 divided by the Repayment Annuity per cent. gives the *present value* of £1 a year.

5.—*Practical * Rules.*—From the preceding table, all other tables can easily be deduced by the following simple rules, which are new :—

Rule i.—*The repayment annuity for any term* divided *by the sinking fund gives the* amount *to which a single £1 would accumulate, with interest, by the end of the same term of years. Such would be the amount to which a debt would accumulate in the time, if the interest and capital were left unpaid.*

EXAMPLE :—Thus, the repayment annuity 8.0177 divided by the sinking fund 1.0177 gives 7.8783, which is the amount of a single £1 in the same time at half-yearly interest. In other words, a debt of £10,000, on which neither interest nor capital was paid, would accumulate to £78,783 in 30 years at 7 per cent.

ii.—*The sinking fund* divided *by the repayment annuity gives the* present value *of a single £1 receivable at the end of the term.*

EXAMPLE :—Thus, 1.0177 divided by 8.0177 gives .1269, which is the present value of £1 receivable at the end of 30 years at the same rate of interest.

---

[* For other Rules see the Memoria Technica, Chapter III., section 1, and the Notes at foot of the Tables appended to this publication.]

Conversely:—

iii.—*The repayment annuity is the* amount *of a sum (equal to the sinking fund)* accumulated *for the term of years.*

EXAMPLE:—Thus, 8.0177 is the amount of 1.0177 accumulated at 7 per cent. for 30 years.

iv.—*The sinking fund is the* present value *of a sum (equal to the repayment annuity) discounted for the term of years.*

EXAMPLE:—Thus, 1.0177 is the present value at 7 per cent. of 8.0177 payable at the end of 30 years.

v.—When a table of the amounts of an annuity gives the figures for only a limited number of years, it can be used to find the *amounts of an annuity* for intervening or longer periods (whether it be yearly, half-yearly, or otherwise), as in the following example:—

*The amount of £1 a year for a term of 30 years is equal to the sum of the amounts of £1 a year for 20 years and 10 years respectively, to which is* added *one year's interest on the product of the said amounts for 20 and 10 years. Thus, at 5 per cent. half-yearly,*

| | |
|---|---|
| 1. *Amount of £1 per annum for 20 years is from above* - - - - - - - | 33·7006 |
| 2. ,, ,, 10 ,, - - | 12·7723 |
| Product - - - - - 430·4342 | |
| 3. *One year's interest thereon* - - - - | 21·5217 |
| Sum of (1), (2) and (3) - - - - - | 67·9946 |
| *which is the amount in 30 years of £1 a year.* | |

Conversely, £100 divided by the result gives the *sinking fund* for £100 in 30 years as in the foregoing table.

vi.—*The present value of an annuity for the term of 30 years is, in like manner, the sum of the values of an annuity for 20 years and 10 years respectively, from which is to be* deducted *one year's interest on the product of the two present values. Thus, at 5 per cent. half-yearly,*

1. The present value of £1 per annum for 20 years is    12·5514
2.      ,,          ,,        ,,    10  ,,   -     7·7946
3. Product of (1) multiplied by (2)    -    97·8331
4. Sum of (1) and (2)    -    -    -    -    -    20·3460
5. One year's interest at 5 per cent. on the product    4·8917
6. Sum less the one year's interest, being (4) less (5)    15·4543

This is the present value of an annuity of £1 a year for 30 years, calculated half-yearly.

6.—*Of Loan Repayments and Drawings* —When a debt is redeemed by an annuity it can be viewed—either as gradually liquidated by the increasing surplus of the annuity over the interest required each half-year on the amount unredeemed—or the annuity can be looked upon as chargeable with the same amount of interest for the whole period, leaving the surplus to act as a sinking fund to accumulate through re-investment by the end of the time to the £100 borrowed.

Where a large group of loans of equal amount has to be redeemed, a third system termed "Drawings" is frequently adopted instead of either of the preceding plans, for they are each open to objection in practical working. The one, that each loan has to be written off by instalments; the other, that all would have to wait for re-payment till the end of the full term.

The *Drawing system is in fact a most ingenious mode of gradually paying off in succession the creditors of a Government or of a Trust in full, without the trouble of accumulating the sinking fund throughout the originally specified term of the loan. Instead of treating each bond as a separate debt they are viewed in the aggregate. The redemption fund required to be set aside for the whole of the debt being fixed, drawings of the bonds to be paid off each year are made by lot. As the gross repayment annuity remains undiminished until the expiration of the number of years fixed, the number of bonds drawn each year increases with the re-

---

[* As to various kinds of drawings and a simple rule for estimating the amount available out of the annuity repayment in any year, see Part V.]

duction in the amount required to be paid for interest on the bonds yet unredeemed.

As far as the borrower is concerned it matters not to him that some of the lenders are paid off preferentially. He pays the stipulated annuity, and no more, for the term agreed.

7.—*Misconception as to Sinking Funds.*—A misconception occasionally arises as to the working of sinking funds and drawings. This can be best appreciated by giving an example :—

The prospectus of a leading Trust quotes £5 10s. as the amount per debenture which it proposes to set aside on its £100 bonds for yearly drawings and dividends, so as to pay £5 a year in dividends and return £110 per bond. The first drawing occurring at the end of the first year, and the dividends saved on the bonds drawn being carried to assist in the redemption of the others. This £5 10s. a year is below the amount the Trust would have to set aside.

To redeem by yearly drawings a present debt of £100 in 51 years would require an annuity of 5.45287 (£5 9s. 1d. nearly), which would consist of the dividend of £5 on the £100, and a sinking fund of 9s. 1d.

Now, it appears to be thought that when a bonus of £10 is added to the bonds of £100 redeemed, the only addition to the yearly fund required is to increase the sinking fund by 11d., being one-tenth of the sinking fund of 9s. 1d. mentioned above.

This would be true if the bonus £10 on all the * bonds were only to be paid at the end of the 51 years, while the bonds themselves were redeemed by yearly drawings. The error consists in not calculating the sinking fund for the whole £110 at a rate of interest modified by the fact that the sum to be redeemed is £110 and not £100.

---

[* The above is altogether independent of the circumstance that the bonds are issued at a lower price than par. That difference is separately chargeable on the general profits of the society, which is equivalent to saying that it must make a higher rate of profit than the nominal rate of interest payable on the bonds.]

## 51 YEARS' TABLE.

The preceding is easily tested by the formulæ for annuities, but can be made practically visible by the following table :—

Showing how a Loan of £1,000,000, in 10,000 Bonds of £100 each, bearing £5 a year in *Dividends*, with a Bonus of £10, will *not* be liquidated in 51 years by half-yearly drawings of an Annuity of £55,000 a year, but will leave a *deficiency* of £134,920.920 on the Bonds, and £13,492.092 on the Bonus, total £148,413.012.

[Four years' specimen of the calculation only are given, but if they be continued the results at the end of the 51st year will be as stated. As in practice fractions of Bonds could not be paid off, the *deficiency* at the close of the 51st year would be greater by the increase of interest paid on the fractions of bonds carried over unredeemed. In the Table the Dividends although payable half-yearly are charged by *annual* rests only on the £55,000 a year per bond, set aside for Dividend and Sinking Fund. Otherwise the Surplus available for Drawings each year would be even less, and the deficiency at the 51st year greater.]

*The last three figures in each column are decimal fractions.*

| Years. | Amount of Bonds unredeemed at the end of each year. | Dividend at £5 a year on amount of Bonds unredeemed. | Surplus out of £55,000 over the Dividends paid available for Drawings yearly. | Number and proportion of Bonds that could be drawn each year. | How Surplus could be applied. | |
|---|---|---|---|---|---|---|
| | | | | | To Bonds at £100 each. | To Bonus at £10 per Bond redeemed. |
| | £ | £ | £ | | £ | £ |
| 0 | 1,000,000 | 50,000. | 5,000. | 45.455 | 4,545.455 | 454.545 |
| 1 | 995,454.545 | 49,772.727 | 5,227.273 | 47.521 | 4,752.066 | 475.207 |
| 2 | 990,702.479 | 49,535.124 | 5,464.876 | 49.681 | 4,968.069 | 496.807 |
| 3 | 985,734.410 | 49,286.721 | 5,713.279 | 51.939 | 5,193.890 | 519.389 |
| 4 | 980,540.520 | : | : | : | : | : |
| 50 | : | 8,844.044 | 46,155.956 | 419.600 | 41,959.960 | 4,195.996 |
| End of 51st year | 134,920.920 | | 951,586.993 | 8,650.787 | | |

**8.**—*As to an ultimate deficiency of* £148,413.—The preceding table draws attention to a point of importance in the consideration of sinking funds and repayment annuities. It affords an excellent illustration of the peril resulting from premature bonus payments. The setting aside of £5 10s. per bond or £55,000 a year to redeem a debt of one million in bonds (with £5 interest and a bonus of 10 per cent. or £100,000 thereon, total £1,100,000) causes about £951,587 of that amount to be paid in the 51 years, and leaves £148,413 unprovided for at the end. Now we have said already that £54,528 14s. a year (which is £471 6s. a year less) would suffice to discharge in the same time the whole debt of one million bearing a like £5 interest, but carrying no bonus. The cause of the lesser effect in the first case being the application of a portion of the larger allowance, £55,000 a year, to the payment of bonuses, by which a smaller sum is left available each year to cancel bonds themselves than would happen if there were no bonus. The result is that of the 10,000 bonds there will remain over 1349 unprovided for, allowing for the decimal fractions.

The bond debt balance remaining larger, the interest still payable thereon continues larger, and, additionally, causes a smaller surplus to be applicable each year for the liquidation of bonds and bonus.

If, however, all the bonuses were not paid till the end as by a coupon of reversion, the same annuity of £55,000 separated into two parts, £54,528 14s., and £471 6s., would suffice,—the £54,528 14s. a year as a repayment annuity, to redeem the million of debt in the time by drawings,—and the £471 6s. as a sinking fund, to accumulate to somewhat more than £100,000 for bonus by the close of the 51 years.

*Section* 2.—*Of Foreign Debts, with illustrations of the Cost thereof to the State borrowing.*

ART. 9.—In a previous section we have described the investments made by existing Trusts as being of a varied character, viz., Railway shares and debentures, Municipal and Corporation bonds, &c., and, to a large extent, the * debt-bonds of Foreign Governments. With respect to the latter, a disposition is sometimes shown to disregard the question of security, and to purchase such as offer a large pecuniary return.

Foreign countries, when borrowing money, usually find it necessary to issue their stock at prices below par. In addition, a large number adopt systems of repayment which select the recipients by drawings of an attractive character. While the State thus avoids the impracticable responsibility of having to repay its bonds all at once at the end of the term, it is not prevented, if it has sufficient spare money, from also cancelling stock by purchases in the open market when the price is advantageously low.

---

[* The debts of Foreign Governments are no longer a small matter, nor is an interest in its stability confined to any one country. Holdings in Turkish Stocks, as in those of Egypt and some other States, are spread over Europe. Stocks are bought and sold, and have become a sort of international currency, affecting the exchanges as well as performing many other functions in account. The bondholders of all countries are united in common interest to a degree that renders presumably certain the adoption of a portion of the debt, for example, of a vast country like Turkey, by the provinces, if the autonomy of any portions were conceded, or if any section of the territory became incorporated with another Kingdom. The principle of the settlement of a proportion of the debt of a country upon its territory has been recognized more than once in the last quarter of a century. In the case of Rome and the other Italian States, the whole debt went with the soil of the annexed territories. Whatever may happen to the Mahomedan rulers of Turkey in Europe, no new distribution of territory nor adjustment of rights is likely to be effected without a proportionate allotment and recognition of the existing foreign debts.—*From a Paper by Mr. W. H. Bishop.*]

When the bond is issued at a large discount and is to be repaid at par, or even above par, the amount of discount on the issue is often a serious item, and materially affects the repayment annuity required to be set aside. The bonus returned on the cash received is equivalent to a further interest paid in a single sum. It represents to the person receiving it a rate of profit on his lending, largely differing according to the number of years the drawing of his bond happens to be deferred.

10.—We subjoin a few specimens of the terms upon which two of the largest borrowers amongst foreign States have raised loans:—

| Particulars of Loans. | TURKISH. | | | EGYPTIAN. | |
|---|---|---|---|---|---|
| | 1865. | 1869. | 1871. | 1868. | 1870. Khedive. |
| Nominal amount of loan | £ s. d.<br>6,000,000 0 0 | £ s. d.<br>22,222,220 0 0 | £ s. d.<br>5,700,000 0 0 | £ s. d.<br>11,890,000 0 0 | £ s. d.<br>7,142,860 0 0 |
| Price of issue per £100 bond | 65 10 0 | 60 10 0 | 73 0 0 | 75 0 0 | 78 10 0 less div. |
| Yearly dividend on the £100 bond | 6 0 0 | 6 0 0 | 6 0 0 | 7 0 0 | 7 0 0 |
| Nearest rate of interest corresponding to the price of issue, exclusive of bonus | 9 3 2 | 9 18 4 | 8 4 5 | 9 6 8 | 9 6 8 |
| Bonus to be paid by the half-yearly drawings of the bonds at par | 34 10 0 | 39 10 0 | 27 0 0 | 25 0 0 | 25 0 0 |
| Original annual rate of sinking fund per £100 bond | 2 8 9 | 1 0 0 | 1 0 0 | 1 0 4½ | 2 7 3 |
| Repayment annuity | 8 8 9 | 7 0 0 | 7 0 0 | 8 0 4½ | 9 7 3 |
| Number of years the loan is to last | 21 years. | 33 years. | 34 years. | 30 years. | 20 years. |
| Special security given | Sheep taxes, Tokah mines, Syrian indemnity. | Tithes, etc. | Egyptian Tribute. | | Private domains |

## THE COST OF THE EGYPTIAN LOAN OF 1868.

In the above specimens of Foreign debts, if we take for example the Egyptian loan of 1868 (as one convenient for illustration by figures), it is observed that in return for £75 paid, the bondholder is to receive £7 a year in dividends until the bond shall be drawn for repayment, and that it is to be paid off at par (£100) by a system of drawings which are to take place half-yearly, from the beginning throughout a term of 30 years. To meet these drawings a * sinking fund of 1.0177 is added to the dividends throughout the term, so that to liquidate each million of bonds issued, an annual cost of £80,177 is incurred for 30 years, payable half-yearly, which by the table in Section 1 is the repayment rate at £7 per cent. per annum. This £80,177 a year for 30 years represents an aggregate of £2,405,310 to be paid for the loan of £750,000 cash received on each million in bonds. Had the loans been an ordinary borrowing at 7 per cent. the £750,000 would require only £60,132 15s. a year for 30 years to repay it, principal and interest; the total payments would be only £1,803,982 10s.

As only £750,000 cash was received for the bonds this † annuity represents about 10⅛ per cent. per annum as the mean cost to the State for interest each year, which is equivalent to the £7 dividends and the £25 bonus.

---

[* The sinking fund on this loan is generally spoken of as £1 per cent., but when four places of decimals are used the correct figure would be 1.0177, or slightly over £1 0s. 4¼d. per cent. The nominal amount of the loan of 1868 was £11,890,000, and the annuity set aside is £953,297, being within a few pounds of the tabular rate. The necessity for great precision, in compound interest calculations relating to large sums of money, is seen by what would be the effect if the 4¼d., or the decimals, were omitted in the annuity. They represent £177 per million, or £2,104 10s. 7d. a year on the £11,890,000 of debt. This amount, measured in connection with the repayment annuity, would give rise to a deficiency exceeding £200,000 in bonds unredeemed.]

[† At 10 per cent. interest an annuity of £79,242 a year, paid half-yearly, would repay a loan of £750,000 in 30 years.]

## Section 3.—*As to profit to lenders*

Art. 11.—If the lender of £75 above received back only £75 at the end of the term, then the £7 a year dividend would be producing to him £9 6s. 8d. per cent. interest per annum; but as he is to obtain, in addition, a bonus of £25 when his bond is drawn, this is a further profit.

For all practical purposes it might be sufficient to regard the profit from the £25 bonus on the £75 separately from the £7 a year dividend, especially as the bonus itself is increased or diminished, and the rate of interest varied by the price paid for the bond in the market, according as it is less or more than £75.

There would be a further convenience in viewing the bonus as a distinct rate of interest or profit, on account of its being dependent on the chance of a drawing, which chance increases each year, while the value of the additional profit so made by an investor decreases with the length of time the drawing is deferred.

12.—But, if the calculations be made with strict arithmetical precision, the cost in dividends and bonuses to the State, as we have remarked above, will be found to be equal to an average rate of interest on all the bonds of about * $10\frac{1}{4}$ per cent per annum.

The investor will, however, make much more, or a little less, than $10\frac{1}{4}$ per cent., according to the year in which his bond happens to be drawn. Thus, if his bond be one of the last repaid, viz., at the end of the period of 30 years, then his dividends and bonus afford to him a mean rate of interest of $9\frac{1}{4}$ per cent. per annum. In other words, the bonus in that year only raises the rate of interest on his £75 from $9\frac{1}{3}$ per cent. per annum (the

---

[* The curious in such matters, who may not be familiar with mathematical formulæ, can verify the above and other like statements by constructing a Table, similar to the one on page 135, in which the interest is added at the rate specified, and the annuity deducted half-yearly or yearly, as the case may be.]

interest which the dividend alone would pay) to 9¼ per cent. per annum. The tabular value of the dividend and bonus together being £75 6s. 2¼d., in this case.

On the other hand the bondholder, who had his bond drawn in the first year, received £7 and £100. This £107 for £75 paid was equivalent to a rate of £42 13s. 4d. per cent. interest, apart from the fact that half the £7 was received in the middle of the year.

If the bond be drawn in the 15th or mean year, the average profit per annum made for the 15 years is about 10¼ per cent.

*Section 4.—On the cost to borrowing States*, continued.

ART. 13.—It will be noticed in the preceding that we have spoken as if the Egyptian treasury had actually received £75 per bond issued; but, in raising money, Governments have to pay large sums to agents, and frequently have to sell many of the bonds below the ostensible price of issue.

If we pass to other countries a lamentable state of things is seen, indicating a great want of prudence in the borrowers, and much foolish cupidity for gain in the lenders.

Taking an illustration from the Turkish loans, we find that the 6 per cent. loan of 1865 (familiarly termed the "Muttons") was for six millions, issued at the price of £65 10s. per cent., redeemable at par by half-yearly drawings in 21 years. The lender was thus offered for his £65 10s. an income of £6 a year and a bonus of £34 10s. Now, until repaid, the dividend alone affords him £9 3s. 2d. a year interest per cent. for the money, while in some year, at the latest 21 years after 1865, he was to receive a bonus of £34 10s., or over 50 per cent. on the cash paid by him to the Turkish Government.

Although these terms were so unusually heavy yet care was taken to provide for the repayment, for it was stipulated that all the sheep taxes of Anatolia, Roumelia and the Archipelago, the produce of the Tokah mines, and the balance of the Syrian indemnity should be reserved as a special security for this debt.

The (Cohen) 6 per cent. loan of Turkey raised in 1869 for over twenty-two millions was not less imprudent. The terms were £60 10s. as the price of issue, for which the dividend of 6 per cent. afforded near £10 per cent. to the purchaser, while a bonus of £39 10s. per bond was promised at the latest in 33 years, or in the interval by half-yearly drawings.

In other words, by way of contrasting example, if a lender had placed £605 in ten bonds of the "Cohen" loan at its price of issue, he expected to reap (without exertion or risk) an income of £60 a year from dividends and £1,000 in repayment of the £605 in the 33 years.

If the same person had placed his money in English Stock, the income for his £605 would not have reached £20 a year; if in Russian or French Stock the annual produce would have been under £35. In neither of these cases would there have been a Bonus of £395 on repayment.

14.—It will occur to the reader that if the lenders themselves had bargained for such terms, they could scarcely be entitled to much sympathy. But they did not do so, for they had no part in the contract upon which the bonds were issued. The reckless nature of the loans made to struggling foreign States has been ably discussed by Mr. Arthur Crump, so well known by his articles as city editor of the *Times*. He remarks that "when a loan is issued at a certain price redeemable within a given time by a sinking fund, the redemption price at par, or any other figure above par, adds to the glitter of the bait in the eyes of the public. As the drawings based upon this sinking fund begin sometimes 3, sometimes 6, and, at the outside, 12 months after the issue of the loan, it is obvious that, in proportion to the lowness of the issue price, is the attractiveness of the lure which places it in every bondholder's chance to have his bonds drawn at a premium on the sum paid by him of 20, 40, or 50 per cent., as the case may be. If the bonds held by the public be taken to represent the lottery ticket, we have in the annual or semi-annual drawings an exact reproduction of the old lottery business. The only difference is that, so long as the borrower is solvent, lenders obtain usurious interest for the loan of the capital which they invested in these tickets until their numbers are drawn."

He recognises that the system of redeeming at par, on which this lottery drawing is based, may contrast favourably for example with the English practice of funding debts for an indefinite period, or for ever.

The one system appears to show a laudable desire to keep open a clear way out of debt, the other evinces an apparently total disregard for the good of posterity, and, what is perhaps more important, for the dictates of common prudence. But a glance at the list of defaulting securities will show how frequently this specious show of thrift is fallacious. When the loans redeemed are issued in the first instance at a discount, the par drawings constitute a large premium, which a Government or a company is either forced or is content to pay for the use of a decreasing sum of money for a given time. He argues that,—

"The true way to use a sinking fund, of whatever percentage, is to apply it in redemption of the bonds by buying them in at market price, just as the English Government buys up Consols with surplus revenue," occasionally.

No doubt such a system is sound where the money saved in interest on the bonds bought is steadily applied to increase the amount available to redeem bonds in succeeding years.

This is the design of the Act of Parliament of 1875, whereby a permanent annual sum, which will be 28 millions a year in 1878, is to be applied to pay interest and buy up bonds of the English debt, independently of the action of the old sinking fund. The effect, however, will still be very small on the large English debt.

15.—Where repayment is seriously designed, Mr. Crump contends that,—

"If the credit of a Government is likely to improve, so that what money it now has to pay highly for, it could by-and-by get cheaply, then the sensible plan for those who wish to provide for getting out of debt, or for easing the charges of debt when the better days come, is to issue bonds in series, redeemable at fixed dates and prices. This is good for the Government, who at such dates can probably substitute a low interest-bearing stock for a high, if not able to repay the principal, and it is good for the public, because everybody knows what he is lending upon, and for how long he lends. The gambling element is removed from the transaction, and if it be provided that the redemption of such bonds shall be effected at par price, there is ample security for everybody. The holder knows that, given the solvency of the Government, he will not have to take less than he gave, and the Government knows that it cannot be forced to take back its obligations at a high premium. These are simple and natural provisions, to which no one can make any serious objection."

16.—The same writer points out two defects of many of the lottery drawings: the one that they are eminently usurious in many cases; the other that the drawings begin too soon, so soon, in fact, that the Governments have not time to benefit by the money borrowed. This last objection could, however, be removed by deferring the first drawing for 5 or 7 years. He says:—

"The half-yearly lottery drawing loans, and their* Sinking Fund arrangements are of a most onerous kind for the borrower. As the announcement is usually made upon a prospectus, the plan looks at the worst a mere offer of Bonus by the borrower, greater or less according to his credit. The sinking fund is 1, 2, or 3 per cent., as the case may be, by which the incidence of that bonus is distributed over the whole period of the loan. When a country ostensibly borrows at 70, and begins its paying-off arrangements at 100 the next year, it strikes mere outsiders as tolerably heavy terms, but not probably as in any way disastrous. * * * But one loan is not half utilized before another is needed to pay the remainder of the first. Taking into account the number of years which the borrower gets the use of the money for, the best-priced and longest-running loans mentioned below are, obviously, extravagantly dear, some of them ruinously so. They would be dear had the borrower the use of the whole of the money throughout the entire period,

---

[\* On this subject the following letter appeared in a financial paper, which shows that the writer shared a misconception that occasionally prevails with regard to compound interest calculations:—

"Sir,—The *Times* of to-day, in its Money Article, has given the public the benefit of its ideas upon the effects of Foreign Loans carrying Drawings, as being demoralising to the lenders, and ruinous to the borrowing States. To make out its theory, however, the *Times* makes the unhappy borrower pay interest upon the *full* amount of the Loan during the whole time of its operation, not being aware, apparently, that upon the drawn Bonds the interest ceases, and the yearly charge consequently becomes less and less. The *Times*' mode of financing would certainly be a ruinous one. It is to be hoped the writer of this homily will employ his next holiday moments to better advantage, and, before engaging to teach the public, take a few lessons himself in common arithmetic.—Yours, &c., "A. B.]
"City, May 18th, 1875."]

and the amount of capital left in his hands were not a diminishing quantity year by year.

"It may, of course, be urged that in some instances the borrowing party would pay more to the lender did the capital lent simply remain in his hands, to be repaid at a fixed time, bearing interest at 5, 6, or 7 per cent., as the case may be, till that time was up. That is doubtless true. In 20 years' time, for example, interest at 5 per cent. will amount to the capital of a loan, and if added to the capital paid back, we shall suppose, at the end of that period, will make the amount paid altogether by the borrower seem a very large sum. But the drawing loans, it cannot be too clearly explained, are not of this nature at all. The\* borrower does not keep the capital for the whole period; on the contrary, he begins paying it off at once, and to anyone who knows how long it takes capital in most instances to fructify so as to reproduce itself with usury —how rarely, in fact, it ever does so—it will at once be evident that capital borrowed on these terms for reproductive purposes must in 19 cases out of 20

---

[\* The above remarks seem founded on an impression that the payment of the sinking fund with the interest makes the loan specially onerous. This is not always the case. Referring to the example before given of the Egyptian Loan of 1868 which costs £80,177 a year per million in £100 bonds for £750,000 cash received, covering interest and sinking fund.

Here, if no bonds were drawn, the annual cost would be £70,000 for interest alone throughout the 30 years, when the million to pay off the bonds at the end would have to be forthcoming. It is probable, therefore, that it is better for the government (which entered into so improvident a bargain) to set aside £10,177 a year more for the 30 years rather than have to find £1,000,000 in cash at the end.

It is for a like reason that the recent suggestion that Peru should postpone the sinking fund on its 5 per cent. loan, would not help that country sufficiently.

If relief be given it must be by the creditors consenting to treat the borrowers with less usury, and to accept such a rate of interest on their bonds, as more fairly corresponds to the cash received, and to what is usually demanded from States which are treated as honest in their intentions. Granting that the lenders have claims, so, also, is consideration expedient to the struggling populations of the countries that have borrowed. In most cases the burdens they have already to bear are very heavy, and out of their small earnings there is little margin to pay an extravagant debt. If, however, moderation be exercised in the present, the future may contain resources to meet a just arrangement.]

prove a mere delusion and a snare. If reproductive works are prospering, their tendency is to require more capital, not less. There is no different law regulating the business of a State from that which controls the growth of the operations of a private firm. Our English Railways—the most prosperous of them—are not in a position to pay back capital; they are, instead, constantly needing more, just because they are for the most part flourishing. Yet we find foreign States, companies, Trusts, corporations of all kinds proceeding on an assumption contrary to all facts, borrowing at heavy rates only to begin paying back, without giving the chance to capital to take root and fructify. It needs no demonstration to prove that business done in this way is most unsound; too often it proves most ruinous."

17.—This writer gives a list of certain public debts which, he remarks :—

" Were chosen simply as the securities came, and with a view to give recent examples in the prominent foreign State loans that are launched on the improvident system deprecated. There is, therefore, nothing exceptional in the figures. The best are there, and, perhaps, the worst, and of even the best it is not too much to say that they do not give a pleasing prospect in the future to those States who have committed themselves to this fallacious mode of raising sums of money for temporary or 'reproductive' purposes. It should in fairness be stated, however, that the debts of some of the States here given are not entirely contracted after this fashion. Both Russia and Turkey, for example, have a great deal more than we have set down below, and much of this debt is not subject to the lottery principle. [See also our specimen table in section 2.]

| Name of Loan. | Issue Price. | Repayment Annuity, or Interest and Sinking Fund, per cent. per annum. | Nominal Amount of Loan. | No. of Years to run. |
|---|---|---|---|---|
| Argentine 6 per cent., 1871 | 88½ | 8½ | £6,122,400 | 21 |
| Bolivian 6 per cent., 1872 | 68 | 8 | 1,700,000 | 24 |
| Brazilian 5 per cent., 1865 | 74 | 6 | 6,963,500 | 37 |
| Chilian 5 per cent., 1873 | 94 | 7 | 2,276,500 | 26 |
| „ 5 per cent., 1875 | 88¼ | 7 | 1,000,000 | 26 |
| Egyptian 7 per cent., 1868 | 75 | 8 | 11,890,000 | 30 |
| „ 7 per cent., 1873 | 84½ | 8 | 32,000,000 | 30 |
| Hungarian 5 per cent., 1871 | 81 | 6½ | 3,000,000 | 32 |
| „ 5 per cent., 1873 | 80 | 6½ | 5,400,000 | 30 |
| Italian State Domain, 1865 | 77½ | 11½ | 8,000,000 | 16 |
| Japanese 9 per cent., 1870 | 98 | 19 | 1,000,000 | 10 |
| „ 7 per cent., 1873 | 92½ | 9 | 2,400,000 | 22 |
| Peruvian 6 per cent., 1870 | 82½ | 8 from 1880 | 11,920,000 | 34 |
| „ 5 per cent., 1872 | 77½ | 7 | 23,215,000 | 26 |
| Spanish (Quicksilver) 5 per cent., 1871 | 80 | 6½ | 2,318,100 | 30 |
| Turkish 6 per cent., 1869 | 60¼ | 7 | 22,222,220 | 33 |
| „ 6 per cent., 1873 | 58½ | 7 | 14,000,000 | 33 |
| Uruguay 6 per cent., 1871 | 72 | 8½ | 3,500,000 | 21 |

| Name of Loan. | *Net Produce to Borrower. | Annual Charge throughout. | Total Cost to Borrower, including Capital repaid at Redemption. |
|---|---|---|---|
| Argentine 6 per cent., 1871 | £5,418,324 | £520,404 | £10,928,484 |
| Bolivian 6 per cent., 1872 | 1,156,000 | 136,000 | 3,235,440 |
| Brazilian 5 per cent., 1865 | 5,152,990 | 417,810 | 15,341,983 |
| Chilian 5 per cent., 1873 | 2,139,910 | 159,355 | 4,992,236 |
| „ 5 per cent., 1875 | 882,500 | 70,000 | 1,797,600 |
| Egyptian 7 per cent., 1868 | 8,917,500 | †951,200 | 29,230,376 |
| „ 7 per cent., 1873 | 26,960,000 | 2,560,000 | 78,568,500 |
| Hungarian 5 per cent., 1871 | 2,430,000 | 190,000 | 6,133,290 |
| „ 5 per cent., 1873 | 4,320,000 | 351,000 | 10,547,550 |
| Italian State Domain, 1865 | 6,200,000 | 906,666 | 14,506,666 |
| Japanese 9 per cent., 1870 | 980,000 | 190,000 | 2,080,000 |
| „ 7 per cent., 1873 | 2,220,000 | 216,000 | 4,801,680 |
| Peruvian 6 per cent., 1870 | 9,834,000 | 1,013,200 | 24,104,028 |
| „ 5 per cent., 1872 | 17,491,625 | 1,625,050 | 41,730,584 |
| Spanish (Quicksilver) 5 per cent., 1871 | 1,854,480 | 150,676 | 4,527,813 |
| Turkish 6 per cent., 1869 | 13,444,443 | 1,553,555 | 51,939,981 |
| „ 6 per cent., 1873 | 8,190,000 | 930,000 | 32,722,200 |
| Uruguay 6 per cent, 1871 | 2,520,000 | 297,500 | 6,247,500 |

18.—Another financial ‡ Journal points, however, to a deeper moral in the arguments of Mr. Crump than is obvious at first sight :—

"He furnishes a list which shows the hard terms of some 18 loans brought out during the last 10 years (1865-75). Thus the Egyptian Loan of 1868, which yielded a little short of £9,000,000 *net* to the Government, will cost for redemption upwards of £29,000,000, while the Turkish 6 per Cent. of 1873, which yielded rather more than £8,000,000, will cost for redemption upwards of £32,000,000. These are terrible terms for the borrowers, but the cases quoted are selected at random, and are all on conditions substantially as onerous.

"We have recently been calling defaulting States severely to task for their poverty and their faithlessness. The Council of Foreign Bondholders finds its *raison d'être* in these unhappy defaults; but all the time we ourselves have been rank usurers, and are only now suffering a penalty which we have deliberately provoked. We have no sympathy with 'West End usurers,' because of their extortions. What claim can City usurers have on our sympathies, when they find their debtors in default ? And it is on behalf of this abominable usury, and of those who practise it, that we are called to arouse the

---

[* "Net," that is exclusive of commissions paid by borrower to loan agents varying from 2 per cent. in the case of good financial houses, to 5, 10, or more where the borrower is weak and the agents unscrupulous.]

[† The actual figure according to the prospectus is £953,297.]

[‡ The *Monetary Gazette*.]

national indignation against the wretched States that are crushed beneath the burden of our covetousness! Surely if the terms of these loans are not misstated, even the defaulters among the poor South American Republics are 'more sinned against than sinning.' The lust of our avarice has imposed on them burdens which from the first it was impossible for them to bear, and the *lenders are responsible and as much to be blamed for the inevitable collapse as the borrowers.* Nay, much more, for the borrowers may at least put in the extenuating plea that they entered unwillingly on a bad bargain under the overwhelming pressure of straitened circumstances—a plea of which the lenders cannot possibly avail themselves. We are now taught to denounce these loans as prodigious engines for draining a country of its resources, or a means of dragging a corporation to ruin. But these terms, if ruinous to the borrower, are demoralizing and degrading to the lenders. There is no escape from that."

*Section 5.—Alternative Measures.*

ART. 19.—Supposing, then, a Government to find it convenient to raise money on the annuity system of repayment, it must yet be recognised that the mere applying of it by drawings does not increase the cost. It is the rate of interest involved and the amount of bonus that have to be looked to. If in future loans all drawing of bonds were omitted (as the recent parliamentary committee almost recommends) it is doubtful whether the change would meet the views of the public at the present time. In this, as in other* countries, the system has become very popular and

---

[* Abroad a system of prizes has been superadded, which is quite a distinct thing from mere repayment of debt with a moderate bonus by drawings. For example, on the 26th drawing of prizes, May 15th, 1874, in the city of Brussels loan of 1867, there was one prize of 25,000f. one of 2,000f., and two of 1,000f. Again, the Communal Council of Antwerp, September, 1874, ratified a contract entered into with Messrs. Errera, Oppenheim, Cassel and Basenwitz, for a loan to the city of Antwerp of 60,000,000f. redeemable by 66 annual drawings. The loan to be issued in lottery bonds bearing interest at the rate of 3 per cent.

any attempt to discourage it here would only drive loans for issue abroad, but would not prevent their being bought and sold in the London market afterwards. The fact exists that corporations and foreign States, at home and elsewhere, which borrow money, find it to their advantage to seek the passing favour of investors by announcing periodic drawings.

20.—The rate of interest receivable is not now always the main attraction. The prospective or contingent advantage is an element agreeable to many purchasers, who are not in any sense speculators. A loan of £100 carrying 6 per cent. interest, issued at par and repayable at par, would not be so attractive as another loan bearing

---

In the Austrian Government loans of 1854 and 1860, Raab-Gratz Railway loan (guaranteed by the Austro-Hungarian Government), Russian Government (Internal) loans of 1864 and 1866, and in the loans of the following European cities, viz. :—Paris, Amsterdam, Brussels, Antwerp, Naples and Florence, the Debentures bear interest at from 3 to $5\frac{1}{2}$ per cent. per annum, and are redeemable within a stated period by drawings at par. On each occasion a certain proportion is drawn with premiums, varying in amount from 4,000fl. to 30,000fl., the principle adopted being the payment of a small rate of interest on the bonds, while a further 1 per cent. per annum—more or less, as the case may be—is divided amongst the bondholders. Instead of each bond receiving its fractional participation, a few bonds are drawn with large sums representing that additional amount of interest upon the *whole loan*. The period for which they are issued is generally fifty or sixty years, by the expiration of which time it is promised that all shall be drawn at par, or higher.

The Debentures of the Austrian Government loan of 1839, for 250fl. each, or £25 are sold at 720fl. or £72 each, as the final drawing takes place in 1878.

It is stated that there are various Government and Municipal Debentures, which do not carry interest or dividends; the entire available amount of interest being appropriated to the operations of the sinking fund and to premiums. Amongst these loans are the following :—Austrian Government loan of 1864, Hungarian Government loan of 1870, Swedish Government loan of 1860, Finland loan of 1867, and loans of the undermentioned cities—viz., Vienna, Genoa, Milan, Venice, Bucharest, &c.]

## EXPENSIVE NATURE OF THE EGYPTIAN LOAN. 151

only 5 per cent., and having the additional £1 a year to form a Bonus drawing fund.

The question then arises whether the dividend rate of interest should not, as a rule, be put somewhat lower than is the practice, and the money (otherwise payable in interest) be saved, so as to be used to keep up the half-yearly funds for drawings or repayment of stock.

21.—Taking the example of the Egyptian loan of 1868, even if the interest alone be looked at, the transaction was a costly one; for without the bonus of £25, the rate of interest afforded by £7 a year * dividend on £75 is $9\frac{1}{3}$ per cent. Such an offer to borrowers by a Government that has every element of soundness, apart from a repute for habitual integrity, was unnecessarily profuse. The whole mean equivalent cost of $10\frac{1}{8}$ per cent. per annum in itself would not be a very large rate of interest for a country in the situation of Egypt to pay for an advance if the present time by itself be considered; but to pledge its credit for the payment of $10\frac{1}{8}$ per cent. a year for so long a term of years as 30, was to ignore all probable improvement in its finances in the future, when money would be obtainable at a percentage more in accordance with the equitable usages of other countries. How greatly the length of time, as well as the rate, affects the question is seen by remembering that, as money would double in about 7 years at

---

[* In long terms of years selected for a loan, where the dividend on the stock is such as to give a high rate of interest on the cash received by the borrower the payment of a bonus on redemption does not add to the expensiveness of the loan, so much as at first sight might be imagined.

A striking illustration of this is shown by the above case of Egypt; for supposing no £25 bonus were payable per bond at all, the redemption in 30 years of the cash received, £750,000, carrying only a dividend of £7 per bond (or $9\frac{1}{3}$ per cent.) interest half yearly, would cost £74,854.275 (£74,854 5s. 6d.) a year—yet with a bonus of £250,000 the redemption annuity for the debt of one million is, as we have stated, but £80,177 or £5,322 14s. 6d. a year more.]

10¾ per cent. per annum half-yearly, a million would be multiplied nineteen-fold in the 30 years. For in 28 years, or 4 times 7 years, one million would accumulate with such a rate of interest to nearly sixteen-fold, and by the close of two years more, the further interest would make up nineteen millions. [*See further on the Memoria Technica Tables and the property of the Number* 70.]

Now, if the dividend instead of £7 had been £4 10s. on the stock issued at £75, it would have given to investors a very high rate of interest viz., 6 per cent. per annum; while if the present repayment annuity had still been set aside, then a loan of £750,000, with all the bonuses of £250,000, would have been capable of liquidation by drawings (reckoning interest half-yearly) in little over 18½ years instead of 30 years.

Both parties would have had reason to be satisfied with the arrangement described. The purchasers of the Egyptian stock would, indeed, have had less interest—viz., 6 per cent. per annum, —but they would be all repaid with their bonuses of £25 in the 18½ years. The State would have 30 years less 18½, that is 11½ years' payments fewer to make. The total loan was £11,890,000 and £953,297 a year is the annuity the Government sets aside. The aggregate of the payment saved would be £953,297 multiplied by 11½ or £10,962,915 10s.

## CHAPTER II.

OF DIVIDENDS AND DRAWINGS IN FOREIGN STOCKS.

---

*Section 1.—The relative values of Dividends and Drawings.*

ART. 22.—The various stocks of a Foreign Government can rarely be compared with each other on precisely the same footing. Many, being ostensibly guaranteed by some particular security, have had until lately a higher value in the market which is not likely, after recent events, to continue. A difference of price has also been observable in stocks of an earlier issue as compared with those of later dates. The relative values of different loans is affected by the amounts of the sinking funds applied to drawings. Ten years ago there were only a few stocks that possessed the drawing privilege, and the character and value of the arrangement were very imperfectly understood. Consequently at that time there was scarcely any difference in the market prices of stocks having different allowances for drawings.

In general, the term of years for the redemption of the earlier loans is shorter than in the later ones, thus giving to the first the largest rate of repayments. Moreover, the chance of a drawing to each investor increases each year, from the fraction, which measures it, depending on the amount available for paying off bonds, and the reduced balance of the whole debt outstanding.

As some guide we give the following table, which shows how much of the outlay in the purchase of bonds or other securities, repayable by drawings and carrying 6 and 7 per cent. interest, corresponds to the dividend income receivable, and how much to the par value £100 of the bond, according to the number of years that elapse before it is drawn :—

## DIVIDENDS AND DRAWINGS TABLE

*Showing the* VALUES OF BONDS *carrying* £6 *and* £7 *dividends a year respectively, with* £100 *par value receivable by Drawings at the end of uncertain periods of years.* [*Discounted half-yearly at* 6 *and* 7 *per cent. per annum respectively.*]

| Years. | Present value discounted at 6 per cent. of | | Present value discounted at 7 per cent. of | |
|---|---|---|---|---|
| | £6 a year Dividend. | £100. | £7 a year Dividend. | £100. |
| 1 | 5.740 | 94.260 | 6.649 | 93.351 |
| 2 | 11.151 | 88.849 | 12.856 | 87.144 |
| 3 | 16.252 | 83.748 | 18.650 | 81.350 |
| 4 | 21.059 | 78.941 | 24.059 | 75.941 |
| 5 | 25.591 | 74.409 | 29.108 | 70.892 |
| 6 | 29.862 | 70.138 | 33.822 | 66.178 |
| 7 | 33.888 | 66.112 | 38.222 | 61.778 |
| 8 | 37.683 | 62.317 | 42.329 | 57.671 |
| 9 | 41.261 | 58.739 | 46.164 | 53.836 |
| 10 | 44.632 | 55.368 | 49.743 | 50.257 |
| 11 | 47.811 | 52.189 | 53.085 | 46.915 |
| 12 | 50.807 | 49.193 | 56.204 | 43.796 |
| 13 | 53.631 | 46.369 | 59.116 | 40.884 |
| 14 | 56.292 | 43.708 | 61.835 | 38.165 |
| 15 | 58.801 | 41.199 | 64.372 | 35.628 |
| 16 | 61.166 | 38.834 | 66.741 | 33.259 |
| 17 | 63.396 | 36.604 | 68.952 | 31.048 |
| 18 | 65.497 | 34.503 | 71.017 | 28.983 |
| 19 | 67.477 | 32.523 | 72.944 | 27.056 |
| 20 | 69.344 | 30.656 | 74.743 | 25.257 |
| 21 | 71.104 | 28.896 | 76.422 | 23.578 |
| 22 | 72.763 | 27.237 | 77.990 | 22.010 |
| 23 | 74.326 | 25.674 | 79.453 | 20.547 |
| 24 | 75.800 | 24.200 | 80.819 | 19.181 |
| 25 | 77.189 | 22.811 | 82.095 | 17.905 |
| 26 | 78.499 | 21.501 | 83.285 | 16.715 |
| 27 | 79.733 | 20.267 | 84.397 | 15.603 |
| 28 | 80.896 | 19.104 | 85.434 | 14.566 |
| 29 | 81.993 | 18.007 | 86.402 | 13.598 |
| 30 | 83.027 | 16.973 | 87.307 | 12.693 |
| 31 | 84.001 | 15.999 | 88.151 | 11.849 |
| 32 | 84.919 | 15.081 | 88.938 | 11.062 |
| 33 | 85.785 | 14.215 | 89.674 | 10.326 |
| 34 | 86.601 | 13.399 | 90.360 | 9.640 |
| 35 | 87.370 | 12.630 | 91.001 | 8.999 |

VALUES OF DIVIDENDS AND DRAWINGS. 155

In the preceding table as the figures, for the present value of a £100 at 6 and 7 per cent. at the end of any number of years, are only given up to 35, it may incidentally be mentioned that, if the number of years exceeds the last in the table, the desired figures can be obtained thus :—Say the number of years is 50—the present value of £100 at the end of 50 years is the product of the present values for any two or more numbers of years which make up 50. Thus the present value of £100 in 20 years multiplied by that for 30 years, or 25.257 multiplied by 12.693, gives 3.206, the present value of £100 in 50 years at 7 per cent.

The present value of an *annuity* for any number of years beyond 35 can also be found from this table by the Rule given in Chap. I., Sect. 1, No. 6 of this Part.

23.—When the cost of a bond is compared with the preceding table, it will be found that frequently the market price is under the present value of the dividend alone, even for the whole unexpired time. Thus, the "Cohen" Turkish loan of 1869, which has about 27 years to run, has a nominal £6 a year in dividend, of which the value for that time is by the table 79.733 or £79 14s. 8d. The market price of the stock in October 1875 fell to £32 10s. or £47 4s. 8d. below the measure of the dividend; and no worth was attached to the £100 receivable per bond; showing reasonable anticipations that a Government, which has raised money on such terms, would probably be unable to continue the stipulated repayments.

Again, the Egyptian Stock of 1868, which has, in 1875, about 23 years unexpired, produces £7 a year dividend, of which the value would be 79.453 or £79 9s. 1d. Even when no panic influence has been at work, the market price was but two or three pounds over the value of the dividend, leaving little for the £100 bond itself, which is receivable at latest by the end of the 23 years.

The table shows, as it should, that the present value of a dividend receivable for any number of years, added to the present value of the £100 on the bond at the end, is equal to £100.

Supposing the Egyptian bond to be drawn at the end of 10 years, the relative values are nearly equal, viz., £49.743 for the £7 a year dividends, and £50.257 for the £100 drawing.

---

Section 2.—*As to Stocks at a Premium, which are redeemable at par.*

ART. 24.—The following table, calculated at half-yearly interest, will serve for the correct assessment of the prices of stocks at a premium, when they pay a high interest-dividend, but are subject to the condition of being paid off at par.

Thus, suppose a stock paying £7 a year dividend half-yearly is redeemable by £100 at the end of 10 years, what the premium should be will depend upon the * purchaser's notion of how much

---

[* On this subject the *Financier* in 1874 had some observations of much practical value :—

"Stocks, redeemable at par, which are quoted at a premium in the market, present a peculiar feature to intending investors, inasmuch as the premium paid must be allowed for in calculating the rate of interest returned, assuming that the Stock be held until its maturity. The market price would experience a gradual decline until the final year before redemption, when it would probably be quoted only so much above par as would represent one year's interest. The gradual decline in the quotations of Securities from this cause may be traced by comparing the prices current from one year to another. One example will show this. In 1869 India Five per Cents., redeemable in 1880, were quoted at 114. The Stock being redeemable in 11 years from 1869, should have declined about 1¼ per cent. each year afterwards. The price now, after four and a half years, is 107¾, so that it has declined 6¼ per cent., or more than the 1¼ in each year. This decline has not, however, taken place regularly each year to the extent of 1¼ per cent., although the result after four and a half years shows

less than 7 per cent. a year he will be satisfied to be making for his money.

If it be 5 per cent., then the present value of £100 of such stock would be £115.590 or £115 11s. 10d.

---

that the influence was at work. The following average price for each year shows how the downward movement went on:—

Average prices in—

| 1868. | 1869. | 1870. | 1871. | 1872. | 1873. |
|---|---|---|---|---|---|
| 114 | 113 | 110 | 111 | 110 | 109 |

Similarly, the prices of the different Colonial Government Bonds vary considerably, according to the dates of their redemption. For instance, Canadian Six per Cents., redeemable in 1876, are quoted at 104, whilst the Six per Cents. of the same Colony, redeemable in 1881 to 1884, are quoted at 110; and, amongst South Australian Bonds, the Six per Cents. redeemable between 1881 and 1890 are quoted at 114, and those redeemable between 1901 and 1918 are quoted at 123.

"In the case of Foreign Government Loans quoted above par, where the redemption takes place by drawings, the investor has to calculate his chance of having Bonds drawn as reducing his income. Loans quoted above par and subject to periodical drawings, pay in interest more than Loans quoted below par in which the drawings raise instead of reducing the return. An instance of this may be found in the Egyptian Viceroy Loans. The Nine per Cent. Loan is quoted at 101, and, at that price, pays the investor nearly 9 per cent. On the other hand, the Seven per Cent. Loan, at 90, pays less than 8 per Cent., but then the holder has the chance of a bonus of 10 per cent. each year, and the certainty of it in the course of a defined number of years. The recent advance in Russian Five per Cent. Stocks to par has not only reduced the rate of interest offered to an investor at the market price, but has also done away with the bonus obtainable on redemption, which, three years ago, amounted to nearly 20 per cent."]

## STOCKS AT A PREMIUM.—TABLE

Showing the prices of Stock, corresponding to the rate of interest desired to be made on Stocks above par, and which produce half-yearly dividends at 5, 6, and 7 per cent. per annum. The Stock being redeemable at par or £100.

| Years to run. | Dividend, 5 per cent. | | Dividend, 6 per cent. | | | | | Dividend, 7 per cent. | | | |
|---|---|---|---|---|---|---|---|---|---|---|---|
| | 4 per cent. | 4½ per cent. | 4 per cent. | 4½ per cent. | 5 per cent. | 4 per cent. | 4½ per cent. | 5 per cent. | 5½ per cent. | 6 per cent. |
| | | | | | while the interest required per annum is:— | | | | | | |
| 5  | 104.491 | 102.217 | 108.982 | 106.650 | 104.376 | 113.473 | 111.093 | 108.752 | 106.480 | 104.265 |
| 10 | 106.176 | 103.991 | 116.352 | 111.973 | 107.795 | 124.528 | 119.965 | 115.590 | 111.421 | 107.439 |
| 15 | 111.198 | 105.412 | 122.396 | 116.234 | 110.465 | 133.594 | 127.067 | 120.930 | 115.188 | 109.800 |
| 20 | 113.578 | 106.549 | 127.366 | 119.646 | 112.551 | 141.034 | 132.743 | 125.102 | 118.069 | 111.657 |
| 25 | 115.712 | 107.469 | 131.424 | 122.376 | 114.181 | 147.136 | 137.293 | 128.362 | 120.249 | 112.865 |
| 30 | 117.380 | 108.187 | 134.760 | 124.561 | 115.454 | 152.140 | 140.935 | 130.908 | 121.917 | 113.838 |
| 35 | 118.749 | 108.771 | 137.496 | 126.312 | 116.449 | 156.247 | 143.853 | 132.898 | 123.190 | 114.562 |
| 40 | 119.872 | 109.238 | 139.744 | 127.713 | 117.226 | 159.616 | 146.188 | 134.452 | 124.159 | 115.100 |
| 45 | 120.793 | 109.611 | 141.586 | 128.833 | 117.833 | 162.379 | 148.056 | 135.666 | 124.900 | 115.501 |
| 50 | 121.549 | 109.911 | 143.098 | 129.732 | 118.307 | 164.647 | 149.553 | 136.614 | 125.464 | 115.799 |

\*\*\* The figures for intervening years in the above table can be calculated by the Rule given in Chap. 1., Sect. I., Number 6 of this Part.

Section 3.—*On the effect of the surplus of Dividends, over a security rate of 4 per cent. per annum, in replacing Capital paid for Stocks.*

Art. 25.—When investments are made in securities bearing a large rate of dividend, the prudent purchaser is aware that a reserve should be made of a certain proportion of the dividend received.

It is generally admitted that, as a rule, 4 per cent. is the highest rate of interest obtainable by private individuals, not engaged in monetary business, for money invested with a view of security; while associations can make more. This point is not always remembered by persons, who, having received a large rate of interest for many years, are yet ready to complain of the risk on their capital;—If loss arise it can scarcely be viewed, in such a case, as other than partial in respect to the capital originally invested.

The surplus received above £4 per cent. (which we will term the security rate) should be treated by the purchaser as being *de facto* a return of the capital invested; and the money which he would have outstanding (and for which the undiminished dividends would be receivable) would decrease each year as shown by the following table, in which the first column shows how much of £100 invested can be written off each year by means of a surplus dividend of £1 a year, which is the excess of £5 over £4 per cent. That column will serve, therefore, for other calculations where the dividend produced by a purchase does not happen to fall into either of the columns.

## SURPLUS OF DIVIDENDS OVER 4 PER CENT.—TABLE.

*If £100 be laid out in a purchase of stock producing equal dividends half-yearly, and the surplus of dividends over £4 INTEREST be applied half-yearly to write off capital, then the amounts of capital returned will be as follows, according to the amount of dividend received for the £100.*

### Capital Received Back out of—

| In Years | £5 a year.<br>£ s. d. | £6 a year.<br>£ s. d. | £7 a year.<br>£ s. d. | £8 a year.<br>£ s. d. | £9 a year.<br>£ s. d. | £10 a year.<br>£ s. d. | £11 a year.<br>£ s. d. | £12 a year.<br>£ s. d. | £13 a year.<br>£ s. d. | £14 a year.<br>£ s. d. | £15 a year.<br>£ s. d. |
|---|---|---|---|---|---|---|---|---|---|---|---|
| 1 | 1 0 2 | 2 0 5 | 3 0 7 | 4 0 10 | 5 1 0 | 6 1 2 | 7 1 5 | 8 1 7 | 9 1 10 | 10 2 0 | 11 2 2 |
| 2 | 2 1 1 | 4 2 5 | 6 3 8 | 8 4 11 | 10 6 1 | 12 7 4 | 14 8 7 | 16 9 9 | 18 10 11 | 20 12 2 | 22 13 5 |
| 3 | 3 2 1 | 6 6 2 | 9 9 3 | 12 12 4 | 15 15 5 | 18 18 6 | 22 1 7 | 25 4 7 | 28 7 9 | 31 10 10 | 34 13 10 |
| 4 | 4 5 10 | 8 11 8 | 12 17 6 | 17 3 3 | 21 9 1 | 25 14 11 | 30 0 9 | 34 6 7 | 38 12 6 | 42 18 4 | 47 4 2 |
| 5 | 5 9 6 | 10 19 0 | 16 8 6 | 21 18 0 | 27 7 6 | 32 17 0 | 38 6 6 | 43 16 0 | 49 5 6 | 54 15 0 | 60 4 6 |
| 6 | 6 14 1 | 13 8 3 | 20 2 4 | 26 16 6 | 33 10 7 | 40 4 9 | 46 18 10 | 53 13 0 | 60 7 1 | 67 1 2 | 73 15 4 |
| 7 | 7 19 9 | 15 19 6 | 23 19 2 | 31 18 11 | 39 18 8 | 47 18 5 | 56 18 2 | 63 17 11 | 71 17 8 | 79 17 5 | 87 17 2 |
| 8 | 9 6 5 | 18 12 10 | 27 19 2 | 37 5 7 | 46 12 0 | 55 18 5 | 65 4 10 | 74 11 2 | 83 17 6 | 93 3 11 | £100 in 7 years |
| 9 | 10 14 1 | 21 8 0 | 32 2 2 | 42 16 6 | 53 10 7 | 64 4 9 | 74 18 10 | 85 13 0 | 96 7 1 | £100 in 8 years | 43 weeks |
| 10 | 12 3 0 | 24 6 0 | 36 8 11 | 48 11 11 | 60 14 11 | 72 17 10 | 85 0 10 | 97 3 9 | £100 in 9 years | 26 weeks | |
| 11 | 13 13 0 | 27 5 5 | 40 19 8 | 54 12 0 | 68 5 1 | 81 18 0 | 95 10 11 | £100 in 10 years | 16 weeks | | |
| 12 | 16 4 3 | 30 6 5 | 45 12 1 | 60 16 10 | 76 1 0 | 91 5 4 | £100 in 11 years | 12 weeks | | | |
| 13 | 16 16 6 | 33 13 6 | 50 10 1 | 67 6 10 | 74 3 6 | £100 in 12 years | 21 weeks | | | | |
| 14 | 18 10 6 | 37 1 0 | 55 11 7 | 74 2 1 | 92 12 7 | 12 years | | | | | |
| 15 | 20 5 8 | 40 11 4 | 60 17 0 | 81 2 9 | £100 in 14 years | 47 weeks | | | | | |
| 16 | 22 2 3 | 44 4 7 | 66 6 10 | 88 9 1 | 44 weeks | | | | | | |
| 17 | 24 0 4 | 48 0 8 | 72 1 0 | 96 1 4 | | | | | | | |
| 18 | 25 19 11 | 51 19 10 | 77 19 10 | £100 in 17 years | | | | | | | |
| 19 | 28 1 2 | 56 2 3 | 84 3 5 | 26 weeks | | | | | | | |
| 20 | 30 4 0 | 60 8 0 | 90 12 1 | | | | | | | | |
| 21 | 32 8 8 | 64 17 3 | 97 5 10 | | | | | | | | |
| 22 | 34 15 0 | 69 10 0 | £100 in 21 years | | | | | | | | |
| 23 | 37 3 4 | 74 6 7 | 20 weeks | | | | | | | | |
| 24 | 39 13 6 | 79 7 1 | | | | | | | | | |
| 25 | 42 5 10 | 84 11 7 | | | | | | | | | |
| 26 | 45 0 2 | 90 0 4 | | | | | | | | | |
| 27 | 47 16 7 | 95 13 6 | | | | | | | | | |
| 28 | 50 15 7 | £100 in 27 years | | | | | | | | | |
| 29 | 53 16 10 | 39 weeks | | | | | | | | | |
| 30 | 57 0 6 | | | | | | | | | | |
| 31 | 60 6 10 | | | | | | | | | | |
| 32 | 63 15 9 | | | | | | | | | | |
| 33 | 67 7 7 | | | | | | | | | | |
| 34 | 71 2 1 | | | | | | | | | | |
| 35 | 74 19 9 | | | | | | | | | | |
| 36 | 79 0 7 | | | | | | | | | | |
| 37 | 83 4 8 | | | | | | | | | | |
| 38 | 87 12 1 | | | | | | | | | | |
| 39 | 92 3 1 | | | | | | | | | | |
| 40 | 96 17 9 | | | | | | | | | | |
|  | £100 in 40 yrs. 33 wks. | | | | | | | | | | |

EXAMPLE:—Suppose £100 to have been invested in Stock producing £10 a year in Dividends, then, at the end of five years £32 17s. can be written off as capital returned, and after 12 years 47 weeks all the £100 will have been received back out of the surplus of the £10 a year over the £4 security rate of interest. £100 would produce.

# THE ARGENTINE AND DANUBIAN LOANS. 161

**26.—*Illustrations of Capital returned by surplus dividends.*—**
(i.)—Suppose a private individual or a Trust to have purchased, on its first issue, some of the Argentine 6 per cent. loan of 1868, issued at 72½; the dividend of £6 a year is equal to interest at the rate of over 8¼ per cent. per annum. In addition, the investors have participated in accumulative drawings at the rate of 2½ per cent. per annum, giving a bonus of 27½ per cent. The present price of 90 shows a rise of 17½ per cent. on the price of issue.

If the sum invested was £725 in the purchase of ten bonds of £100 in 1868, the surplus of the dividends £60 a year over £29, which is 4 per cent. on the £725, has been £31 a year, *half-yearly*.

These surplus dividends, treated as capital received back, have in seven years to 1875 returned £247 12s. 3d. The balance of the £725 outstanding is reduced to £477 7s. 9d.

If the Argentine Government should be able to continue to pay the onerous dividends of this loan for 9 years 8 months longer (making altogether 16 years 8 months since the time of issue), the purchaser will have received all his capital back by the surplus dividends, and will stand in the free enjoyment of £60 dividends in the future, without any capital invested, and until the ten bonds are repaid by £1,000.

(ii.)—Taking the Danubian 8 per cent. loan issued at 71 in 1867, the recent price was 104, or a rise of 33. The original subscribers to this loan have received interest at the rate of over 11¼ per cent. per annum, and have participated in accumulative drawings at the rate of 1⅝ per cent. per annum, giving a bonus of 29 per cent.

In this case, if £710 had been invested in ten bonds, the surplus would be £51 12s. arising from the £80 a year dividends over £28 8s. a year, which is the 4 per cent. on the £710.

In 11 years 1 month in 1878 this surplus would enable the whole £710 to be written off, and the Trust would stand free of any capital outstanding, although the £80 a year would be still receivable until the ten bonds are drawn, and payment received of £1,000.

27.—Both these examples, if advantageous to the purchaser, show the exceedingly improvident terms on which the Argentine Confederation and the Danubian Government raised the loans referred to. Hence the importance cannot be too much insisted upon, of regarding all surplus received over 4 per cent., and all bonuses, as capital returned, or as premiums to be set against the risk attending high dividend securities.

"If an investor receives 8 per cent. for his money and spends the whole, he is, in effect, living upon capital, or, at any rate, running the risk of doing so, as a portion of the amount is really received as insurance against contingent loss."

The * journal from which those words are quoted points out further that securities yielding high interest rise and fall to a larger extent than those yielding small interest, and, the difference in interest afforded is a measure of the difference in liability to variation according to the opinion of the market, a result which would naturally be expected. In other words *the liability of stocks to fluctuation in value is proportionate to the excess of interest above the rate obtainable on undoubted security* :

"If there be two stocks, each paying 5 per cent. on the nominal capital, one of which is quoted at par and the other at 50, and if it be assumed that the former will fluctuate in value to the extent of 5 per cent. in the course of a year, then it follows that, in the estimation of the market, the latter will fluctuate in value 30 per cent. during the same time, because the rates of interest yielded by the two stocks are 5 per cent. and 10 per cent. respectively, and the excess of interest above 4 per cent. is 1 per cent. and 6 per cent. respectively; so that the fluctuation in the latter case may be expected to be six times that in the former."

---

[* *Financier*, 1874.]

## CHAPTER III.

TABLES—*continued.*

### *Section 1.—Memoria Technica Tables.*

ART. 28.—For calculations connected with "Trust" operations the following curious property may be useful, which relates to the *doubling* of *money* at compound interest. It is convenient as being one easily remembered.

When a sum of money increases to double its value by the accumulation of compound interest, the analytical investigations assume a peculiar form, from which the following Rule arises :—

For all rates of interest not exceeding 10 per cent. :—*The Number of years, in which a Single sum will become double in amount by accumulation of compound interest, may be found in round numbers by dividing* 70 *by the rate of interest per cent.*, and taking that whole number which is ***nearest*** to the quotient obtained.

The accuracy of this Rule may be judged of by the following table, wherein the results agree very closely with the figures in the half-yearly interest column :—

| £100 or any other sum will double itself in | | |
|---|---|---|
| Rate of interest per cent. per annum. | Approximate time of doubling shown by the number 70 divided by the interest. | Accurate time of doubling when interest is compounded half-yearly. |
| 2 per cent. | 35 years | $34\frac{5}{6}$ years |
| $2\frac{1}{2}$ ,, | 28 ,, | $27\frac{8}{9}$ ,, |
| 3 ,, | $23\frac{1}{3}$ ,, | $23\frac{5}{18}$ ,, |
| $3\frac{1}{2}$ ,, | 20 ,, | 20 ,, |
| 4 ,, | $17\frac{1}{2}$ ,, | $17\frac{1}{2}$ ,, |
| $4\frac{1}{2}$ ,, | $15\frac{1}{2}$ ,, | $15\frac{7}{12}$ ,, |
| 5 ,, | 14 ,, | $14\frac{1}{30}$ ,, |
| 6 ,, | $11\frac{2}{3}$ ,, | $11\frac{3}{4}$ ,, |
| 7 ,, | 10 ,, | $10\frac{3}{40}$ ,, |
| 8 ,, | $8\frac{3}{4}$ ,, | $8\frac{5}{6}$ ,, |
| 9 ,, | $7\frac{7}{9}$ ,, | $7\frac{8}{9}$ ,, |
| 10 ,, | 7 ,, | $7\frac{1}{10}$ ,, |

164   DOUBLING PERIODS AND SAVINGS FUNDS.

The * Rule may be applied to the converse question ;—given the number of years, to find the rate of interest required to be made in order that money may become doubled. Thus, let the number of years be 17½, then the rate of interest required would be 70 divided by 17½ or 4 per cent.

29.—The foregoing table is also useful as a means of remembering the approximate periods in which annuities accumulate to certain amounts.

Thus, since in *one* doubling period, £100 invested accumulates—(by the interest annuity on it being compounded) to £200
Then :—in 2 periods it accumulates to  -   -   400
       in 3      „          „         -   -   800
       in 4      „          „         -   -   1,600, and so on.

In other words, the annuity (derived in the form of *interest* on the original £100) accumulates, by being itself invested, to £100, £300, £700, &c., in the various periods mentioned. Thus, taking for example interest at 5 per cent. a year and deducting the original £100 investment, an annuity of £5 per annum (by being compounded at the same rate, 5 per cent) would accumulate in—

|  |  | £ |
|---|---|---|
| 1 period (14₁₀ years accurate time) to | | 100 |
| 2    „    or twice that time    „ | | 300 |
| 3    „    or thrice       „     „ | | 700 |
| 4    „    or four times   „     „ | | 1,500 |

Similarly for other rates in the respective periods corresponding to those rates.

30.—Hence, if the *rate of interest* per cent. be divided by the *number* of hundred pounds that would correspond to the accumu-

---

[* For the mathematical demonstration of this property of the number 70, which we first noticed and published in 1847, see the Appendix to our Treatise on Building Societies. The Rule has since been copied by some writers without acknowledgment, among others by M. Fédor Thoman, etc.]

lations in the above, we have the *savings* per annum invested half-yearly, which will amount to £100 at the end of the respective terms of years.

Thus for example * 14s. 3d. a year set aside half-yearly, at 5 per cent. compound interest, will amount to £100 in three periods of doubling. This corresponds to the above, where it is shown that £5 a year would amount to £700 in that time (14s. 3d. being equal to £5 divided by 7) as shown by the following Table :—

| Number of Doubling Periods. | Divisor. | At £3 per cent. | At £4 per cent. | At £5 per cent. | At £6 per cent. | At £7 per cent. |
|---|---|---|---|---|---|---|
| | | \multicolumn{5}{c}{Interest per Annum.} | | | | |
| | | \multicolumn{5}{c}{£100 will be produced by a yearly saving of} | | | | |
| In 1 | — | £3 a year | £4 a year | £5 a year | £6 a year | £7 a year |
| In 2 | 3 | £ s. d.<br>1 0 0 | £ s. d.<br>1 6 8 | £ s. d.<br>1 13 4 | £ s. d.<br>2 0 0 | £ s. d.<br>2 6 8 |
| In 3 | 7 | 0 8 7 | 0 11 5 | 0 14* 3 | 0 17 2 | 1 0 0 |
| In 4 | 15 | 0 4 0 | 0 5 4 | 0 6 8 | 0 8 0 | 0 9 4 |
| In 5 | 31 | 0 1 11 | 0 2 7 | 0 3 3 | 0 3 10 | 0 4 6 |

*Section 2.—Suggestions with respect to Loans.*

ART. 31.—The preceding properties suggest some alternatives, which might be adopted for raising money at par on temporary or perpetual stocks, so as to produce either fixed or increasing incomes.

Thus, for £100 received, the cost to the borrower, by either of the following nine alternatives, would be the same at 5 per cent. interest:—

(1.) In Perpetual Stock:—£100 would be worth £5 a year for ever.

(2.) In Temporary Stock:—for £100 £10 a year could be paid for 14 years.

(3.) In Perpetual Deferred Stock:—£10 a year for ever, but not beginning till the end of 14 years.

(4.) In Mixed Stock:—the payments could be £5 a year for the first 14 years and then increased to £10 a year for 14 years more.

(5.) ,, or £2 10s. a year for 14 years, then £7 10s. a year for ever.

(6.) ,, or £4 a year for 14 years, then £6 a year for ever.

(7.) ,, or £6 a year for 14 years, then only £4 a year for ever.

(8.) ,, or £3 a year for 14 years, then £7 a year for ever.

(9.) ,, or £7 a year for 14 years, and £3 a year for ever.

And so on, provided always that the sum of the two figures equals £10. Fourteen years is quoted as the time involved, that being the number of years nearly in which money will double at 5 per cent.

Other rates of interest may be used as the basis for calculating the equivalents. All that is necessary is that the sum of the figures should be twice the rate of interest.

Thus, on a basis of 6 per cent., the time of doubling being $11\frac{3}{4}$ years (half-yearly interest), a Government or other borrower could pay (modifying the numbers above), 8 per cent. for $11\frac{3}{4}$ years, and 4 per cent. afterwards for ever, or 7 per cent. for $11\frac{3}{4}$ years and 5 per cent. for ever. Either would cost the same as 6 per cent. all through for ever.

In the above alternatives the loans are supposed to be obtained at par. The £100 could be redeemed by drawings each year throughout a doubling term of years with interest until redemption, by setting aside each year twice the interest. Thus, a Government could redeem 7 per cent. bonds in a little over 10 years by £14 a year for interest and sinking fund. In like manner, £8 would suffice at 4 per cent. interest in $17\frac{1}{2}$ years.

## Section 3.—*Of the present values of Decreasing and Increasing Annuities.*

Art. 32.—The above annuities arise in Trust calculations occasionally. The following new rules, which will probably be best understood by examples, afford the means of easy calculations where they decrease or increase uniformly :—

(i). *Decreasing.*—Let the annuity be one for 10 years payable yearly, commencing at £10 the first year, and decreasing £1 a year, until it is £1 in the last year; let the rate of interest be 6 per cent. yearly.

Then, the present value of such a Decreasing annuity is equal to the difference (between £10 and the value of an ordinary £1 a year annuity for 10 years) divided by .06.

Thus, the value of £1 a year for 10 years at 6 per cent. is 7.36. Subtracted from £10, the difference is 2.64. This 2.64 divided by .06 gives £44, which is the value of the decreasing annuity. (When four places of decimals are used the result is £43.9983).

(ii). *Increasing.*—Suppose the Increasing annuity be for 10 years, beginning at £1 the first year, and rising £1 a year till it is £10 in the 10th year.

Then, the value of the Increasing annuity is found by subtracting the value of the above Decreasing annuity from 11 times the value of an ordinary £1 a year for 10 years.

| | |
|---|---|
| Thus, 11 times £7.36 is equal to .. | £80.96 |
| The value of a Decreasing Annuity is | £44.00 |
| Difference is     ..    .. | £36.96 |

which is the value of the Increasing annuity.

For other annuities and rates of interest the process of calculation would be similar.

If the Decreasing or Increasing annuity be half-yearly, with half-yearly decrements or increments of 10s., calculate the value of a yearly £1 decreasing or increasing annuity for double the term at half the rate of interest, and half the result found will be the value required.

# TABLES.

## TABLE I.

Shewing the *Decimal* corresponding to every Penny in the *Pound*.

| s. | d. | Decimal. | s. | d. | Decimal. | s. | d. | Decimal. | s. | d. | Decimal. | s. | d. | Decimal. |
|---|---|---|---|---|---|---|---|---|---|---|---|---|---|---|
| 0 | 1 | .004 | 4 | 1 | .204 | 8 | 1 | .404 | 12 | 1 | .604 | 16 | 1 | .804 |
| 0 | 2 | .008 | 4 | 2 | .208 | 8 | 2 | .408 | 12 | 2 | .608 | 16 | 2 | .808 |
| 0 | 3 | .012 | 4 | 3 | .212 | 8 | 3 | .412 | 12 | 3 | .612 | 16 | 3 | .812 |
| 0 | 4 | .017 | 4 | 4 | .217 | 8 | 4 | .417 | 12 | 4 | .617 | 16 | 4 | .817 |
| 0 | 5 | .021 | 4 | 5 | .221 | 8 | 5 | .421 | 12 | 5 | .621 | 16 | 5 | .821 |
| 0 | 6 | .025 | 4 | 6 | *.225 | 8 | 6 | .425 | 12 | 6 | .625 | 16 | 6 | .825 |
| 0 | 7 | .029 | 4 | 7 | .229 | 8 | 7 | .429 | 12 | 7 | .629 | 16 | 7 | .829 |
| 0 | 8 | .033 | 4 | 8 | .233 | 8 | 8 | .433 | 12 | 8 | .633 | 16 | 8 | .833 |
| 0 | 9 | .037 | 4 | 9 | .237 | 8 | 9 | .437 | 12 | 9 | .637 | 16 | 9 | .837 |
| 0 | 10 | .042 | 4 | 10 | .242 | 8 | 10 | .442 | 12 | 10 | .642 | 16 | 10 | .842 |
| 0 | 11 | .046 | 4 | 11 | .246 | 8 | 11 | .446 | 12 | 11 | .646 | 16 | 11 | .846 |
| 1 | 0 | .050 | 5 | 0 | .250 | 9 | 0 | .450 | 13 | 0 | .650 | 17 | 0 | .850 |
| 1 | 1 | .054 | 5 | 1 | .254 | 9 | 1 | .454 | 13 | 1 | *.654 | 17 | 1 | *.854 |
| 1 | 2 | .058 | 5 | 2 | .258 | 9 | 2 | .458 | 13 | 2 | .658 | 17 | 2 | .858 |
| 1 | 3 | .062 | 5 | 3 | .262 | 9 | 3 | .462 | 13 | 3 | .662 | 17 | 3 | .862 |
| 1 | 4 | .067 | 5 | 4 | .267 | 9 | 4 | .467 | 13 | 4 | .667 | 17 | 4 | .867 |
| 1 | 5 | .071 | 5 | 5 | .271 | 9 | 5 | .471 | 13 | 5 | .671 | 17 | 5 | .871 |
| 1 | 6 | *.075 | 5 | 6 | .275 | 9 | 6 | .475 | 13 | 6 | .675 | 17 | 6 | .875 |
| 1 | 7 | .079 | 5 | 7 | .279 | 9 | 7 | .479 | 13 | 7 | .679 | 17 | 7 | .879 |
| 1 | 8 | .083 | 5 | 8 | .283 | 9 | 8 | .483 | 13 | 8 | .683 | 17 | 8 | .883 |
| 1 | 9 | .087 | 5 | 9 | .287 | 9 | 9 | .487 | 13 | 9 | .687 | 17 | 9 | .887 |
| 1 | 10 | .092 | 5 | 10 | .292 | 9 | 10 | .492 | 13 | 10 | .692 | 17 | 10 | .892 |
| 1 | 11 | .096 | 5 | 11 | .296 | 9 | 11 | .496 | 13 | 11 | .696 | 17 | 11 | .896 |
| 2 | 0 | .100 | 6 | 0 | .300 | 10 | 0 | .500 | 14 | 0 | .700 | 18 | 0 | .900 |
| 2 | 1 | .104 | 6 | 1 | .304 | 10 | 1 | .504 | 14 | 1 | .704 | 18 | 1 | .904 |
| 2 | 2 | .108 | 6 | 2 | .308 | 10 | 2 | .508 | 14 | 2 | .708 | 18 | 2 | .908 |
| 2 | 3 | .112 | 6 | 3 | .312 | 10 | 3 | .512 | 14 | 3 | .712 | 18 | 3 | .912 |
| 2 | 4 | .117 | 6 | 4 | .317 | 10 | 4 | .517 | 14 | 4 | .717 | 18 | 4 | .917 |
| 2 | 5 | .121 | 6 | 5 | .321 | 10 | 5 | .521 | 14 | 5 | .721 | 18 | 5 | .921 |
| 2 | 6 | .125 | 6 | 6 | .325 | 10 | 6 | *.525 | 14 | 6 | .725 | 18 | 6 | .925 |
| 2 | 7 | .129 | 6 | 7 | .329 | 10 | 7 | .529 | 14 | 7 | .729 | 18 | 7 | .929 |
| 2 | 8 | .133 | 6 | 8 | .333 | 10 | 8 | .533 | 14 | 8 | .733 | 18 | 8 | .933 |
| 2 | 9 | .137 | 6 | 9 | .337 | 10 | 9 | .537 | 14 | 9 | .737 | 18 | 9 | .937 |
| 2 | 10 | .142 | 6 | 10 | .342 | 10 | 10 | .542 | 14 | 10 | .742 | 18 | 10 | .942 |
| 2 | 11 | .146 | 6 | 11 | .346 | 10 | 11 | .546 | 14 | 11 | .746 | 18 | 11 | .946 |
| 3 | 0 | .150 | 7 | 0 | .350 | 11 | 0 | .550 | 15 | 0 | .750 | 19 | 0 | .950 |
| 3 | 1 | .154 | 7 | 1 | .354 | 11 | 1 | .554 | 15 | 1 | *.754 | 19 | 1 | *.954 |
| 3 | 2 | .158 | 7 | 2 | .358 | 11 | 2 | .558 | 15 | 2 | .758 | 19 | 2 | .958 |
| 3 | 3 | .162 | 7 | 3 | .362 | 11 | 3 | .562 | 15 | 3 | .762 | 19 | 3 | .962 |
| 3 | 4 | .167 | 7 | 4 | .367 | 11 | 4 | .567 | 15 | 4 | .767 | 19 | 4 | .967 |
| 3 | 5 | .171 | 7 | 5 | .371 | 11 | 5 | .571 | 15 | 5 | .771 | 19 | 5 | .971 |
| 3 | 6 | .175 | 7 | 6 | *.375 | 11 | 6 | .575 | 15 | 6 | .775 | 19 | 6 | .975 |
| 3 | 7 | .179 | 7 | 7 | .379 | 11 | 7 | .579 | 15 | 7 | .779 | 19 | 7 | .979 |
| 3 | 8 | .183 | 7 | 8 | .383 | 11 | 8 | .583 | 15 | 8 | .783 | 19 | 8 | .983 |
| 3 | 9 | .187 | 7 | 9 | .387 | 11 | 9 | .587 | 15 | 9 | .787 | 19 | 9 | .987 |
| 3 | 10 | .192 | 7 | 10 | .392 | 11 | 10 | .592 | 15 | 10 | .792 | 19 | 10 | .992 |
| 3 | 11 | .196 | 7 | 11 | .396 | 11 | 11 | .596 | 15 | 11 | .796 | 19 | 11 | .996 |
| 4 | 0 | .200 | 8 | 0 | .400 | 12 | 0 | .600 | 16 | 0 | .800 | 20 | 0 | 1.000 |

*Example.*—The value of the Decimal .075, is 1s. 6d.—.225, is 4s. 6d.—.375, is 7s. 6d.—.525, is 10s. 6d.—.654, is 13s 1d.—.754, is 15s. 1d.—.854, is 17s. 1d.—.954, is 19s. 1d.

# TABLES.

## TABLE II.

(A.) *Shewing the sum per Pound to which a Rate of Interest per cent. is equivalent.*

|  |  |  |  | s. | d. |  |
|---|---|---|---|---|---|---|
| 2 per cent interest is equal to | nearly | 0 | 5 | in the pound. |
| 2½ | ,, | ,, | exactly | 0 | 6 | ,, |
| 3 | ,, | ,, | nearly | 0 | 7¼ | ,, |
| 3½ | ,, | ,, | ,, | 0 | 8½ | ,, |
| 4 | ,, | ,, | ,, | 0 | 9¾ | ,, |
| 4½ | ,, | ,, | ,, | 0 | 11 | ,, |
| 5 | ,, | ,, | exactly | 1 | 0 | ,, |
| 5½ | ,, | ,, | nearly | 1 | 1¼ | ,, |
| 6 | ,, | ,, | ,, | 1 | 2½ | ,, |
| 7 | ,, | ,, | ,, | 1 | 5 | ,, |
| 8 | ,, | ,, | ,, | 1 | 7¼ | ,, |
| 9 | ,, | ,, | ,, | 1 | 9¾ | ,, |
| 10 | ,, | ,, | exactly | 2 | 0 | ,, |

(B.) *To calculate the Interest for One Year on any sum.*

If the rate be 2 per cent. } multiply the sum by $.02$ or $\frac{1}{50}$ } and the product is the interest required

| If 2½ | ,, | by $.025$ or $\frac{1}{40}$ | ,, | ,, |
| If 3 | ,, | by $.03$ or $\frac{3}{100}$ | ,, | ,, |
| If 3½ | ,, | by $.035$ or $\frac{7}{200}$ | ,, | ,, |
| If 4 | ,, | by $.04$ or $\frac{1}{25}$ | ,, | ,, |
| If 4½ | ,, | by $.045$ or $\frac{9}{200}$ | ,, | ,, |
| If 5 | ,, | by $.05$ or $\frac{1}{20}$ | ,, | ,, |
| If 6 | ,, | by $.06$ or $\frac{3}{50}$ | ,, | ,, |
| If 7 | ,, | by $.07$ or $\frac{7}{100}$ | ,, | ,, |
| If 8 | ,, | by $.08$ or $\frac{2}{25}$ | ,, | ,, |
| If 9 | ,, | by $.09$ or $\frac{9}{100}$ | ,, | ,, |
| If 10 | ,, | by $.1$ or $\frac{1}{10}$ | ,, | ,, |

REMARK.—To perform the above, it will be remembered that to multiply a quantity by a fraction it must be first multiplied by the numerator, and then the result divided by the denominator of the fraction. The division by 100 can be effected by dividing twice by 10. Similarly the other divisors can be separated, and the quotient obtained by successive divisions.

---

## Note to Table IV., page 4.

*Table IV. can, by means of the following Formulæ, be made to give the results generally required from Tables of Discount or Annuities.*

1. Table IX. The *present value* of £100 due at the end of any number of years } is equal to { £100 divided by the *Amount*, in Table IV., of £1 at the end of the same time.

2. Table X. The *Amount* of an *Annuity* of £100 in any number of years } is equal to { The quotient of: (the *Amount* in Table IV., of a *single* £100 in the same time, less £100,) (divided by the rate of interest per pound) involved in the calculation.

3. Table XI. The *present value* of an Annuity of £100 for any number of years } is equal to { The quotient of £100 *diminished* by the *present value* of a single £100, (due at the end of the same time) divided by the rate of interest per pound.*

4. Tables X and XI may be calculated from each other, if either be known, by the property, that

$$\frac{1}{\text{Present Value of an Annuity}} \text{ less } \frac{1}{\text{Amount of an Annuity}} \text{ is equal } \begin{cases} \text{a year's} \\ \text{to} \\ \text{interest.} \end{cases}$$

* (The present value required for the division being found from Table IV., by the formula of (1).)

## TABLE III.

Shewing the RATE OF INTEREST obtainable from £3 per cent. Stock for £100 cash invested according to the price of the day.

| Price of Stock. (1.) | Interest which £100 cash obtains. (2.) | | | Amount of Stock £100 will purchase, or amount of Stock required to be sold to produce £100. (3.) | | | *Most recent years in which the average price of Consols was that of (1.) |
|---|---|---|---|---|---|---|---|
| | £ | s. | d. | £. | s. | d. | |
| 60 | 5 | 0 | 0 | 166 | 13 | 4 | 1815 |
| 61 | 4 | 18 | 9 | 163 | 18 | 9 | 1813 |
| 62 | 4 | 16 | 9 | 161 | 5 | 10 | 1816 |
| 63 | 4 | 15 | 3 | 158 | 14 | 8 | |
| 64 | 4 | 13 | 9 | 156 | 5 | 0 | 1811 |
| 65 | 4 | 12 | 3 | 153 | 16 | 11 | |
| 66 | 4 | 10 | 11 | 151 | 10 | 4 | 1808 |
| 67 | 4 | 9 | 7 | 149 | 5 | 1 | 1814 |
| 68 | 4 | 8 | 3 | 147 | 1 | 2 | 1820 |
| 69 | 4 | 7 | 0 | 144 | 18 | 7 | |
| 70 | 4 | 5 | 9 | 142 | 17 | 2 | |
| 71 | 4 | 4 | 6 | 140 | 16 | 11 | |
| 72 | 4 | 3 | 4 | 138 | 17 | 8 | 1819 |
| 73 | 4 | 2 | 2 | 136 | 19 | 9 | 1817 |
| 74 | 4 | 1 | 1 | 135 | 2 | 9 | 1821 |
| 75 | 4 | 0 | 0 | 133 | 6 | 8 | 1788 |
| 76 | 3 | 18 | 11 | 131 | 11 | 7 | 1793 |
| 77 | 3 | 17 | 11 | 129 | 17 | 5 | |
| 78 | 3 | 16 | 11 | 128 | 4 | 1 | 1777 |
| 79 | 3 | 15 | 11 | 126 | 11 | 8 | 1826 |
| 80 | 3 | 15 | 0 | 125 | 0 | 0 | 1831 |
| 81 | 3 | 14 | 1 | 123 | 9 | 2 | |
| 82 | 3 | 13 | 2 | 121 | 19 | 0 | 1760 |
| 83 | 3 | 12 | 4 | 120 | 9 | 8 | 1827 |
| 84 | 3 | 11 | 5 | 119 | 0 | 11 | 1832 |
| 85 | 3 | 10 | 7 | 117 | 12 | 11 | 1848 |
| 86 | 3 | 9 | 9 | 116 | 5 | 7 | 1847 |
| 87 | 3 | 9 | 0 | 114 | 18 | 10 | 1773 |
| 88 | 3 | 8 | 2 | 113 | 12 | 9 | 1833 |
| 89 | 3 | 7 | 5 | 113 | 7 | 2 | 1841 |
| 90 | 3 | 6 | 8 | 111 | 2 | 3 | 1855 |
| 91 | 3 | 5 | 11 | 109 | 17 | 10 | 1856 |
| 92 | 3 | 5 | 3 | 108 | 13 | 11 | 1842 |
| 93 | 3 | 4 | 6 | 107 | 10 | 7 | 1849 |
| 94 | 3 | 3 | 10 | 106 | 7 | 8 | 1744 |
| 95 | 3 | 3 | 2 | 105 | 5 | 3 | 1843 |
| 96 | 3 | 2 | 6 | 104 | 3 | 4 | 1853 |
| 97 | 3 | 1 | 10 | 103 | 1 | 10 | 1850 |
| 98 | 3 | 1 | 3 | 102 | 0 | 10 | 1851 |
| 99 | 3 | 0 | 7 | 101 | 0 | 3 | 1852 |
| 100 | 3 | 0 | 0 | 100 | 0 | 0 | 1751 |
| 101 | 2 | 19 | 4 | 99 | 0 | 2 | 1743 |

* [The average price of Consols for the whole of the 100 years, 1759 to 1858, is about 78¼. During that period the average price for the whole of a year was never at or above par. The average for several months of the year 1852 was above 100. It is curious, however, that during several years previous to 1759, the average price for the whole of the year was at or above par: thus, in 1733, '42, '50, and '51, it was 100; in 1739 and '43, 101; in '36, 102; '54, 103; '38, '52, and '53, 104; and in 1737 it was as high as 106. On the other hand, between 1781 and 1815, there were ten years in which the average fell below 60. Between 1822 and 1831, a medium price of about 80 was kept to.]

*From the* TREATISE ON SAVINGS BANKS.

## TABLE IV.

*Shewing the Amount to which £100 Principal will increase at various Rates of Compound yearly Interest. (See Note, page 2.)*

| At the end of Years. | 3 per cent. | 4 per cent. | 5 per cent. | 6 per cent. | 7 per cent. | 8 per cent. |
|---|---|---|---|---|---|---|
| 1  | 103.00 | 104.00 | 105.00 | 106.00 | 107 00 | 108.00 |
| 2  | 106.09 | 108.16 | 110.25 | 112.36 | 114.49 | 116.64 |
| 3  | 109.27 | 112.48 | 115.76 | 119.10 | 122.50 | 125.97 |
| 4  | 112.55 | 116.98 | 121.55 | 126.24 | 131.07 | 136.04 |
| 5  | 115.92 | 121.66 | 127.62 | 133.82 | 140.25 | 146.93 |
| 6  | 119.40 | 126.53 | 134.00 | 141.85 | 150.07 | 158.68 |
| 7  | 122.98 | 131.59 | 140.71 | 150.36 | 160.57 | 171.38 |
| 8  | 126.67 | 136.85 | 147.74 | 159.38 | 171.81 | 185.09 |
| 9  | 130.47 | 142.33 | 155.13 | 168.94 | 183.84 | 199.90 |
| 10 | 134.39 | 148.02 | 162.88 | 179.08 | 196.71 | 215.89 |
| 11 | 138.42 | 153.94 | 171.03 | 189.82 | 210.48 | 233.16 |
| 12 | 142.57 | 160.10 | 179.58 | 201.21 | 225.21 | 251.81 |
| 13 | 146.85 | 166.50 | 188.56 | 213.29 | 240.98 | 271.96 |
| 14 | 151.25 | 173.16 | 197.99 | 226.09 | 257.85 | 293.71 |
| 15 | 155.79 | 180.09 | 207.89 | 239.65 | 275.90 | 317.21 |
| 16 | 160.47 | 187.29 | 218.28 | 254.03 | 295.21 | 342.59 |
| 17 | 165.28 | 194.79 | 229.20 | 269.27 | 315.88 | 370.00 |
| 18 | 170.24 | 202.58 | 240.66 | 285.43 | 337.99 | 399,60 |
| 19 | 175.35 | 210.68 | 252.69 | 302.55 | 361.65 | 431,57 |
| 20 | 180.61 | 219.11 | 265.32 | 320.71 | 386.96 | 466 09 |
| 21 | 186.02 | 227.87 | 278.59 | 339.95 | 414.05 | 503,38 |
| 22 | 191.61 | 236.99 | 292.52 | 360.35 | 443.04 | 543,65 |
| 23 | 197.35 | 246.47 | 307.15 | 381.97 | 474.95 | 587,14 |
| 24 | 203.27 | 256.33 | 322.50 | 404.89 | 507.23 | 634.11 |
| 25 | 209.37 | 266.58 | 338.63 | 429.18 | 542.74 | 684.84 |
| 26 | 215.65 | 277.24 | 355.56 | 454.93 | 580.73 | 739.63 |
| 27 | 222.12 | 288 33 | 373.34 | 482.23 | 621.38 | 798.80 |
| 28 | 228.79 | 299.87 | 392.01 | 511.16 | 664.88 | 862.71 |
| 29 | 235.65 | 311.86 | 411.61 | 541.83 | 711.42 | 931.72 |
| 30 | * 242.72 | 324.34 | * 432.19 | 574.34 | 761.22 | 1006.26 |
| 31 | 250.00 | 337.31 | 453.80 | 608.81 | 814.51 | 1086.76 |
| 32 | 257.50 | 350.80 | 476.49 | 645.33 | 871.52 | 1173.70 |
| 33 | 265.23 | 364.83 | 500.31 | 684.05 | 932.53 | 1267.60 |
| 34 | 273.19 | 379.43 | 525.33 | 725.10 | 997.81 | 1369.01 |
| 35 | 281.38 | 394.60 | 551.60 | 768.60 | 1067.65 | 1478.53 |
| 36 | 289.82 | 410.39 | 579.18 | 814.72 | 1142.39 | 1596.81 |
| 37 | 298.52 | 426.80 | 608.14 | 863.60 | 1222.36 | 1724.56 |
| 38 | 307.47 | 443.88 | 638.54 | 915.42 | 1307.92 | 1862.52 |
| 39 | 316.70 | 461.63 | 670.47 | 970.35 | 1399.48 | 2011.52 |
| 40 | 326.20 | 480.10 | 703.99 | 1028.57 | 1497.44 | 2172.45 |
| 41 | 335.99 | 499.30 | 739.19 | 1090.28 | 1602.26 | 2346.24 |
| 42 | 346.06 | 519.27 | 776.15 | 1155.70 | 1714.42 | 2533.94 |
| 43 | 356.45 | 540.04 | 814.96 | 1225.04 | 1834.43 | 2736.66 |
| 44 | 367.14 | 561.65 | 855.71 | 1298.54 | 1962.84 | 2955.59 |
| 45 | 378.15 | 584.11 | 898.50 | 1376.46 | 2100.24 | 3192.04 |
| 46 | 389.50 | 607.48 | 943.42 | 1459.04 | 2247.26 | 3447.40 |
| 47 | 401.18 | 631.78 | 990.59 | 1546.59 | 2404.57 | 3723.20 |
| 48 | 413.22 | 657.05 | 1040.12 | 1639.38 | 2572.89 | 4021.05 |
| 49 | 425.62 | 683.33 | 1092.13 | 1737.75 | 2752.99 | 4342.74 |
| 50 | 438.39 | 710.66 | 1146.74 | 1842.01 | 2945.70 | 4690.16 |

\* EXAMPLE.—£100 will amount at the end of 30 years to £242. 14s. 5d., if interest be made at the rate of 3 per cent. per annum, or to £432. 3s. 10d. at 5 per cent.

*Notes:*—1.—To find the *present value* of a sum of money payable at the end of any number of years, divide that sum by the amount in the above Table and multiply by 100.

2.—To find the amount *of £100 at the end of any number of years not given in the above Table, take the product of the figures opposite any two terms in the Table, which, added together, would make up the term required, and divide by 100. Thus, the amount of £100 at the end of 53 years, (50 years and 3 years), is, at 5 per cent*, (£1146.74 × 115.76) or £1327.47. *Again, the amount of £100 at 3 per cent. at the end of 100 years (50 + 50) is* (£438.39 × 438.39), *or £1921.86. See also Note, page* 2.

## TABLE V.

*Shewing the Rates of Interest payable only* once *a-year, which are equivalent to* nominal *annual rates of Interest actually paid at frequent intervals in each year.*

| Nominal Annual Rate per cent. | Real yearly interest, to which the nominal rates are equivalent when paid :— | | | | | | | | | | | | | | |
|---|---|---|---|---|---|---|---|---|---|---|---|---|---|---|---|
| | Yearly. | | | Half-yearly. | | | Quarterly. | | | Monthly. | | | Momently. | | |
| | £. | s. | d. | £. | s. | d. | £. | s. | d. | £. | s. | d. | £. | s. | d. |
| 3 per cent. | 3 | 0 | 0 | 3 | 0 | 5½ | 3 | 0 | 8¼ | 3 | 0 | 10 | 3 | 0 | 11 |
| 4 per cent. | 4 | 0 | 0 | 4 | 0 | 9¾ | 4 | 1 | 2½ | 4 | 1 | 6 | 4 | 1 | 7¾ |
| 5 per cent. | 5 | 0 | 0 | *5 | 1 | 3 | 5 | 1 | 10¾ | 5 | 2 | 4 | 5 | 2 | 6½ |
| 6 per cent. | 6 | 0 | 0 | 6 | 1 | 9¾ | 6 | 2 | 8¾ | 6 | 3 | 4 | 6 | 3 | 8¼ |
| 7 per cent. | 7 | 0 | 0 | 7 | 2 | 5½ | 7 | 3 | 8¾ | 7 | 4 | 7 | 7 | 5 | 0¼ |
| 8 per cent. | 8 | 0 | 0 | 8 | 3 | 2½ | 8 | 4 | 10½ | 8 | 6 | 0 | 8 | 6 | 7 |

* *Example.*—If a person receives interest half-yearly, after the *nominal* annual rate of 5 per cent., the actual interest derived by him by one year's investment is £5. 1*s.* 3*d.*

## TABLE VI.

*Shewing the nominal Annual Rates of Interest paid* momently, *which are equivalent to rates paid at the* end *of each year.*

| Yearly Rate | Corresponding momentaneous Rate. | | £. | s. | d. | Yearly Rate. | Corresponding momentaneous Rate. | | £. | s. | d. |
|---|---|---|---|---|---|---|---|---|---|---|---|
| 2 per cent. | £1.9802 | or | 1 | 19 | 7½ | 7 per cent. | £6.7658 | or | 6 | 15 | 4 |
| 3 " | 2.9558 | | 2 | 19 | 1½ | 8 " | 7.6791 | | 7 | 13 | 11¼ |
| 4 " | 3.9220 | | 3 | 18 | 5½ | 9 " | 8.6177 | | 8 | 12 | 4¼ |
| 5 " | 4.8790 | | *4 | 17 | 7 | 10 " | 9.5310 | | 9 | 10 | 7½ |
| 6 " | 5.8268 | | 5 | 16 | 6½ | | | | | | |

* *Example.*—The amount to which a sum of money will accumulate in any number of years at *yearly* interest 5 per cent., is the same as the amount to which it would accumulate at *momentaneous* interest, after the nominal annual rate of £4. 17*s.* 7*d.* per cent.

## TABLE VII.

*Shewing the Amount to which £100 will increase at Compound Interest, according as it is paid yearly, half-yearly, quarterly, or momently.* [*See Table IV.*]

| Nominal rate of Interest. | Payable. | The Amount of £100 in | | | |
|---|---|---|---|---|---|
| | | 1 Year. | 5 Years. | 25 Years. | 50 Years. |
| 3 per cent. | yearly | 103.000 | 115.927 | 209.378 | 438.391 |
| | half-yearly | 103.022 | 116.054 | 210.524 | 443.204 |
| | quarterly | 103.034 | 116.119 | 211.108 | 445.667 |
| | momently | 103.045 | 116.183 | 211.700 | 448.169 |
| 4 per cent. | yearly | 104.000 | 121.665 | 266.584 | 710.668 |
| | half-yearly | 104.040 | 121.899 | 269.159 | 724.465 |
| | quarterly | 104.060 | 122.019 | 270.481 | 731.602 |
| | momently | 104.081 | 122.140 | 271.828 | 738.906 |
| 5 per cent. | yearly | 105.000 | 127.628 | 338.634 | 1146.740 |
| | half-yearly | 105.062 | 128.008 | 343.711 | 1181.372 |
| | quarterly | 105.095 | 128.204 | 346.340 | 1199.517 |
| | momently | 105.127 | 128.402 | 349.034 | 1218.249 |
| 6 per cent. | yearly | 106.000 | 133.823 | 429.187 | 1842.015 |
| | half-yearly | 106.090 | 134.392 | 438.391 | 1921.863 |
| | quarterly | 106.136 | 134.685 | 443.204 | 1964.303 |
| | momently | 106.184 | 134.986 | 448.169 | 2008.553 |
| 7 per cent. | yearly | 107.000 | 140.255 | 542.743 | 2945.703 |
| | half-yearly | 107.122 | 141.060 | 558.493 | 3119.141 |
| | quarterly | 107.186 | 141.478 | 566.816 | 3212.799 |
| | momently | 107.251 | 141.907 | 575.460 | 3311.545 |
| 8 per cent. | yearly | 108.000 | 146.933 | 684.847 | 4690.161 |
| | half-yearly | 108.160 | 148.024 | 710.668 | 5050.495 |
| | quarterly | 108.243 | 148.595 | 724.465 | 5248.490 |
| | momently | 108.329 | 149.182 | 738.906 | 5459.815 |

## TABLE VIII.

*Time in which Money will double itself at Simple or Compound yearly Interest.*

| Rate Per cent. | | At Simple Interest. | At Compound Interest. | | |
|---|---|---|---|---|---|
| | | Years. | Years. | Years. | Days. |
| 2 | | 50.0000 | 35.00278878 = | 35 | 2 |
| 2½ | | 40.0000 | 28.07103453 = | 28 | 26 |
| 3 | | 33.3333 | 23.44977225 = | 23 | 165 |
| 3½ | £1 or any | 28.5714 | 20.14879169 = | 20 | 55 |
| 4 | other sum | 25.0000 | 17.67298769 = | 17 | 246 |
| 4½ | will dou- | 22.2222 | 15.74730184 = | 15 | 272 |
| 5 | ble itself | 20.0000 | 14.20669908 = | 14 | 76 |
| 6 | in | 16.6666 | 11.89566105 = | 11 | 327 |
| 7 | | 14.2857 | 10.24476835 = | 10 | 90 |
| 8 | | 12.5000 | 9.00646834 = | 9 | 3 |
| 9 | | 11.1111 | 8.04323173 = | 8 | 16 |
| 10 | | 10.0000 | 7.27254090 = | 7 | 100 |

As to the time in which Money Doubles, see Chapter 2, and the Appendix, for our remarkable theorem, that—for all rates per cent. under 10 per cent, the number of years in which a sum of money will Double Itself at compound Interest, is simply 70 divided by the rate per cent.

EXAMPLES.—1.—*Divide 70 by the rate of interest per cent*, and take that whole number which is *nearest* to the quotient obtained. Thus, if the rate of Interest be—

2 per cent. then the number of years will be $\frac{70}{2}$ or 35 years nearly.

3½ ,, ,, ,, $\frac{70}{3\frac{1}{2}}$ ,, 20 ,, ,,

5 ,, ,, ,, $\frac{70}{5}$ ,, 14 ,, ,,

8 ,, ,, ,, $\frac{70}{8}$ ,, 9 ,, ,,

10 ,, ,, ,, $\frac{70}{10}$ ,, 7 ,, ,,

2.—The time in which money *doubles* being thus ascertained, to find the further time in which it will become *threefold*, divide the doubling period by 1.70; *fourfold*, by 2.40; *fivefold*, by 3.10; *sixfold*, by 3.80; and so on, the divisor increasing in arithmetical progression by .70 each time.

Thus, since money *doubles* at 5 *per cent*. in 14 years, it would become *threefold* in $\frac{14}{1.70}$ or eight years more, making 22 together; *fourfold*, in $\frac{14}{2.40}$ or six years more, or 28 years altogether; and so on.

TABLES. 7

## TABLE IX.

*Shewing the present Value of £100 payable at the end of any number of Years, at various Rates of Interest.*

This Table will serve to determine the *present value* of Shares in a Building Society, or the sum which must be given at once to obtain a *paid-up* Share, which is to be received at the end of a specified number of years.

| Years. | 3 per cent. | 4 per cent. | 5 per cent. | 6 per cent. | 7 per cent. | 8 per cent. |
|---|---|---|---|---|---|---|
| 1  | 97.08 | 96.15 | 95.23 | 94.33 | 93.45 | 92.59 |
| 2  | 94.25 | 92.45 | 90.70 | 88.99 | 87.34 | 85.73 |
| 3  | 91.51 | 88.89 | 86.38 | 83.96 | 81.62 | 79.38 |
| 4  | 88.84 | 85.48 | 82.27 | 79.20 | 76.28 | 73.50 |
| 5  | 86.26 | 82.19 | 78.35 | 74.72 | 71.29 | 68.05 |
| 6  | 83.74 | 79.03 | 74.62 | 70.49 | 66.63 | 63.01 |
| 7  | 81.30 | 75.99 | 71.06 | 66.50 | 62.27 | 58.34 |
| 8  | 78.94 | 73.06 | 67.68 | 62.74 | 58.20 | 54.02 |
| 9  | 76.64 | 70.25 | 64.46 | 59.18 | 54.39 | 50.02 |
| 10 | 74.40 | 67.55 | *61.39 | 55.83 | 50.83 | 46.31 |
| 11 | 72.24 | 64.95 | 58.46 | 52.67 | 47.50 | 42.88 |
| 12 | 70.13 | 62.45 | 55.68 | 49.69 | 44.40 | 39.71 |
| 13 | 68.09 | 60.05 | 53.03 | 46.88 | 41.49 | 36.76 |
| 14 | 66.11 | 57.74 | 50.50 | 44.23 | 38.78 | 34.04 |
| 15 | 64.18 | 55.52 | 48.10 | 41.72 | 36.24 | 31.52 |
| 16 | 62.31 | 53.39 | 45.81 | 39.36 | 33.87 | 29.18 |
| 17 | 60.50 | 51.33 | 43.62 | 37.13 | 31.65 | 27.02 |
| 18 | 58.73 | 49.36 | 41.55 | 35.03 | 29.58 | 25.02 |
| 19 | 57.02 | 47.46 | 39.57 | 33.05 | 27.65 | 23.17 |
| 20 | 55.36 | 45.63 | 37.68 | 31.18 | 25.84 | 21.45 |
| 21 | 53.75 | 43.88 | 35.89 | 29.41 | 24.15 | 19.86 |
| 22 | 52.18 | 42.19 | 34.18 | 27.75 | 22.57 | 18.39 |
| 23 | 50.66 | 40.57 | 32.55 | 26.18 | 21.09 | 17.03 |
| 24 | 49.19 | 39.01 | 31.00 | 24.69 | 19.71 | 15.77 |
| 25 | 47.76 | 37.51 | 29.53 | 23.30 | 18.42 | 14.60 |
| 26 | 46.36 | 36.06 | 28.12 | 21.98 | 17.21 | 13.52 |
| 27 | 45.01 | 34.68 | 26.78 | 20.73 | 16.09 | 12.51 |
| 28 | 43.70 | 33.34 | 25.50 | 19.56 | 15.04 | 11.59 |
| 29 | 42.43 | 32.06 | 24.29 | 18.45 | 14.05 | 10.73 |
| 30 | 41.19 | 30.83 | 23.13 | 17.41 | 13.13 | 9.93 |
| 31 | 39.99 | 29.64 | 22.03 | 16.42 | 12.27 | 9.20 |
| 32 | 38.83 | 28.50 | 20.98 | 15.49 | 11.47 | 8.52 |
| 33 | 37.70 | 27.40 | 19.98 | 14.61 | 10.72 | 7.88 |
| 34 | 36.60 | 26.35 | 19.03 | 13.79 | 10.02 | 7.30 |
| 35 | 35.53 | 25.34 | 18.12 | 13.01 | 9.36 | 6.76 |
| 36 | 34.50 | 24.36 | 17.26 | 12.27 | 8.75 | 6.26 |
| 37 | 33.49 | 23.42 | 16.44 | 11.57 | 8.18 | 5.79 |
| 38 | 32.52 | 22.52 | 15.66 | 10.92 | 7.64 | 5.36 |
| 39 | 31.57 | 21.66 | 14.91 | 10 30 | 7.14 | 4.97 |
| 40 | 30.65 | 20.82 | 14.20 | 9 72 | 6.67 | 4.60 |
| 41 | 29.76 | 20.02 | 13.52 | 9.17 | 6.24 | 4.26 |
| 42 | 28.89 | 19.25 | 12.88 | 8.65 | 5.83 | 3.94 |
| 43 | 28.05 | 18.51 | 12.27 | 8.16 | 5.45 | 3.65 |
| 44 | 27.23 | 17.80 | 11.68 | 7.70 | 5.09 | 3.38 |
| 45 | 26.44 | 17.12 | 11.12 | 7.26 | 4.76 | 3.13 |
| 46 | 25.67 | 16.46 | 10.59 | 6.85 | 4.45 | 2.90 |
| 47 | 24.92 | 15.82 | 10.09 | 6.46 | 4.15 | 2.68 |
| 48 | 24.20 | 15.21 | 9.61 | 6.10 | 3.88 | 2.48 |
| 49 | 23.49 | 14.63 | 9.15 | 5.75 | 3.63 | 2.30 |
| 50 | 22.81 | 14.07 | 8.72 | 5.42 | 3.39 | 2.13 |

\* *Example.*—If a member of a Building Society desire to purchase by a single payment a Share, whose amount is £100, to be received at the end of 10 years, and the rate of interest be 5 per cent., he must pay £61.39 or £61. 7s. 11d. for the same; a modification of course being made in the case of *monthly* payments

[*Refer to Note No. 2, at foot of Table IV, page 4, for any time beyond 50 years.*]

## TABLE X.

See Remarks, No. 2, at foot of page 2.]

*Shewing the Amount to which an Annuity of £100, paid at the end of each year, will accumulate at Compound Interest.*

This Table will serve to determine the yearly subscription requisite to purchase an investing share in a Building Society

| Years. | 3 per cent. | 4 per cent. | 5 per cent. | 6 per cent. | 7 per cent. | 10 per cent. |
|---|---|---|---|---|---|---|
| 1 | 100.00 | 100.00 | 100.00 | 100.00 | 100.00 | 100.00 |
| 2 | 203.00 | 204.00 | 205.00 | 206.00 | 207.00 | 210.00 |
| 3 | 309.09 | 312.16 | 315.25 | 318.36 | 321.49 | 331.00 |
| 4 | 418.36 | 424.64 | 431.01 | 437.46 | 443.99 | 464.10 |
| 5 | 530.91 | 541.63 | 552.56 | 563.70 | 575.07 | 610.51 |
| 6 | 646.84 | 663.29 | 680.19 | 697.53 | 715.32 | 771.56 |
| 7 | 766.24 | 789.82 | 814.20 | 839.38 | 865.40 | 948.71 |
| 8 | 889.23 | 921.42 | 954.91 | 989.74 | 1025.98 | 1143.58 |
| 9 | 1015.91 | 1058.27 | 1102.65 | 1149.13 | 1197.79 | 1357.94 |
| 10 | 1146.38 | 1200.61 | 1257.78 | 1318.07 | 1381.64 | 1593.74 |
| 11 | 1280.77 | 1348.63 | *1420.67 | 1497.16 | 1578.35 | 1853.11 |
| 12 | 1419.20 | 1502.58 | 1591.71 | 1686.99 | 1788.84 | 2138.42 |
| 13 | 1561.77 | 1662.68 | 1771.29 | 1888.21 | 2014.06 | 2452.27 |
| 14 | 1708.63 | 1829.19 | 1959.86 | 2101.50 | 2255.04 | 2797.49 |
| 15 | 1859.89 | 2002.35 | 2157.85 | 2327.59 | 2512.90 | 3177.24 |
| 16 | 2015.68 | 2182.45 | 2365.74 | 2567.25 | 2788.80 | 3594.97 |
| 17 | 2176.15 | 2369.75 | 2584.03 | 2821.28 | 3084.02 | 4054.47 |
| 18 | 2341.44 | 2564.54 | 2813.23 | 3090.56 | 3399.90 | 4559.91 |
| 19 | 2511.68 | 2767.12 | 3053.90 | 3375.99 | 3737.89 | 5115.90 |
| 20 | 2687.03 | 2977.80 | 3306.59 | 3678.55 | 4099.54 | 5727.49 |
| 21 | 2867.64 | 3196.92 | 3571.92 | 3999.27 | 4486.51 | 6400.24 |
| 22 | 3053.67 | 3424.79 | 3850.52 | 4339.22 | 4900.57 | 7140.27 |
| 23 | 3245.28 | 3661.78 | 4143.04 | 4699.58 | 5343.61 | 7954.30 |
| 24 | 3442.64 | 3908.26 | 4450.19 | 5081.55 | 5817.66 | 8849.73 |
| 25 | 3645.92 | 4164.59 | 4772.70 | 5486.45 | 6324.90 | 9834.70 |
| 26 | 3855.30 | 4431.17 | 5111.34 | 5915.63 | 6867.64 | 10918.17 |
| 27 | 4070.96 | 4708.42 | 5466.91 | 6370.57 | 7448.38 | 12109.99 |
| 28 | 4293.09 | 4996.75 | 5840.25 | 6852.81 | 8069.76 | 13420.99 |
| 29 | 4521.88 | 5296.62 | 6232.27 | 7363.97 | 8734.65 | 14863.09 |
| 30 | 4757.54 | 5608.49 | 6643.88 | 7905.81 | 9446.07 | 16449.40 |
| 31 | 5000.26 | 5932.83 | 7076.07 | 8480.16 | 10207.30 | 18194 84 |
| 32 | 5250.27 | 6270.14 | 7529.88 | 9088.97 | 11021.81 | 20113.77 |
| 33 | 5507.78 | 6620.95 | 8006.37 | 9734.31 | 11898.34 | 22225.15 |
| 34 | 5773.01 | 6985.79 | 8506.69 | 10418.37 | 12825.87 | 24547.66 |
| 35 | 6046.20 | 7365.22 | 9032.03 | 11143.47 | 13823.68 | 27102.43 |
| 36 | 6327.59 | 7759.83 | 9583.63 | 11912.08 | 14891.34 | 29912 68 |
| 37 | 6617.42 | 8170.22 | 10162.81 | 12726.81 | 16033.74 | 33003.94 |
| 38 | 6915.94 | 8597.03 | 10770.95 | 13590.42 | 17256.10 | 36404.34 |
| 39 | 7223.42 | 9040.91 | 11409.50 | 14505.84 | 18564.02 | 40144.77 |
| 40 | 7540.12 | 9502.55 | 12079.97 | 15476.19 | 19963.51 | 44259.25 |
| 41 | 7866.32 | 9982.65 | 12783.97 | 16504.76 | 21460.95 | 48785.18 |
| 42 | 8202.31 | 10481.95 | 13523.17 | 17595.05 | 23068.22 | 53763.69 |
| 43 | 8548.38 | 11001.23 | 14299.33 | 18750.75 | 24777.64 | 59240.06 |
| 44 | 8904.84 | 11541.28 | 15114.30 | 19975.80 | 26612.08 | 65264.07 |
| 45 | 9271.98 | 12102.93 | 15970.01 | 21274.35 | 28574.93 | 71890.48 |
| 46 | 9650.14 | 12687.05 | 16868.51 | 22650.81 | 30675.17 | 79179.53 |
| 47 | 10039.65 | 13294.53 | 17811.94 | 24109.86 | 32922.43 | 87197.48 |
| 48 | 10440.84 | 13926.32 | 18802.53 | 25656.45 | 35327.00 | 96017.23 |
| 49 | 10854.06 | 14583.31 | 19842.66 | 27295.84 | 37899.90 | 105718.95 |
| 50 | 11279.68 | 15266.70 | 20934.79 | 29033.59 | 40652 89 | 116390.85 |

[NOTE.—The above Table will also serve to determine the amount of an Annuity paid at the *beginning* of each year.

For the amount of an Annuity for *n* years paid } = { the amount of an Annuity (for *n* + 1) years at the *beginning* of each year. } = { from above Table — 100.

* *Example.*—The amount of an Annuity of £100 at 5 per cent. for 10 years paid at the beginning of each year = £1420.67—£100.
= £1320.67.]

TABLES.

## TABLE XI.

[See Remarks No. 3, at foot of page 2.]

*Shewing the present Value of an Annuity of £100 at the end of each Year.*

| Years. | 3 per cent. | 4 per cent. | 5 per cent. | 6 per cent. | 7 per cent. | 8 per cent. |
|---|---|---|---|---|---|---|
| 1 | 97.08 | 96.15 | 95.23 | 94.33 | 93.45 | 92.59 |
| 2 | 191.34 | 188.60 | 185.94 | 183.33 | 180.80 | 178.32 |
| 3 | 282.86 | 277.50 | 272.32 | 267.30 | 262.43 | 257.70 |
| 4 | 371.70 | 362.98 | 354.59 | 346.51 | 338.72 | 331.21 |
| 5 | 457.97 | 445.18 | 432.94 | 421.23 | 410.01 | 399.27 |
| 6 | 541.71 | 524.21 | 507.56 | 491.73 | 476.65 | 462.28 |
| 7 | 623.02 | 600.20 | 578.63 | 558.23 | 538.92 | 520.63 |
| 8 | 701.96 | 673.27 | 646.32 | 620.97 | 597.12 | 574.66 |
| 9 | 778.61 | 743.53 | *710.78 | 680.16 | 651.52 | 624.68 |
| 10 | 853.02 | 811.08 | 772.17 | 736.00 | 702.35 | 671.00 |
| 11 | 925.26 | 876.04 | 830.64 | 788.68 | 749.86 | 713.89 |
| 12 | 995.40 | 938.50 | 886.32 | 838.38 | 794.26 | 753.60 |
| 13 | 1063.49 | 998.56 | 939.35 | 885.26 | 835.76 | 790.37 |
| 14 | 1129.60 | 1056.31 | 989.86 | 929.49 | 874.54 | 824.42 |
| 15 | 1193.79 | 1111.83 | 1037.96 | 971.22 | 910.79 | 855.94 |
| 16 | 1256.11 | 1165.22 | 1083.77 | 1010.58 | 944.66 | 885.13 |
| 17 | 1316.61 | 1216.56 | 1127.40 | 1047.72 | 976.32 | 912.16 |
| 18 | 1375.35 | 1265.92 | 1168.95 | 1082.76 | 1005.90 | 937.18 |
| 19 | 1432.37 | 1313.39 | 1208.53 | 1115.81 | 1033.55 | 960.35 |
| 20 | 1487.74 | 1359.03 | 1246.22 | 1146.99 | 1059.40 | 981.81 |
| 21 | 1541.50 | 1402.91 | 1282.11 | 1176.40 | 1083.55 | 1001.68 |
| 22 | 1593.69 | 1445.11 | 1316.30 | 1204.15 | 1106.12 | 1020.07 |
| 23 | 1644.36 | 1485.68 | 1348.85 | 1230.33 | 1127.21 | 1037.10 |
| 24 | 1693.55 | 1524.69 | 1379.86 | 1255.03 | 1146.93 | 1052.87 |
| 25 | 1741.31 | 1562.20 | 1409.39 | 1278.33 | 1165.35 | 1067.47 |
| 26 | 1787.68 | 1598.27 | 1437.51 | 1300.31 | 1182.57 | 1080.99 |
| 27 | 1832.70 | 1632.95 | 1464.30 | 1321.05 | 1198.67 | 1093.51 |
| 28 | 1876.41 | 1666.30 | 1489.81 | 1340.61 | 1213.71 | 1105.10 |
| 29 | 1918.84 | 1698.37 | 1514.10 | 1359.07 | 1227.76 | 1115.84 |
| 30 | 1960.04 | 1729.20 | 1537.24 | 1376.48 | 1240.90 | 1125.77 |
| 31 | 2000.04 | 1758.84 | 1559.28 | 1392.90 | 1253.18 | 1134.97 |
| 32 | 2038.87 | 1787.35 | 1580.26 | 1408.40 | 1264.65 | 1143.49 |
| 33 | 2076.57 | 1814.76 | 1600.25 | 1423.02 | 1275.37 | 1151.38 |
| 34 | 2113.18 | 1841.11 | 1619.29 | 1436.81 | 1285.40 | 1158.69 |
| 35 | 2148.72 | 1866.46 | 1637.41 | 1449.82 | 1294.76 | 1165.45 |
| 36 | 2183.22 | 1890.68 | 1654.68 | 1462.09 | 1303.52 | 1171.71 |
| 37 | 2216.72 | 1914.25 | 1671.12 | 1473.67 | 1311.70 | 1177.51 |
| 38 | 2249.24 | 1936.78 | 1686.78 | 1484.60 | 1319.34 | 1182.88 |
| 39 | 2280.82 | 1958.44 | 1701.70 | 1494.90 | 1326.49 | 1187.85 |
| 40 | 2311.47 | 1979.27 | 1715.90 | 1504.62 | 1333.17 | 1192.46 |
| 41 | 2341.24 | 1999.30 | 1729.43 | 1513.80 | 1339.41 | 1196.72 |
| 42 | 2370.13 | 2018.56 | 1742.32 | 1522.45 | 1345.24 | 1200.66 |
| 43 | 2398.19 | 2037.07 | 1754.59 | 1530.61 | 1350.69 | 1204.32 |
| 44 | 2425.42 | 2054.88 | 1766.27 | 1538.31 | 1355.79 | 1207.70 |
| 45 | 2451.87 | 2072.00 | 1777.40 | 1545.58 | 1360.55 | 1210.84 |
| 46 | 2477.54 | 2088.46 | 1788.00 | 1552.43 | 1365.00 | 1213.74 |
| 47 | 2502.47 | 2104.29 | 1798.10 | 1558.90 | 1369.16 | 1216.42 |
| 48 | 2526.67 | 2119.51 | 1807.71 | 1565.00 | 1373.04 | 1218.91 |
| 49 | 2550.16 | 2134.14 | 1816.87 | 1570.76 | 1376.67 | 1221.21 |
| 50 | 2572.07 | 2148.21 | 1825.59 | 1576.18 | 1380.07 | 1223.34 |
| Perpetuity | 3333.33 | 2500.00 | 2000.00 | 1666.67 | 1428.57 | 1250.00 |

[NOTE.—The above Table will serve to determine the present value of an Annuity paid at the *beginning* of each year,

For, the present value of an annuity of £100, paid at the beginning of each year, for *n* years } = { the present value of an annuity for (*n*−1) years + 100

* *Example.*—The present value at 5 per cent. of £100 a year paid at the beginning of each year for ten years = £710.78 + £100.
= £810.78.]

## TABLE XII.

*Shewing the Annuity which £100 will purchase for a given number of Years.*

This Table will serve to determine the Annuity to be paid by a **borrowing** member of a Building Society in repayment of a given advance.

| Years. | 3 per cent. | 5 per cent. | 7 per cent. | 8 per cent. | 9 per cent. | 10 per cent. |
|---|---|---|---|---|---|---|
| 1 | 103.00 | 105.00 | 107.00 | 108.00 | 109.00 | 110.00 |
| 2 | 52.26 | 53.78 | 55.31 | 56.08 | 56.85 | 57.62 |
| 3 | 35.35 | 36.72 | 38.11 | 38.80 | 39.51 | 40.21 |
| 4 | 26.90 | 28.20 | 29.52 | 30.19 | 30.87 | 31.55 |
| 5 | 21.84 | 23.10 | 24.39 | 25.05 | 25.71 | 26.38 |
| 6 | 18.46 | 19.70 | 20.98 | 21.63 | 22.29 | 22.96 |
| 7 | 16.05 | 17.28 | 18.56 | 19.21 | 19.87 | 20.54 |
| 8 | 14.25 | 15.47 | 16.75 | 17.40 | 18.07 | 18.74 |
| 9 | 12.84 | 14.07 | 15.35 | 16.01 | 16.68 | 17.36 |
| 10 | 11.72 | 12.95 | *14.24 | 14.90 | 15.58 | 16.27 |
| 11 | 10.81 | 12.04 | 13.34 | 14.01 | 14.69 | 15.40 |
| 12 | 10.05 | 11.28 | 12.59 | 13.27 | 13.97 | 14.68 |
| 13 | 9.40 | 10.65 | 11.97 | 12.65 | 13.36 | 14.08 |
| 14 | 8.85 | 10.10 | 11.43 | 12.13 | 12.84 | 13.58 |
| 15 | 8.37 | 9.63 | 10.98 | 11.68 | 12.41 | 13.15 |
| 16 | 7.96 | 9.23 | 10.59 | 11.30 | 12.03 | 12.78 |
| 17 | 7.60 | 8.87 | 10.24 | 10.96 | 11.70 | 12.47 |
| 18 | 7.27 | 8.55 | 9.94 | 10.67 | 11.42 | 12.19 |
| 19 | 6.98 | 8.27 | 9.68 | 10.41 | 11.17 | 11.95 |
| 20 | 6.72 | 8.02 | 9.44 | 10.19 | 10.95 | 11.75 |
| 21 | 6.49 | 7.80 | 9.23 | 9.98 | 10.76 | 11.56 |
| 22 | 6.28 | 7.60 | 9.04 | 9.80 | 10.59 | 11.40 |
| 23 | 6.08 | 7.41 | 8.87 | 9.64 | 10.44 | 11.26 |
| 24 | 5.91 | 7.25 | 8.72 | 9.50 | 10.30 | 11.13 |
| 25 | 5.74 | 7.10 | 8.58 | 9.37 | 10.18 | 11.02 |
| 26 | 5.59 | 6.96 | 8.46 | 9.25 | 10.07 | 10.92 |
| 27 | 5.46 | 6.83 | 8.34 | 9.15 | 9.97 | 10.83 |
| 28 | 5.33 | 6.71 | 8.24 | 9.05 | 9.89 | 10.75 |
| 29 | 5.21 | 6.60 | 8.15 | 8.96 | 9.81 | 10.67 |
| 30 | 5.10 | 6.51 | 8.06 | 8.88 | 9.73 | 10.61 |
| 31 | 5.00 | 6.41 | 7.98 | 8.81 | 9.67 | 10.55 |
| 32 | 4.90 | 6.33 | 7.91 | 8.74 | 9.61 | 10.50 |
| 33 | 4.82 | 6.25 | 7.84 | 8.68 | 9.56 | 10.45 |
| 34 | 4.73 | 6.18 | 7.77 | 8.63 | 9.51 | 10.40 |
| 35 | 4.65 | 6.11 | 7.72 | 8.58 | 9.46 | 10.37 |
| 36 | 4.58 | 6.04 | 7.67 | 8.53 | 9.42 | 10.33 |
| 37 | 4.51 | 5.98 | 7.62 | 8.49 | 9.39 | 10.30 |
| 38 | 4.45 | 5.93 | 7.58 | 8.45 | 9.35 | 10.27 |
| 39 | 4.38 | 5.88 | 7.54 | 8.42 | 9.32 | 10.25 |
| 40 | 4.33 | 5.83 | 7.50 | 8.39 | 9.30 | 10.23 |
| 41 | 4.27 | 5.78 | 7.47 | 8.36 | 9.27 | 10.21 |
| 42 | 4.22 | 5.74 | 7.43 | 8.33 | 9.25 | 10.19 |
| 43 | 4.17 | 5.70 | 7.40 | 8.30 | 9.23 | 10.17 |
| 44 | 4.12 | 5.66 | 7.38 | 8.28 | 9.21 | 10.15 |
| 45 | 4.08 | 5.63 | 7.35 | 8.26 | 9.19 | 10.14 |
| 46 | 4.04 | 5.59 | 7.33 | 8.24 | 9.17 | 10.13 |
| 47 | 4.00 | 5.56 | 7.30 | 8.22 | 9.16 | 10.11 |
| 48 | 3.96 | 5.53 | 7.28 | 8.20 | 9.15 | 10.10 |
| 49 | 3.92 | 5.50 | 7.26 | 8.19 | 9.13 | 10.09 |
| 50 | 3.89 | 5.48 | 7.25 | 8.17 | 9.12 | 10.08 |
| Perpetuity | 3.00 | 5.00 | 7.00 | 8.00 | 9.00 | 10.00 |

*Example.*—If a member borrow £100 for 10 years to be repaid by equal instalments, including principal and interest, at 7 per cent., in that time, he must pay £14.24 or nearly £14. 5s. a year in repayment for the same.

☞ From this Table may also be calculated the annual sinking fund to accumulate to £100 in any number of years. *Ex*: The sinking fund to produce £100 in 12 years at 5 per cent. is equal to £11.28 less the interest, or to £6.28, which is £6. 5s. 6d. nearly.

11

| | Present Value of £100 (payable at end of any number of years), Discounted at | | Amount of £100 at the end of any number of years, Accumulated with Compound Interest at | | Present Value of an Annuity of £100 (payable at end of each year), Discounted at | | Amount of an Annuity of £100 (payable at end of each year), Accumulated at Compound Interest. | |
|---|---|---|---|---|---|---|---|---|
| Years. | $2\frac{1}{2}$ Per Cent. | $3\frac{1}{2}$ Per Cent. | $2\frac{1}{2}$ Per Cent. | $3\frac{1}{2}$ Per Cent. | $2\frac{1}{2}$ Per Cent. | $3\frac{1}{2}$ Per Cent. | $2\frac{1}{2}$ Per Cent. | $3\frac{1}{2}$ Per Cent. |
| 1 | 97.560 | 96.618 | 102.50 | 103.50 | 97.561 | 96.618 | 100.000 | 100.000 |
| 2 | 95.181 | 93.351 | 105.06 | 107.12 | 192.742 | 189.969 | 202.500 | 203.500 |
| 3 | 92.859 | 90.194 | 107.68 | 110.87 | 285.602 | 280.163 | 307.562 | 310.622 |
| 4 | 90.595 | 87.144 | 110.38 | 114.75 | 376.197 | 367.307 | 415.251 | 421.491 |
| 5 | 88.385 | 84.197 | 113.14 | 118.76 | 464.582 | 451.505 | 525.632 | 536.246 |
| 6 | 86.229 | 81.350 | 115.96 | 122.92 | 550.812 | 532.855 | 638.773 | 655.015 |
| 7 | 84.126 | 78.599 | 118.86 | 127.22 | 634.939 | 611.454 | 754.745 | 777.940 |
| 8 | 82.074 | 75.941 | 121.84 | 131.68 | 717.013 | 687.395 | 873.611 | 905.168 |
| 9 | 80.072 | 73.373 | 124.88 | 136.28 | 797.086 | 760.768 | 995.451 | 1036.849 |
| 10 | 78.119 | 70.891 | 128.00 | 141.05 | 875.206 | 831.660 | 1120.338 | 1173.139 |
| 11 | 76.214 | 68.494 | 131.20 | 145.99 | 951.420 | 900.155 | 1248.316 | 1314.189 |
| 12 | 74.355 | 66.178 | 134.48 | 151.10 | 1025.776 | 966.333 | 1379.555 | 1459.196 |
| 13 | 72.542 | 63.940 | 137.85 | 156.39 | 1098.318 | 1030.273 | 1514.011 | 1611.303 |
| 14 | 70.773 | 61.778 | 141.29 | 161.86 | 1169.091 | 1092.052 | 1651.805 | 1767.698 |
| 15 | 69.048 | 59.689 | 144.82 | 167.53 | 1238.137 | 1151.741 | 1793.112 | 1929.568 |
| 16 | 67.362 | 57.670 | 149.15 | 173.39 | 1305.500 | 1209.411 | 1938.022 | 2097.103 |
| 17 | 65.719 | 55.724 | 152.16 | 179.45 | 1371.219 | 1265.132 | 2086.173 | 2270.501 |
| 18 | 64.116 | 53.836 | 155.96 | 185.71 | 1435.336 | 1318.968 | 2238.634 | 2449.969 |
| 19 | 62.552 | 52.015 | 159.86 | 192.25 | 1497.883 | 1370.983 | 2394.600 | 2635.718 |
| 20 | 61.027 | 50.256 | 163.86 | 198.97 | 1558.916 | 1421.240 | 2554.465 | 2827.968 |
| 21 | 59.538 | 48.557 | 167.95 | 205.91 | 1618.454 | 1469.797 | 2718.327 | 3026.947 |
| 22 | 58.086 | 46.915 | 172.15 | 213.15 | 1676.541 | 1516.712 | 2886.285 | 3232.830 |
| 23 | 56.669 | 45.328 | 176.46 | 220.61 | 1733.211 | 1562.041 | 3058.442 | 3446.011 |
| 24 | 55.287 | 43.795 | 180.87 | 228.33 | 1788.498 | 1605.836 | 3234.903 | 3666.652 |
| 25 | 53.939 | 42.311 | 185.39 | 236.32 | 1842.437 | 1648.151 | 3415.776 | 3894.985 |

From the above Tables can be calculated the *Present Value*, or the *Amount* of an Annuity, at nominal rates of 5 and 7 per Cent. Interest per annum, on the principle of half-yearly compounding of such Interest. (See also, Tables V. and VII.)

# TABLE XIV.

PRESENT VALUE of an Annuity of £100 per annum, for a given number of years certain, supposing the Purchaser TO TAKE OUT OF THE ANNUITY 5 per Cent., 6 per Cent., or 7 per Cent. per Annum as INTEREST on his Purchase Money, while he is enabled to Reinvest the Surplus of the Annuity beyond the Interest, so as to make 3 per Cent., 4 per Cent., and 5 per Cent. thereon, in order to replace the Purchase Money by the end of the number of years.

| | INTEREST to be 5 % | | INTEREST to be 6 % | | INTEREST to be 7 % | | |
|---|---|---|---|---|---|---|---|
| | The Reinvestments to replace Capital to be made at the rate of | | The Reinvestments to replace Capital to be made at the rate of | | The Reinvestments to replace Capital to be made at the rate of | | |
| Years. | 3 Per Cent. | 4 Per Cent. | 3 Per Cent. | 4 Per Cent. | 3 Per Cent. | 4 Per Cent. | 5 Per Cent. |
| | £ | £ | £ | £ | £ | £ | £ |
| 1 | 95 | 95 | 94 | 94 | 93 | 93 | 93 |
| 2 | 184 | 185 | 181 | 182 | 178 | 178 | 179 |
| 3 | 268 | 270 | 261 | 263 | 254 | 256 | 258 |
| 4 | 346 | 350 | 334 | 338 | 323 | 327 | 331 |
| 5 | 419 | 426 | 402 | 409 | 387 | 393 | 398 |
| 6 | 489 | 498 | 466 | 474 | 445 | 453 | 461 |
| 7 | 554 | 566 | 524 | 536 | 499 | 508 | 518 |
| 8 | 615 | 631 | 572 | 593 | 548 | 560 | 572 |
| 9 | 674 | 692 | 631 | 647 | 594 | 608 | 622 |
| 10 | 729 | 750 | 679 | 698 | 636 | 652 | 669 |
| 11 | 781 | 805 | 724 | 745 | 675 | 694 | 712 |
| 12 | 830 | 858 | 766 | 790 | 712 | 732 | 753 |
| 13 | 877 | 908 | 806 | 832 | 746 | 768 | 791 |
| 14 | 921 | 955 | 844 | 872 | 778 | 802 | 826* |
| 15 | 963 | 1000 | 879 | 909 | 808 | 834 | 859 |
| 16 | 1004 | 1043 | 912 | 945 | 836 | 863 | 891 |
| 17 | 1042 | 1085 | 944 | 978 | 862 | 891 | 920 |
| 18 | 1079 | 1124 | 973 | 1010 | 887 | 917 | 947 |
| 19 | 1113 | 1161 | 1002 | 1040 | 910 | 942 | 973 |
| 20 | 1146 | 1196 | 1028 | 1068 | 932 | 965 | 997 |
| 21 | 1178 | 1230 | 1054 | 1095 | 953 | 987 | 1020 |
| 22 | 1208 | 1262 | 1078 | 1121 | 973 | 1008 | 1042 |
| 23 | 1237 | 1293 | 1101 | 1145 | 992 | 1028 | 1062 |
| 24 | 1265 | 1323 | 1123 | 1168 | 1009 | 1046 | 1081 |
| 25 | 1291 | 1351 | 1144 | 1190 | 1026 | 1064 | 1099 |
| 26 | 1317 | 1378 | 1164 | 1211 | 1042 | 1080 | 1116 |
| 27 | 1341 | 1404 | 1182 | 1231 | 1057 | 1096 | 1132 |
| 28 | 1364 | 1428 | 1200 | 1253 | 1072 | 1111 | 1148 |
| 29 | 1387 | 1452 | 1218 | 1268 | 1085 | 1125 | 1162 |
| 30 | 1408 | 1474 | 1234 | 1285 | 1099 | 1138 | 1176 |

EXAMPLE.—If £100 a year for 14 years be bought for £826, the annuity will suffice to pay 7 per Cent. on the £826, and give a surplus, which, laid out at only 5 per Cent. interest, will in 14 years reproduce the purchase money, £826.

## TABLE XV.

*Specimen of New Deposit Tables, for Savings Banks and Industrial Associations, shewing—*

1.—The Amount to which a Deposit of £100 will accumulate at the end of any number of years up to 10.
2.—The Amount to which a Deposit of £10 per annum will accumulate at the end of any number of years up to 10.

On the condition that, after the first Year, One Half (or One Fourth) of the Sum deposited may be withdrawn, *without interest*, on giving one week's notice; the balance of the Deposit and the accumulated compound Interest remaining unwithdrawable till the end of the period, unless six months' notice of withdrawal be given.

Rates of Interest £3. 10s. and £2. 10s. per cent., as explained at foot.

| | Deposit of £100. | | Deposit of £10 per annum. | | |
|---|---|---|---|---|---|
| No. of Years. | One Half withdrawable. | One Fourth withdrawable. | One Fourth withdrawable. | One Half withdrawable. | No. of Years. |
| | £. s. d. | £. s. d. | £. s. d. | £. s. d. | |
| 1  | 103 0 0   | 103 5 0    | 10 6 6     | 10 6 0     | 1  |
| 2  | 106 2 1   | 106 12 4   | 20 19 9    | 20 18 2    | 2  |
| 3  | 109 6 5   | 110 1 11   | 31 19 11   | 31 16 10   | 3  |
| 4  | 112 12 11 | 113 13 11  | 43 7 4     | 43 2 1     | 4  |
| 5  | 116 1 9   | 117 8 7    | 55 2 2     | 54 14 3    | 5  |
| 6  | 119 13 0  | 121 5 9    | 67 4 9     | 66 13 7    | 6  |
| 7  | 123 6 9   | 125 5 8    | 79 15 4    | 79 0 3     | 7  |
| 8  | 127 3 1   | 129 8 4    | 92 14 2    | 91 14 7    | 8  |
| 9  | 131 2 1   | 133 14 0   | 106 1 7    | 104 16 10  | 9  |
| 10 | 135 3 11  | 138 2 7    | 119 17 10  | 118 7 2    | 10 |

N.B.—This Table is computed according to formulæ Nos. 1 and 13, Arts. 67, 75, in the Appendix to "*Treatise on Associations for Provident Investment,*" on the supposition that the *lower* rate of 2½ per cent. is allowed on the withdrawable portion of the Deposit, and 3½ per cent. on the unwithdrawable portion, as also upon the entire amount of the interest as it accumulates from year to year.

*Example:* 1.—A person having deposited £100 will be entitled, at any time after the first year, to draw out £50, or £25, as the case may be, at a week's notice. Say he has retained the power to withdraw one-half, and that he exercises this power at the end of the 5th year. The amount at his credit at that moment is £116. 1s. 9d., from which deducting the £50 withdrawn, there will remain £66. 1s. 9d. to accumulate for the remaining 5 years (or until withdrawn under a six months' notice) at 3½ per cent. compound interest. If, on the other hand, the whole amount of the Deposit be left undisturbed by the Depositor during the term, then the accumulated amount at the end of 10 years will be £135. 3s. 11d.

2.—A person having deposited £10 per annum, say for 5 years, will be entitled at the end of that year to withdraw one-half or one-fourth of the aggregate of his deposits to that time (viz., £25 or £12. 10s.) as the case may be, at a week's notice; the remainder, together with the interest, being left to accumulate at 3½ per cent. till the end of the term, or until withdrawn under a six months' notice.

## TABLE XVI.
*Extract from the Tables of Logarithms.*

| Number. | Hyperbolic or Neperian Logarithms. | Ordinary Logarithms. | Number. | Hyperbolic or Neperian Logarithms. | Ordinary Logarithms. |
|---|---|---|---|---|---|
| 1.01 | .0099503 | .0043214 | 47.00 | 3.8501476 | 1.6720979 |
| 1.02 | .0198026 | .0086002 | 48.00 | 3.8712010 | .6812412 |
| 1.03 | .0295588 | .0128372 | 49.00 | 3.8918203 | .6901961 |
| 1.04 | .0392207 | .0170333 | 50.00 | 3.9120230 | .6989700 |
| 1.05 | .0487902 | .0211893 | 51.00 | 3.9318256 | .7075702 |
| 1.06 | .0582689 | .0253059 | 52.00 | 3.9512437 | .7160033 |
| 1.07 | .0676586 | .0293838 | 53.00 | 3.9702919 | .7242759 |
| 1.08 | .0769610 | .0334238 | 54.00 | 3.9889840 | .7323938 |
| 1.09 | .0861777 | .0374265 | 55.00 | 4.0073332 | .7403627 |
| 1.10 | .0953102 | .0413927 | 56.00 | 4.0253517 | .7481880 |
| 2.00 | .6931472 | .3010300 | 57.00 | 4.0430513 | .7558749 |
| 3.00 | 1.0986123 | .4771213 | 58.00 | 4.0604430 | .7634280 |
| 4.00 | 1.3862943 | .6020600 | 59.00 | 4.0775374 | .7708520 |
| 5.00 | 1.6094379 | .6989700 | 60.00 | 4.0943446 | .7781513 |
| 6.00 | 1.7917594 | .7781513 | 61.00 | 4.1108739 | .7853298 |
| 7.00 | 1.9459101 | .8450980 | 62.00 | 4.1271344 | .7923917 |
| 8.00 | 2.0794415 | .9030900 | 63.00 | 4.1431347 | .7993405 |
| 9.00 | 2.1972245 | .9542425 | 64.00 | 4.1588831 | .8061800 |
| 10.00 | 2.3025851 | 1.0000000 | 65.00 | 4.1743873 | .8129134 |
| 11.00 | 2.3978953 | .0413927 | 66.00 | 4.1896547 | .8195439 |
| 12.00 | 2.4849066 | .0791812 | 67.00 | 4.2046926 | .8260748 |
| 13.00 | 2.5649494 | .1139434 | 68.00 | 4.2195077 | .8325089 |
| 14.00 | 2.6390573 | .1461280 | 69.00 | 4.2341065 | .8388491 |
| 15.00 | 2.7080502 | .1760913 | 70.00 | 4.2484952 | .8450980 |
| 16.00 | 2.7725887 | .2041200 | 71.00 | 4.2626799 | .8512583 |
| 17.00 | 2.8332133 | .2304489 | 72.00 | 4.2766661 | .8573325 |
| 18.00 | 2.8903718 | .2552725 | 73.00 | 4.2904594 | .8633229 |
| 19.00 | 2.9444390 | .2787536 | 74.00 | 4.3040651 | .8692317 |
| 20.00 | 2.9957323 | .3010300 | 75.00 | 4.3174881 | .8750613 |
| 21.00 | 3.0445224 | .3222193 | 76.00 | 4.3307333 | .8808136 |
| 22.00 | 3.0910425 | .3424227 | 77.00 | 4.3438054 | .8864907 |
| 23.00 | 3.1354942 | .3617278 | 78.00 | 4.3567088 | .8920946 |
| 24.00 | 3.1780538 | .3802112 | 79.00 | 4.3694479 | .8976271 |
| 25.00 | 3.2188758 | .3979400 | 80.00 | 4.3820266 | .9030900 |
| 26.00 | 3.2580965 | .4149733 | 81.00 | 4.3944492 | .9084850 |
| 27.00 | 3.2958369 | .4313638 | 82.00 | 4.4067192 | .9138139 |
| 28.00 | 3.3322045 | .4471580 | 83.00 | 4.4188406 | .9190781 |
| 29.00 | 3.3672958 | .4623980 | 84.00 | 4.4308168 | .9242793 |
| 30.00 | 3.4011974 | .4771213 | 85.00 | 4.4426513 | .9294189 |
| 31.00 | 3.4339872 | .4913617 | 86.00 | 4.4543473 | .9344985 |
| 32.00 | 3.4657359 | .5051500 | 87.00 | 4.4659081 | .9395193 |
| 33.00 | 3.4965076 | .5185139 | 88.00 | 4.4773368 | .9444827 |
| 34.00 | 3.5263605 | .5314789 | 89.00 | 4.4886364 | .9493900 |
| 35.00 | 3.5553481 | .5440680 | 90.00 | 4.4998097 | .9542425 |
| 36.00 | 3.5835189 | .5563025 | 91.00 | 4.5108595 | .9590414 |
| 37.00 | 3.6109179 | .5682017 | 92.00 | 4.5217886 | .9637878 |
| 38.00 | 3.6375862 | .5797836 | 93.00 | 4.5325995 | .9684829 |
| 39.00 | 3.6635616 | .5910646 | 94.00 | 4.5432948 | .9731279 |
| 40.00 | 3.6888795 | .6020600 | 95.00 | 4.5538769 | .9777236 |
| 41.00 | 3.7135721 | .6127839 | 96.00 | 4.5643482 | .9822712 |
| 42.00 | 3.7376696 | .6232493 | 97.00 | 4.5747110 | .9867717 |
| 43.00 | 3.7612001 | .6334685 | 98.00 | 4.5849675 | .9912261 |
| 44.00 | 3.7841896 | .6434527 | 99.00 | 4.5951199 | .9956352 |
| 45.00 | 3.8066625 | .6532125 | 100.00 | 4.6051702 | 2.0000000 |
| 46.00 | 3.8286414 | .6627578 | | | |

*Rem.*—Hyperbolic Logarithms can be deduced from the ordinary tables of Logarithms to the base 10, by multiplying the latter by Log° 10 or 2.302851.

See "Callet's Logarithms."—*Firmin Didot, Paris.*

TABLES. 15

## TABLE XVII.

*English Life Table No. 3. Interest 3 per cent.*

(Calculated by the Registrar-General from the Returns for 17 Years.)

| Age. | Expectation of Life. | | Present Value of £100 a-year, Annuity due. | | Present Value of £100 payable at Death. | |
|---|---|---|---|---|---|---|
| | Males. | Females. | Males. | Females. | Males. | Females. |
| | Years. | Years. | | | | |
| 0  | 39.9 | 41.9 | £1915 | £1985 | £44.2 | £42.2 |
| 1  | 46.7 | 47.3 | 2235 | 2244 | 34.9 | 34.6 |
| 2  | 48.8 | 49.4 | 2350 | 2354 | 31.5 | 31.4 |
| 3  | 49.6 | 50.2 | 2403 | 2407 | 30.0 | 29.9 |
| 4  | 49.8 | 50.4 | 2430 | 2435 | 29.2 | 29.1 |
| 5  | 49.7 | 50.3 | 2444 | 2448 | 28.8 | 28.7 |
| 6  | 49.4 | 50.0 | 2447 | 2451 | 28.7 | 28.6 |
| 7  | 48.9 | 49.5 | 2444 | 2447 | 28.8 | 28.7 |
| 8  | 48.4 | 49.0 | 2437 | 2440 | 29.0 | 28.9 |
| 9  | 47.7 | 48.4 | 2425 | 2429 | 29.4 | 29.3 |
| 10 | 47.1 | 47.7 | 2411 | 2415 | 29.8 | 29.7 |
| 11 | 46.3 | 47.0 | 2393 | 2398 | 30.3 | 30.2 |
| 12 | 45.5 | 46.2 | 2374 | 2380 | 30.8 | 30.7 |
| 13 | 44.8 | 45.4 | 2354 | 2360 | 31.4 | 31.3 |
| 14 | 44.0 | 44.7 | 2332 | 2340 | 32.1 | 31.8 |
| 15 | 43.2 | 43.9 | 2311 | 2319 | 32.7 | 32.4 |
| 16 | 42.4 | 43.1 | 2289 | 2299 | 33.3 | 33.0 |
| 17 | 41.6 | 42.4 | 2267 | 2278 | 34.0 | 33.6 |
| 18 | 40.9 | 41.7 | 2246 | 2258 | 34.6 | 34.2 |
| 19 | 40.2 | 41.0 | 2226 | 2239 | 35.2 | 34.8 |
| 20 | 39.5 | 40.3 | 2206 | 2221 | 35.7 | 35.3 |
| 21 | 38.8 | 39.6 | 2187 | 2203 | 36.3 | 35.8 |
| 22 | 38.1 | 39.0 | 2168 | 2186 | 36.8 | 36.3 |
| 23 | 37.5 | 38.3 | 2149 | 2168 | 37.4 | 36.9 |
| 24 | 36.8 | 37.7 | 2129 | 2150 | 38.0 | 37.4 |
| 25 | 36.1 | 37.0 | 2109 | 2131 | 38.6 | 37.9 |
| 26 | 35.4 | 36.4 | 2089 | 2112 | 39.2 | 38.5 |
| 27 | 34.8 | 35.8 | 2067 | 2093 | 39.8 | 39.0 |
| 28 | 34.1 | 35.1 | 2046 | 2074 | 40.4 | 39.6 |
| 29 | 33.4 | 34.5 | 2024 | 2054 | 41.1 | 40.2 |
| 30 | 32.8 | 33.8 | 2001 | 2034 | 41.7 | 40.8 |
| 31 | 32.1 | 33.2 | 1978 | 2013 | 42.4 | 41.4 |
| 32 | 31.4 | 32.5 | 1955 | 1992 | 43.1 | 42.0 |
| 33 | 30.7 | 31.9 | 1931 | 1970 | 43.8 | 42.6 |
| 34 | 30.1 | 31.2 | 1906 | 1948 | 44.5 | 43.3 |
| 35 | 29.4 | 30.6 | 1881 | 1925 | 45.2 | 43.9 |
| 36 | 28.7 | 29.9 | 1855 | 1902 | 46.0 | 44.6 |
| 37 | 28.1 | 29.3 | 1829 | 1878 | 46.7 | 45.3 |
| 38 | 27.4 | 28.6 | 1802 | 1854 | 47.5 | 46.0 |
| 39 | 26.7 | 28.0 | 1775 | 1829 | 48.3 | 46.7 |
| 40 | 26.1 | 27.3 | 1747 | 1804 | 49.1 | 47.5 |
| 41 | 25.4 | 26.7 | 1719 | 1777 | 49.9 | 48.2 |
| 42 | 24.7 | 26.0 | 1690 | 1750 | 50.8 | 49.0 |
| 43 | 24.1 | 25.4 | 1661 | 1723 | 51.6 | 49.8 |
| 44 | 23.4 | 24.7 | 1631 | 1695 | 52.5 | 50.6 |
| 45 | 22.8 | 24.1 | 1601 | 1666 | 53.4 | 51.5 |
| 46 | 22.1 | 23.4 | 1570 | 1636 | 54.3 | 52.3 |
| 47 | 21.5 | 22.7 | 1539 | 1606 | 55.2 | 53.2 |
| 48 | 20.8 | 22.1 | 1507 | 1574 | 56.1 | 54.1 |
| 49 | 20.2 | 21.4 | 1475 | 1542 | 57.0 | 55.1 |
| 50 | 19.5 | 20.8 | 1442 | 1509 | 58.0 | 56.0 |

## TABLE XVII.—(continued.)
### English Life Table No. 3. Interest 3 per cent.
(Calculated by the Registrar-General from the Returns for 17 Years.)

| Age. | Expectation of Life. | | Present Value of £100 a-year, Annuity due. | | Present Value of £100 payable at Death. | |
|---|---|---|---|---|---|---|
| | Males. | Females. | Males. | Females. | Males. | Females. |
| | Years. | Years. | | | | |
| 51 | 18.9 | 20.1 | £1409 | £1476 | £59.0 | £57.0 |
| 52 | 18.3 | 19.4 | 1376 | 1441 | 59.9 | 58.0 |
| 53 | 17.7 | 18.8 | 1343 | 1405 | 60.9 | 59.1 |
| 54 | 17.1 | 18.1 | 1310 | 1369 | 61.9 | 60.1 |
| 55 | 16.5 | 17.4 | 1276 | 1333 | 62.8 | 61.2 |
| 56 | 15.9 | 16.8 | 1241 | 1297 | 63.8 | 62.2 |
| 57 | 15.3 | 16.2 | 1207 | 1261 | 64.8 | 63.3 |
| 58 | 14.7 | 15.6 | 1172 | 1225 | 65.9 | 64.3 |
| 59 | 14.1 | 14.9 | 1137 | 1189 | 66.9 | 65.4 |
| 60 | 13.5 | 14.3 | 1102 | 1153 | 67.9 | 66.4 |
| 61 | 13.0 | 13.8 | 1067 | 1117 | 68.9 | 67.5 |
| 62 | 12.4 | 13.2 | 1031 | 1080 | 70.0 | 68.5 |
| 63 | 11.9 | 12.6 | 996 | 1044 | 71.0 | 69.6 |
| 64 | 11.3 | 12.1 | 961 | 1008 | 72.0 | 70.6 |
| 65 | 10.8 | 11.5 | 927 | 973 | 73.0 | 71.7 |
| 66 | 10.3 | 11.0 | 892 | 938 | 74.0 | 72.7 |
| 67 | 9.8 | 10.5 | 859 | 903 | 75.0 | 73.7 |
| 68 | 9.3 | 9.8 | 825 | 868 | 76.0 | 74.7 |
| 69 | 8.9 | 9.5 | 793 | 835 | 76.9 | 75.7 |
| 70 | 8.5 | 9.0 | 761 | 802 | 77.8 | 76.7 |
| 71 | 8.0 | 8.6 | 730 | 769 | 78.7 | 77.6 |
| 72 | 7.6 | 8.1 | 700 | 738 | 79.6 | 78.5 |
| 73 | 7.2 | 7.7 | 670 | 707 | 80.5 | 79.4 |
| 74 | 6.9 | 7.3 | 642 | 677 | 81.3 | 80.3 |
| 75 | 6.5 | 6.9 | 614 | 648 | 82.1 | 81.1 |
| 76 | 6.2 | 6.6 | 588 | 620 | 82.9 | 81.9 |
| 77 | 5.8 | 6.2 | 562 | 593 | 83.6 | 82.7 |
| 78 | 5.5 | 5.9 | 538 | 568 | 84.3 | 83.5 |
| 79 | 5.2 | 5.6 | 514 | 543 | 85.0 | 84.2 |
| 80 | 4.9 | 5.3 | 492 | 519 | 85.7 | 84.9 |
| 81 | 4.7 | 5.0 | 470 | 496 | 86.3 | 85.6 |
| 82 | 4.4 | 4.7 | 450 | 474 | 86.9 | 86.2 |
| 83 | 4.2 | 4.5 | 430 | 453 | 87.5 | 86.8 |
| 84 | 4.0 | 4.2 | 412 | 433 | 88.0 | 87.4 |
| 85 | 3.7 | 4.0 | 394 | 414 | 88.5 | 87.9 |
| 86 | 3.5 | 3.8 | 377 | 396 | 89.0 | 88.5 |
| 87 | 3.3 | 3.6 | 361 | 379 | 89.5 | 89.0 |
| 88 | 3.2 | 3.4 | 346 | 363 | 89.9 | 89.4 |
| 89 | 3.0 | 3.2 | 331 | 347 | 90.3 | 89.9 |
| 90 | 2.8 | 3.0 | 318 | 333 | 90.7 | 90.3 |
| 91 | 2.7 | 2.9 | 305 | 319 | 91.1 | 90.7 |
| 92 | 2.6 | 2.7 | 293 | 306 | 91.5 | 91.1 |
| 93 | 2.4 | 2.6 | 281 | 294 | 91.8 | 91.4 |
| 94 | 2.3 | 2.4 | 270 | 282 | 92.1 | 91.8 |
| 95 | 2.2 | 2.3 | 260 | 271 | 92.4 | 92.1 |
| 96 | 2.1 | 2.2 | 250 | 260 | 92.6 | 92.4 |
| 97 | 2.0 | 2.1 | 241 | 251 | 92.9 | 92.7 |
| 98 | 1.9 | 2.0 | 233 | 241 | 93.0 | 93.0 |
| 99 | 1.8 | 1.9 | 224 | 232 | 93.2 | 93.0 |
| 100 | 1.7 | 1.8 | 217 | 224 | 93.1 | 93.3 |

# MEMORANDA

### FOR AN

# AVERAGE INVESTMENT TRUST,

## WITH SHARE CAPITAL;

### AND ISSUING

BONUS INVESTMENT BONDS, and
BONUS INVESTMENT CERTIFICATES.

*\** The within Tables are calculated on the basis of Bonds and Certificates of £100 each, but in many cases Bonds and Certificates of £25 and £30 each may be found more convenient.

# MEMORANDA FOR A PROSPECTUS

## OF AN

# AVERAGE INVESTMENT TRUST.

*Capital.*—The Capital of the Trust to be raised by means of Shares of £   each, called up in the ordinary way.

*Bonus Investment Bonds.*—In addition to the Share Capital, in order to meet the requirements of persons who might desire to invest their money without becoming Members of the Trust, Bonds could be issued in consideration of a single payment, to be called Bonus Investment Bonds, on which interest could be paid half-yearly until they are repaid, which could be effected by Annual Drawings, to commence at the end of a fixed number of years, with a guaranteed bonus.

EXAMPLES:—*Thus, if a Trust makes 6 per cent. per annum clear of expenses, and pays 4 or 4½ per cent. to the Bondholders, it could pay off 1000 Bonds of £100 each, as under, leaving a considerable surplus at the end:—*

CLASS A.—*Interest paid to Bondholders 4 per cent. Whole term 17 years. After the first 3 years, 70 Bonds a-year could be paid off with a bonus of £20. The Bonds drawn each year getting £120.*

CLASS B.—*Interest paid to Bondholders 4½ per cent. Whole term 21 years. After the first 7 years, 70 Bonds a-year could be paid off, commencing at £115 per Bond, and increasing £1 for each year's delay. The Bonds drawn in the last (21st) year getting £128.*

The Bondholder could also be allowed to share in the allotments of surplus profit (if over 6 per cent.) at the Triennial Valuations, payable when the Bond is drawn, in addition to the Guaranteed Bonuses mentioned above.

The two following Tables show how this arrangement would work. They are on the assumption that only 6 per cent. would be made clear of expenses.

## CLASS A.—Bonus Investment Bonds.

Table *shewing how a Trust with a Fund of £100,000, making 6 per cent. per annum, clear of expenses, and paying 4 per cent. to the Bondholders, could after 3 years pay off 70 Bonds a-year, the Bonds drawn getting £120. A considerable surplus will remain, from the Compound Interest not included, available for residuary Allotments to the Shareholders.*

| At end of Years. | Balance of Fund or Bonds to be Redeemed. | Cost of 4 per Cent. a Year paid by Society. | 6 per Cent. made by Society. | Surplus of Simple Interest remaining each Year in favour of Society. | Bonds Paid off. | | Bonuses Paid out. | | Total Payments out. |
|---|---|---|---|---|---|---|---|---|---|
| | | | | | No. | Amount. | Rate. | Amount. | |
| | £ | £ | £ | £ | | | | | |
| 1 | 100,000 | 4,000 | 6,000 | 2,000 | | | | | |
| 2 | 100,000 | 4,000 | 6,000 | 2,000 | | | | | |
| 3 | 100,000 | 4,000 | 6,000 | 2,000 | | | | | |
| | | 12,000 | 18,000 | 6,000 | | | | | |
| | | | | | | £ | | £ | £ |
| 4 | 93,000 | 4,000 | 6,000 | 2,000 | 70 | 7,000 | 20 | 1,400 | 8,400 |
| 5 | 86,000 | 3,720 | 5,580 | 1,860 | 70 | 7,000 | 20 | 1,400 | 8,400 |
| 6 | 79,000 | 3,440 | 5,160 | 1,720 | 70 | 7,000 | 20 | 1,400 | 8,400 |
| 7 | 72,000 | 3,160 | 4,740 | 1,580 | 70 | 7,000 | 20 | 1,400 | 8,400 |
| 8 | 65,000 | 2,880 | 4,320 | 1,440 | 70 | 7,000 | 20 | 1,400 | 8,400 |
| 9 | 58,000 | 2,600 | 3,900 | 1,300 | 70 | 7,000 | 20 | 1,400 | 8,400 |
| 10 | 51,000 | 2,320 | 3,480 | 1,160 | 70 | 7,000 | 20 | 1,400 | 8,400 |
| 11 | 44,000 | 2,040 | 3,060 | 1,020 | 70 | 7,000 | 20 | 1,400 | 8,400 |
| 12 | 37,000 | 1,760 | 2,640 | 880 | 70 | 7,000 | 20 | 1,400 | 8,400 |
| 13 | 30,000 | 1,480 | 2,220 | 740 | 70 | 7,000 | 20 | 1,400 | 8,400 |
| 14 | 23,000 | 1,200 | 1,800 | 600 | 70 | 7,000 | 20 | 1,400 | 8,400 |
| 15 | 16,000 | 920 | 1,380 | 460 | 70 | 7,000 | 20 | 1,400 | 8,400 |
| 16 | 9,000 | 640 | 960 | 320 | 70 | 7,000 | 20 | 1,400 | 8,400 |
| 17 | | 360 | 540 | 180 | 90 | 9,000 | 20 | 1,800 | 10,800 |
| | | 30,520 | 45,780 | 15,260 | 1000 | 100,000 | | | |
| | | 42,520 | 63,780 | 21,260 | 1000 | 100,000 | | 20,000 | 120,000 |

*Obs.*—The balance of the Simple Interest at 6 per cent. over the 4 per cent. paid is £21,260, of which the cost of the Bonus will absorb £20,000, leaving £1,260 over. If the Trust defers all Allotments, out of the Compound Interest not included, till the end of the 17th year, there will be, after paying off the Bonds with the above Bonuses, a surplus of £10,236. 3*s.* 7*d.*, which includes the preceding £1,260.

## CLASS B.—BONUS INVESTMENT BONDS.

TABLE *shewing how a Trust with a Fund of £100,000, making 6 per cent. per annum, clear of expenses, and paying 4½ per cent. to the Bondholders, could after 7 years pay off 70 Bonds a-year, commencing at £115 per Bond, and increasing £1 for each year's delay. The Bonds drawn in the last (21st) year getting £128. A considerable surplus will remain, from the Compound Interest not included, available for residuary Allotments to the Shareholders.*

| At end of Years. | Balance of Fund or Bonds to be Redeemed. | Cost of 4½ per Cent. a Year paid by Society. | 6 per Cent. made by Society. | Surplus remaining each Year in favour of Society. | Bonds Paid off. | | Bonuses Paid out. | | Total Payments out. |
|---|---|---|---|---|---|---|---|---|---|
| | | | | | No. | Amount. | Rate. | Amount. | |
| | £ | £ | £ | £ | | | | | |
| 1 | 100,000 | 4,500 | 6,000 | 1,500 | | | | | |
| 2 | 100,000 | 4,500 | 6,000 | 1,500 | | | | | |
| 3 | 100,000 | 4,500 | 6,000 | 1,500 | | | | | |
| 4 | 100,000 | 4,500 | 6,000 | 1,500 | | | | | |
| 5 | 100,000 | 4,500 | 6,000 | 1,500 | | | | | |
| 6 | 100,000 | 4,500 | 6,000 | 1,500 | | | | | |
| 7 | 100,000 | 4,500 | 6,000 | 1,500 | | | | | |
| | | 31,500 | 42,000 | 10,500 | | | | | |
| | | | | | | £ | | £ | £ |
| 8 | 93,000 | 4,500 | 6,000 | 1,500 | 70 | 7,000 | 15 | 1,050 | 8,050 |
| 9 | 86,000 | 4,185 | 5,580 | 1,395 | 70 | 7,000 | 16 | 1,120 | 8,120 |
| 10 | 79,000 | 3,870 | 5,160 | 1,290 | 70 | 7,000 | 17 | 1,190 | 8,190 |
| 11 | 72,000 | 3,555 | 4,740 | 1,185 | 70 | 7,000 | 18 | 1,260 | 8,260 |
| 12 | 65,000 | 3,240 | 4,320 | 1,080 | 70 | 7,000 | 19 | 1,330 | 8,330 |
| 13 | 58,000 | 2,925 | 3,900 | 975 | 70 | 7,000 | 20 | 1,400 | 8,400 |
| 14 | 51,000 | 2,610 | 3,480 | 870 | 70 | 7,000 | 21 | 1,470 | 8,470 |
| 15 | 44,000 | 2,295 | 3,060 | 765 | 70 | 7,000 | 22 | 1,540 | 8,540 |
| 16 | 37,000 | 1,980 | 2,640 | 660 | 70 | 7,000 | 23 | 1,610 | 8,610 |
| 17 | 30,000 | 1,665 | 2,220 | 555 | 70 | 7,000 | 24 | 1,680 | 8,680 |
| 18 | 23,000 | 1,350 | 1,800 | 450 | 70 | 7,000 | 25 | 1,750 | 8,750 |
| 19 | 16,000 | 1,035 | 1,380 | 345 | 70 | 7,000 | 26 | 1,820 | 8,820 |
| 20 | 9,000 | 720 | 960 | 240 | 70 | 7,000 | 27 | 1,890 | 8,890 |
| 21 | | 405 | 540 | 135 | 90 | 9,000 | 28 | 2,520 | 11,520 |
| | | 34,335 | 45,780 | 11,445 | 1000 | 100,000 | | | |
| Total ... | | 65,835 | 87,780 | 21,945 | 1000 | 100,000 | | 21,630 | 121,630 |

*Obs.*—If the Trust defers all Allotments, out of the Compound Interest not included, till the end of the 21st year, there will be, after paying off the Bonds with the above Bonuses, a surplus of £16,902. 13s. 2d., which includes the £315 difference between the surplus above £21,945, and the cost of the Bonus, £21,630.

## CLASS C.—DOUBLING ACCUMULATIVE BONDS,*

### WITH CONTINGENT BONUSES.

TABLE *shewing how a Trust, which makes only 5 per cent. clear of Expenses, could, out of an Accumulation at Compound Interest, return £200 for each £100 Bond, by Annual Drawings commencing at the end of the 10th Year. If the Trust made a higher rate clear of Expenses, it could set aside the Surplus towards* TRIENNIAL *Allotments of Additional Contingent* BONUSES. *The Table is given on the basis of £100,000 Fund in 1000 Bonds of £100 each, returnable by £200,000 drawn at the rate of 100 Bonds a Year.*

[There is a small unused Annual Surplus of £90·41 arising from the fractions of interest.]

| At end of Years. | Interest at 5 per Cent. on the Balance at the end of the previous Year. | Sum of Balance and Interest. | Deduction each Year. | | Balance of Capital and Interest at end of each Year, less Drawing and Surplus. |
|---|---|---|---|---|---|
| | | | Drawing. | Surplus. | |
| | £ | £ | £ | £ | £ |
| 9 | ... | ... | ... | ... | 155132·82 |
| 10 | 7756·64 | 162889·46 | 20,000 | 90·41 | 142799·05 |
| 11 | 7139·95 | 149939·00 | 20,000 | 90·41 | 129848·59 |
| 12 | 6492·43 | 136341·02 | 20,000 | 90·41 | 116250·61 |
| 13 | 5812·53 | 122063·14 | 20,000 | 90·41 | 101972·73 |
| 14 | 5098·64 | 107071·37 | 20,000 | 90·41 | 86980·96 |
| 15 | 4349·05 | 91330·01 | 20,000 | 90·41 | 71239·60 |
| 16 | 3561·98 | 74801·58 | 20,000 | 90·41 | 54711·17 |
| 17 | 2735·56 | 57446·73 | 20,000 | 90·41 | 37356·32 |
| 18 | 1867·82 | 39224·14 | 20,000 | 90·41 | 19133·73 |
| 19 | 956·68 | 20090·41 | 20,000 | 90·41 | ... |
| | 45771·28 | ... | 200,000 | 904·10 | ... |

* [*See* the Section on the Doubling of Money, and the Properties of the Number 70.]

## Class D.—Investment Certificates,

### Realisable with Bonus by Gradual Subscriptions.

*Bonus Investment Certificates.*—For the convenience of those, who might not be able to pay for a Bonus Investment Bond by a single payment, Bonus Investment Certificates of £100 each could be issued, to be paid up by monthly or other contributions, varying according to the length of the term selected. A guaranteed interest at 4 per cent. per annum, compounded half-yearly, could be credited on these certificates until completion, and they would, also, enjoy the advantage of participating in the triennial allotments of Bonus, out of the surplus profits, payable on completion of the Certificate.

This department would suit the person, who seeks an investment for such regular subscriptions as he can set aside from his income, at a moderate but secured interest for his money, with a chance of bonus periodically.

It would also be accessible to the investor of humble means, who at present has only open to him the Savings' Bank or the Building Society. In the Savings' Bank, at the date of the last return, the deposits had reached the enormous amount of 63½ millions, although the rate of interest allowed therein is only from 2½ to 3 per cent.

It might be anticipated that some portion of this would come to the Trust, which guarantees a better rate of interest, irrespective of the contingent Bonuses.

These Certificates are suitable for the accumulation of money *as Endowments* or *Provision for Children* on attaining a specified age, or to make *Provision for Old Age.*

They are transferable with all the benefits allotted to them, or the money paid to the Society may be withdrawn, with interest at 4 per cent., after the first year, on notice being given.

The following is a specimen Table for paying up a Bonus Investment Certificate by gradual periodic instalments:—

## Class D.—Bonus Investment Certificates,

### Realisable by Monthly or other Periodic Subscriptions.

Table *shewing the Amount that may be received back in* Principal and Interest *(accumulated half-yearly at 4 per cent. per annum), at end of different terms of years, for £100 paid in, apart from the Bonuses to be allotted at Triennial Valuations of Profits, but payable on completion of the Certificates.*

[From £100 not being divisible by the number of years in all cases, there is sometimes a fraction over—So also when dividing by 12 for the monthly contributions.]

| No. of Payments Monthly. | For a term of Years. | By Paying In the Year. | By Paying Monthly. | Total Paid at the end of the Term selected. | The Subscriber can receive for Principal and Interest. | Equivalent present values of the amounts discounted half-yearly at 4 per Cent. | Equivalent present values of Subscriptions discounted half-yearly at 5 per Cent. |
|---|---|---|---|---|---|---|---|
|  |  | £ | £ s. d. | £ | £ s. d. | £ s. d. | £ s. d. |
| 60 | 5 | 20·000 | 1 13 4 | 100 | 109 10 0 | 89 16 5 | 87 10 5 |
| 72 | 6 | 16·667 | 1 7 10 | 100 | 111 15 4 | 88 2 7 | 85 9 8 |
| 84 | 7 | 14·286 | 1 3 10 | 100 | 114 2 0 | 86 9 7 | 83 10 0 |
| 96 | 8 | 12·500 | 1 0 10 | 100 | 116 9 11 | 84 17 1 | 81 12 0 |
| 108 | 9 | 11·111 | 0 18 7 | 100 | 118 19 1 | 83 5 10 | 79 14 10 |
| 120 | 10 | 10·000 | 0 16 8 | 100 | 121 9 9 | 81 15 2 | 77 19 0 |
| 132 | 11 | 9·091 | 0 15 2 | 100 | 124 1 9 | 80 5 2 | 76 4 2 |
| 144 | 12 | 8·333 | 0 13 11 | 100 | 126 15 0 | 78 16 0 | 74 10 3 |
| 156 | 13 | 7·692 | 0 12 10 | 100 | 129 10 0 | 77 7 9 | 72 17 8 |
| 168 | 14 | 7·143 | 0 11 11 | 100 | 132 6 7 | 76 0 2 | 71 6 0 |
| 180 | 15 | 6·667 | 0 11 2 | 100 | 135 4 8 | 74 13 3 | 69 15 5 |
| 192 | 16 | 6·250 | 0 10 5 | 100 | 138 4 2 | 73 6 8 | 68 5 6 |
| 204 | 17 | 5·882 | 0 9 10 | 100 | 141 5 4 | 72 0 11 | 66 16 7 |
| 216 | 18 | 5·556 | 0 9 3 | 100 | 144 8 10 | 70 16 1 | 65 8 9 |
| 228 | 19 | 5·263 | 0 8 10 | 100 | 147 13 4 | 69 11 7 | 64 1 5 |
| 240 | 20 | 5·000 | 0 8 4 | 100 | 151 0 1 | 68 7 10 | 62 15 1 |

Example 1.—*A Member paying for 14 years 11s. 11d. a month, will be entitled to £132. 6s. 7d. at the end, with Bonuses in addition, allotted triennially.*

Example 2.—*If a Member paying 11s. 11d. a month for 14 years, wished (by giving Security) to have cash in advance, instead of waiting for the £132. 6s. 7d., he could be paid £76. 0s. 2d., if the Trust gave the exact equivalent at 4 per cent. discount, or £71. 6s. if it thought proper to require a compensatory margin of 1 per cent., and therefore discounted at 5 per cent.*

## LEGAL CONSTITUTION OF A TRUST.

*Dividends and Profits.*—The Dividends and Drawings received each year from the Stocks and other Securities purchased by the Trust could be applied, after deducting expenses :—

*1.—To crediting interest half-yearly on the Bonus Investment Bonds and Certificates, commencing at the rate per cent. guaranteed.*

*2.—As a Sinking Fund, to pay off the Certificates, with bonus, at the end of selected terms, and the Investment Bonds by Annual Drawings extending over such period of years as might be determined on.*

The surplus profits would be available to pay Dividends each year to the Ordinary shares which constitute the backbone of the Trust, and triennially, after valuations made, could be allotted in the form of augmented Dividends to them, and of Bonus to the Investment Bonds and Certificates.

*Expenses.*—The expenses might be limited to a percentage on the amount to be raised under the Trust.

*Officers.*—The names of the following officers should be printed in the prospectus :—

| DIRECTORS. | INSPECTING COMMITTEE. To be chosen from the Shareholders and Bond and Certificate holders. |
|---|---|
| BANKERS. | BROKERS. |
| CONSULTING ACTUARY. | SOLICITORS. |
| AUDITORS. | SECRETARY. |

As to the *Legal Constitution* of a Trust. It would have to be framed under the Companies' Acts, or by means of a Trust Deed. There is an objection to the latter plan, on account of the contingent liabilities attaching to the position of Trustee, which are known to spring up quite unexpectedly many years afterwards on persons who have held that office; so that few would be willing to undertake such a responsibility in a commercial Trust. Hence, on the whole, the Companies' incorporation seems to be preferable.

www.ingramcontent.com/pod-product-compliance
Lightning Source LLC
Chambersburg PA
CBHW031813220426
43662CB00007B/634